SHARDS & PELLETS & KNIVES

Also by John Fulker

And True Deliverance Make (1985)
The View From Above (1992)
Chickensoup, Cheap Whiskey & Bad Women (2000)

SHARDS & PELLETS & KNIVES *Oh my!*

by John Fulker

ORANGE FRAZER PRESS
Wilmington, Ohio

Additional copies of *Shards & Pellets & Knives, Oh My!* may be ordered directly from:
Orange Frazer Press
P.O. Box 214
Wilmington, OH 45177

Telephone 1.800.852.9332 for price and shipping information.
Website: *www.orangefrazer.com*

cover design and art direction Jeff Fulwiler
interior design Chad DeBoard

Library of Congress Cataloging-in-Publication Data

Fulker, John, 1929-
    Shards & pellets & knives, oh my! / by John Fulker.
        p. cm.
    ISBN 1-933197-27-7
        1. Murder--Ohio--Miami County--Case studies. 2. Trials (Murder)--Ohio--Miami County--Case studies. I. Title. II. Title: Shards and pellets and knives, oh my!

    HV6533.05F85 2007
    364.152'30977148--dc22   2006051133

Once, again, for NJ

SHARDS & PELLETS & KNIVES *oh my!*

SKULL WAS CRUSHED IN MIDNIGHT ASSAULT

June 28
1915

Book 1

S H A R D S

GLAD TIDINGS SELDOM COME to visit in the small hours before dawn. The frenetic rapping at the door or the strident jangle of the telephone—between the hours of two and five in the morning—is certain to occasion, for most of us, either a puckish agitation or an atavistic sense of foreboding. Because these are the trappings with which we expect our troubles to arrive, they are not welcome events.

In the case of William A. Haines, however, the response to such harsh stimuli, while equally Pavlovian, was nonetheless altogether different from the norm. For Haines, who had already earned a considerable reputation as one of southern Ohio's doughtiest criminal lawyers, the unexpected middle-of-the-night summons usually promised a new and potentially exciting challenge—a problem to solve, a windmill to tilt at, or perhaps merely a joust with an adversary worthy of his steel.

Because this sort of thing was commonplace for Bill Haines, he had long since caused his magneto-powered telephone to be mounted on the wall just at his bedside so that he could answer quickly without disturbing either Blanche or their two small daughters who slept in the adjacent bedroom. On a warm Monday morning in June of 1915 he managed to get to it on the first ring. The call came at about 4:30 a.m. and he'd roused instantly from a deep sleep. Blanche, who was more than a little queasy from her current pregnancy, had slept fitfully most of the night and she wakened to the bell also.

"This is Haines," he growled *sotto voce*. He had rolled to his feet to speak into the mouthpiece and was unaware that his wife was awake. He marveled at his own eagerness; he had once reflected that after more than twenty years of this sort of thing he should have been more blasé about such an event. Most likely the call would turn out to be an unruly drunkard or an out-of-control wife beater unwilling to spend the early morning hours in jail and demanding to be bailed out immediately. Haines was fully conversant with the probability curve. There was, however, just the possibility that something really

3

important was afoot and his services might be needed. And the existence of that bare possibility, however remote, is what fed and replenished his enthusiasm for what he did for a living. It was what made him run.

Haines ground the receiver hard against his ear and listened intently to his caller. His excitement, even though professionally restrained, was nonetheless apparent to his wife. She recognized the outward signs, the way he cocked his head to the left, the deeply furrowed brow and the rapt attention he lavished on the caller's obviously distraught recitations.

"All right, Eva," he soothed. "I'll arrange to see him as soon as possible, probably around nine." He waited for her to process his assurance on that score. When she seemed to have that in hand, he pressed her gently concerning the details. "How many were supposed to have been involved?"

Another pause. Then: "Do you know their names?"

"Are they all in custody?"

When it became clear that his caller was at the brink of hysteria, Haines tried to calm her down. "Now take it slow, Eva. It may not be as bad as you think. We'll get through it." He waited until she seemed under control. "Just one more thing," he inquired. "Where'd they say all this happened?"

He was not fully satisfied with her response, and had to try again. Haines recognized the need to curb his impatience; what the lady wanted was just the least modicum of sympathy, not a star chamber grilling. He took a long breath, let it out slowly and prompted, as gently as he could. "I got all that, Eva, but what I want to know is precisely where. Which side of the road? How far from the ticket office? North or south?"

Haines took the response. Then: "I understand all that; really I do. Just tell me what you do know and I'll work it from there, O.K.?"

From Blanche's perspective the conversation had seemed interminable, but it had actually consumed no more than ten minutes. "That's fine, Eva," Haines soothed, trying to close it off. "You go back to bed, try to get some sleep. I'll go see him first thing this morning and I'll drop over to your place before noon. Maybe you could have some coffee ready?"

An interval. Eva seemed to be losing it. Haines eased the conversation to an end. "I know. I know," he comforted. "You need to try anyway; go lie down awhile. There's nothing further you can do now. I'll see you before noon."

Bill Haines broke the connection, replaced the receiver into its cradle and turned into Blanche's inquiring glance. "What is it, Bill?" she asked apprehensively. "It certainly sounds ominous from this end. Who was it? What's happened?"

"Easy, love," he answered. "I don't know all that much yet myself, but that was Eva Burton—I'll explain that later. It seems her son has just been arrested, just a few minutes ago, along with three other of our young blades. They haven't been charged yet, but they're supposed to have beaten Frank Favorite's head in and he's not expected to live. Soon as he dies, they'll likely be charged with murder."

He had dressed rapidly while offering this sketchy information. Now he made for the door. When Blanche asked for further explanation, he put her off. "I'm going to take a short ride. Maybe I can put my own thoughts together and try to get some kind of handle on this thing. After I've worked it through, and maybe asked around a bit, I'll be back for a shave and some breakfast. By that time I should be able to fill in some blanks. For right now, you should try to get some sleep."

IF SLEEP HAD BEEN DIFFICULT for Blanche Haines before Mrs. Burton's early morning call, it was now utterly impossible. She knew better than to try. She was not really a morning person and would normally have expected to remain in bed for another three or four hours, but she could not possibly have done so under the present circumstance.

It was a different matter for her husband, she thought. He had been born on a farm in Staunton Township just outside of town and was raised, there and elsewhere, pretty much as a farm boy. He had acquired early on, and would continue for a lifetime, the habit of rising early in the morning. It was amazing, he'd said, how much a man could accomplish each day while the rest of the world was fast asleep.

As she moved about their bedroom, making herself ready to face the day, she was moderately surprised to note that Haines, upon leaving the house, had not gone to the front curb where their shiny new machine was parked. She had assumed, it seemed, that he had meant to take his "short ride" in the automobile. She now saw that he had actually proceeded in the opposite direction and followed the cement walkway to the small wooden utility shed behind the house. Her interest piqued, she watched him unlock the shed and wheel

Afterward, Bill Haines would say to his wife, Blanche, "The game is not always worth the candle." She was not sure she understood what he meant. He wasn't sure, either.

out his safety bicycle. No longer new, it was nonetheless a thing of beauty. It was a well-cared-for Colonel Pope Special, with pneumatic tires and a fully modern coaster brake. Haines himself had long been an enthusiastic cyclist, had set and still held several records for travel within the county. The fact that he owned the record for the annual nine-mile road race from Troy to nearby Pleasant Hill was the source of considerable pride to him. He had accomplished that feat in twenty-seven minutes nearly twenty years earlier, at age twenty-seven, and no one had yet bettered his mark. Now, at age forty-six, he was still in top physical condition. However lean and diminutive he appeared, he was also trim, sinewy and keenly honed by regular and strenuous physical activity.

Blanche could barely see her husband in the pre-dawn darkness as he lovingly wiped the seat and grips with a soft cloth and oiled the chain with his specially selected lubricant. A moment later he had disappeared up the alley, moving towards the center of town.

Chapter Two

Although she tried to do so, Blanche Haines was unable to delay her own breakfast long enough to share the meal with her husband. She had needed to eat something in order to stave off the anticipated recurrence of her pregnancy-induced morning sickness. She had already broken her fast, finished her coffee, done the dishes and seen the girls off to their play. She had just begun to make the beds when she became aware that Haines had carried his bicycle onto the porch and entered the front door. It was nearly ten o'clock.

"That must have been a long ride," she said. "I wanted to wait breakfast, but I couldn't make it."

"I'm very glad of that, my love; I hadn't intended to be gone so long, but I followed my nose and it led me in a lot of different directions. I've not eaten a thing yet, so maybe you'd fix me an early lunch while I shave and change." He headed towards the bedroom and added, "You'll want to know what's been happening."

Lunch, early or late, was a simple matter for Bill Haines. He was a firm believer in the nutritional and restorative values of fresh fruit. Two apples, a banana and a handful of grapes were set out for him well before his emergence from the bedroom, clean-shaven and properly attired for a day in the office. Blanche joined him at the table with a glass of cold tea.

"Tell me what's happened," she pleaded. "Will this person—a Favorite, you said—will he make it? I don't know who any of these people are."

"Easy now, hon," Haines admonished. "One thing at a time, and we'll get you the whole story. Answer to the first question is the young man died, not an hour ago. No one ever expected he'd make it. His head was stove in like an overripe pumpkin. So the charge will, indeed, be first degree murder.

"Next answer is that the young man was Frank Favorite, a cattle dealer. Lived on a farm up by Eldean. You'd know his father. That's Dan Favorite. He's mostly retired now, but he owns the meat market over on Adams Street where you've been buying our steaks and chops these last couple of years. Anyway, Frank was in his early thirties, unmarried and maybe a little footloose. Seems he drank some, chased after the girls, spent a lot of time at one or the other of those bootleg clubs up on the riverbank. Word is he was considered to be a pretty nice fellow, didn't cause anybody any trouble. I understand he was well thought of and fairly popular among the younger folks who knew him."

Blanche couldn't hold it. "Then who is this Burton person who called this morning? How is she involved? Who else is involved in this thing?"

"Whoa, now," he warned patiently. He drew a deep breath, sighed, and then, "Eva Burton started this life as Eva Knoop. Some years ago—she was only eighteen—she had a child out of wedlock, named him Forrest—Forrest Knoop—she'd never say who the father was. She set out to raise the boy herself; moved off the family farm and into town. She and the boy took an apartment on Main Street, across the street from the Hatfield House, and she worked here and there as a domestic. Hard life for a young girl with a small child. A little while back, when the boy was ten or eleven years old, Eva married Lou Burton. He works at the Hayner Distillery on Water Street, they live practically next door. Burton helped her raise Forrest, but never actually adopted him. Eva might not have permitted it; she may have wanted him to keep the Knoop name."

"The Knoop name? Is Eva one of those Knoops?" Blanche was well aware that pioneer Knoops were among the earliest settlers in the area and that one of their progeny, a Jacob Knoop, was widely recognized as the first white child born in the county. She remembered having attended an affair some ten years earlier when the Daughters of the American Revolution had erected and dedicated a monument commemorating the birth of that first white child on the site of the old Dutch Station. The Knoop family—and the name they shared—was one of considerable local distinction.

Bill Haines nodded soberly. "Yes. She is. She's about four generations down from old Jacob, but she's a direct descendant." He scratched his ear, knitted his brow, and counted. "Let's see if I've got this right. I think Jacob would have been Eva's great-great grandfather." He paused a moment to confirm his calculations. "I think that's right. The original Jacob, the guy on the monument, was born in 1798. Says so on the stone. That's almost a hundred and twenty years ago, roughly five generations. Young Forrest would be the old man's great-great-great grandson. I'd imagine his mother would have wanted him to keep the name."

Blanche's patience was wearing thin. "All right, all right. That's enough genealogy. You've told me who Eva Burton is. Now tell me how she's involved and why she called this morning."

"She called to retain my services on behalf of her son, Forrest Knoop. He was arrested at her home at about 4:30 this morning, just moments before she called. Forrest is to be charged as the principal assailant of Frank Favorite. Now that Frank has died, Forrest, along with his three companions, will probably be charged with murder.

"Now, is that explanation sufficiently concise?" he asked with a touch of asperity.

Blanche Haines touched her husband's cheek as though to dissipate the choler. "Yes, dear. It is." She smiled. "But it gives rise to a whole lot of additional questions."

"It does?" He acknowledged the implicit rebuke. "Such as?"

"Well, apart from his pedigree, you might tell me something about this Forrest Knoop. Since you tell me he was arrested at his mother's home in the wee hours, I will assume he's not married. How old is he? What does he do? Why would he have gotten involved in something as sordid as beating a person to death?"

"Great God, woman!" he sputtered. "Give me a chance. I'm doing the best I can. There's a good deal to tell yet. Let me answer one question at a time.

"First question. Marital status, I think it was. You are, of course, quite correct in your assumption that Forrest Knoop is not married. He does live in the home of his mother and his stepfather. Second question. I should imagine he would be twenty-three years old, maybe twenty-four next birthday, whenever that is. And, as to your third, he's currently employed at the courthouse, in the Miami County Surveyor's office. He's probably the chief deputy in that office. His uncle, L.P. Knoop, I'm sure you'll remember, was just recently elected as county surveyor. And without intending to hark back to the genealogy, I'll cite that fact as an example that blood is, indeed, thicker than water.

"Now then, in order to properly answer your last question, why—

or rather—how he would have gotten involved in this kind of thing, I'll probably have to tell you a lot more than you'd like to hear, but there's really no help for it."

"I'll be good," she promised. "I'm better now."

"I'm glad to hear it." His eyes smiled at her over the rim of his coffee cup as he sipped his after-lunch allotment. "That'll make my job a lot easier."

Bill Haines pushed his plate and empty coffee cup towards the center of the table, leaned forward onto his forearms and made ready to spin a long tale. "You'll form a clearer picture of this young man if I first tell you that virtually no one knows who Forrest Knoop is. Everybody—except maybe his mother—calls him 'Slicker.' Slicker Knoop. And I suppose it fits. Slicker Knoop is pretty much what the name implies.

"He's a good-looking chap, moves easily and dresses well. Add to the mix the fact that he's bright, fairly suave and extremely confident and you'll have a pretty good, apparently complete picture of a young man with good prospects for the future. Backside of the portrait is that he generally seems to be looking out for himself first and foremost. You might say he's one of those fellows whose eye seems always focused on his own main chance. In spite of all that, though, he's been quite popular amongst his own set of our more adventurous young bucks. You know, the sort who take their pleasure in drinking, gambling and chasing after young women. They mostly take their leisure in the local pool halls and in the bootleg joints up along the river."

"Actually," Blanche demurred, "I don't know, but I'll take your word for it."

Haines ignored the interruption. "Well, from what I've managed to piece together so far, there were these five young men who'd spent most of yesterday afternoon and evening at one of the river clubs. That'd be Slicker Knoop, Frank Favorite, and three of their friends. They'd spent most of the time drinking and gambling and then, about eleven o'clock, when the club closed down, they all started back to town together. Couple of hundred yards down the road some kind of fight broke out and Favorite got the worst of it. Everybody's saying they got him out there alone and Slicker broke a beer bottle over his head, practically caved in his skull. Story has it, they took all his money, then just let him lay alongside the road, walked on into town, and went home to bed."

"Oh, Bill, that's ghastly! To steal his money and then to leave him in the way like a slaughtered animal! What kind of monsters are they?"

"Well, now, love, let's not rush too hastily to judgment," Haines admonished. "I've only repeated the rumors heard on the street. I've not spoken with my client yet. Nor, for that matter, with anyone else who might have firsthand knowledge."

"Tell me then," she cajoled. "What have you been up to this morning? You were out of here long before daylight."

"I took a ride on my Colonel Pope," he answered blithely. "Thought it might help organize my thinking. Then, next thing I knew, the Colonel had run me out towards the fairgrounds. Gave me a chance to get oriented, familiarize myself with the 'scene of the crime.' I spent a little time there, just mosied around, got the feel of the place. Then I came back into town, stopped by the pool hall, Ott Smith's grocery and Harmon and Edmunds' restaurant. Talked with some of the people out by the fairgrounds, downtown, and whoever else I could catch at the corner of Main and Elm. Actually, I spent most of the morning just asking around, trying to pick up whatever scuttlebutt I could learn. That really wasn't terribly difficult. It's all anyone wants to talk about, and every version I heard was different.

"Finally, I stopped by the jail to interview the man himself." He snorted, "And Blanche, this never happened to me before, but Sheriff Barnett wouldn't permit me to talk with Slicker. He said they'd just learned that Frank Favorite had died and Doc Ullery was already in process of setting up his Coroner's Inquest. I asked Joe what the hell that had to do with my interviewing my client. He said he was real sorry, but he had his orders from both the coroner and the prosecutor.

"Then, just to add insult to the injury, I was debarred from the inquest, too."

"What will you do?" Blanche wanted to know.

"As a practical matter, there's not much I can do at the moment. They've scheduled him for arraignment tomorrow morning. I expect I'll have a chance to see him this evening."

He pushed his chair away from the table, stood up and pecked Blanche on the cheek. "Meanwhile, I've an appointment with Eva Burton. I'll be home for dinner."

Chapter Three

Because Eva Burton's home was on the east side of town, nearly twelve blocks away, Bill Haines had to take his Colonel Pope again in order to honor his promise to stop by her home before noon. As it was, he arrived no more than five minutes before the hour. It was obvious from her appearance that she had been unable to rest since their early morning telephone conversation. She led Haines into the neatly appointed front parlor of her home, offered him a glass of tea, and explained that her husband was somewhere west of Chicago on a business trip for his employer. Lou Burton was an executive with the Hayner Distillery and was often away on company business. She had managed to reach him by phone and he had promised to start home immediately.

"Have you seen Forrest?" she asked anxiously.

"No, I haven't. Much to my consternation, I've not yet been permitted access," Haines replied. "But I'm quite certain that I'll be able to see him before the end of the day. They cannot, in good conscience, deny him the opportunity to speak with counsel any longer. And," he added, "I have it on very good authority that they have ultimately decided that it would be inappropriate to proceed with the Coroner's Inquest without permitting me to appear on behalf of my client. They convened briefly this morning, but quickly adjourned until tomorrow. I think they finally realized they could not properly proceed without permitting me to attend."

"I just can't believe any of this is happening," she lamented. "Forrest would never intentionally harm anyone. It's simply not his way."

"I'm sure that's true, Eva. There's probably been some mistake, but we'll have to work it through," Haines consoled. "Now, then, let's see if I have it correctly. I think you told me that this other fellow, Clyde Starry, had spent Saturday night here with Slicker and that the two of them left the house Sunday morning at about eight o'clock and that Slicker came home alone shortly after midnight. Is that right?"

"Yes."

"Did you speak with him when he came in?"

"No. I was in bed. I heard him come in, and I believe he went straight to his bedroom," she answered quickly. "Then, at about 4:30 this morning the police arrived. Officers Harris and Landrey, I think. They told me there had been some trouble at the fairgrounds and they had come to arrest Forrest. I made them wait in the parlor while I went to wake him up."

Street talk said Slicker Knoop caved Frank Favorite's head in with a beer bottle. Slicker was surprised at the charges. He said Frank fell down and hit his head.

"What was Slicker's reaction to all this?" asked Haines.

"He was quite surprised. He was sound asleep and I had some difficulty rousing him. Then when I did, he couldn't understand why he was being arrested."

"Did he say anything about what had happened?"

"He told me there'd been some kind of scuffle on the way home from the club and that he'd struck Frank Favorite."

"And?"

"He said that Frank was drunk and that he fell down, maybe hit his head, or passed out, and they'd had to send a taxi back to pick him up. He was sure he hadn't been seriously injured."

Haines nodded. "That's pretty much what you told me this morning. Anything else?"

"That's all we had time for. The officers were becoming impatient. He did ask me to call you right away, and, of course, I did."

BILL HAINES' NEXT STOP THAT DAY took him to the county courthouse. To the unsophisticated observer, his calling upon the prosecuting attorney might have seemed little more than a casual visit. Frank Goodrich waved him past his secretary's desk and into his private office. "Hi Bill. This a social call?"

"Something like that," Haines answered lightly. "Thought you might give me some idea what this charge against Slicker Knoop's all about. Joe Barnett wouldn't let me talk with him this morning."

"Yeah, I know. My orders. Wasn't a good idea. You can see him anytime. I've already passed the word." Not quite forty, Goodrich was not an experienced prosecutor. Now he grimaced as if to acknowledge his initial lapse in judgment. "We also adjourned the Coroner's Inquest. Doc's got that scheduled for tomorrow at 11:00, after the arraignment. You're invited."

"Thank you, Frank. I'll be there. Glad to have that bit straightened out," Haines said easily. "Tell me what my guy's supposed to have done."

"You've probably heard all this before, Bill. But the way I have it is that your guy Slicker is supposed to have cracked poor Frank Favorite on the top of his skull with a beer bottle. Hit him so hard that both Frank's skull and the beer bottle were literally shattered into fragments. Then, it seems that the four of them picked him clean, left his wallet under his body along with a single nickel. Don't know what that means. They probably just lost the nickel in the dark. Anyway, it looks like Slicker hit him one hell of a lick."

Bill Haines glanced at the prosecutor with a look of pure incredulity. "Frank, I can't make myself believe it happened that way. As you know, I haven't had a chance to talk with Slicker yet, but that story just doesn't jibe with anything I've heard. So far as I hear, there was nothing more than a little tussle. A shove maybe, and Frank fell down and hit his head. There's been no mention of any kind of weapon, and certainly nothing about a beer bottle. It'd take a lot of force to actually break a bottle on a man's head."

"Exactly," said Goodrich. "With that much force, it could hardly have been an accident. You hit a man that hard, I'd say you meant to kill him. That makes it murder one."

"Can't argue that," conceded Haines. "But are you sure that's what happened?"

"It's what I've been hearing," answered Goodrich. "We've already talked with some of these miscreants."

"Easy enough to check," Haines answered glumly. "If it happened that way, I s'pose there'd be fragments and bits of glass all over the place. You've probably got most of it in an evidence bag already. May I see it?"

"Well, actually I don't have it yet," admitted Goodrich grudgingly. "The boys haven't had a chance to do a complete search yet. Frank died only a few hours ago."

"I can understand that all right. Maybe it's an opportunity," said Haines.

"An opportunity for what?" asked Goodrich.

"Well," mused Haines. "maybe we might get the sheriff to take us out there now, see what we can learn from the crime site. Joe's got to do it sometime. Sooner the better, I'd think."

"True enough," acknowledged Goodrich.

"And, of course, you and I'll both want to look around too. If we find a whole passel of broken glass, we'll have a pretty good idea what happened. This thing might get to be a lot easier to deal with."

Goodrich grasped the arms of his oaken swivel chair and heaved himself to a standing position. "Let's do it," he pronounced.

Chapter Two.

Bill Haines had arranged to meet with his client that same evening. He arrived at the county jailhouse shortly after seven o'clock. Sheriff Joe Barnett met him at the reception desk and escorted him upstairs to the conference room directly above the kitchen. Barnett was embarrassed over having turned him away earlier and he apologized for the second time.

"I couldn't be sorrier, Bill, but those were my orders. They came straight from Frank."

"I know, Joe. He apologized to me this afternoon. We've got past that all right," assured Haines. "How's Slicker handling life in a cage?"

"Well, I can't imagine he likes it much, but he hasn't complained either. I'll go get him for you and you can ask him about it." And with that the sheriff disappeared down the stairwell.

Less than a minute later, Barnett led the prisoner into the conference room and took his leave. Bill Haines and Slicker Knoop were casually acquainted with one another. Knoop worked at the surveyor's office in the courthouse and Haines had seen him often on his way to the county courts, housed on the upper floors of the building. Despite their passing acquaintanceship, Knoop entered the over-sized cubicle tentatively. He looked cautiously about this new environment until his eyes landed on Haines, seated at a plain deal table on which lay the latter's slightly dog-eared, leather briefcase. The prisoner approached his lawyer with obvious diffidence, uncertain whether, under the circumstances, to offer his hand.

"Hello, Mr. Haines," he said. "Thank you for coming by. I confess to being greatly embarrassed by all this. And," he added, "I hope you'll agree to help me."

Haines tried his best to put Knoop at ease. He clasped his hand firmly and projected as much empathy as he could muster. "It's all right, son," he said amiably. "We've just come to a rough stretch in the road. We'll get by it soon enough."

"It all seems so tawdry," Knoop lamented. "It didn't happen the way they're trying to make it sound. We didn't set out to kill Frank. I'm devastated over that. And nobody tried to rob him either. We were all friends. We'd spent most of the day together...."

Haines waved his hands in the universally recognized stop signal. "Tell you what, son," he said. "There's a whole lot of scuttlebutt out there; mostly rumor and misinformation, I expect. Let me tell you, first, what's on the street, and then you can tell me what's accurate. O.K.?"

"Okay," said Knoop. "Go ahead."

"All right, then," Haines began. "What people are saying is that the five of you—that's you, Clyde Starry, Bob Ellicker, Charlie Heitman and Favorite—had all spent most of Sunday afternoon and evening at this bootleg place up on the riverbank. Not just the five of you, but a whole lot of other young chaps as well. And I'm sure there was considerable drinking and gambling going on. That'd be beer and whiskey, and poker and dice. Am I right so far?"

"Yes. There were quite a few of us there," came the response. "And yes, we were all drinking and most of us were gambling."

"This would have been at the big clubhouse? The one Ed Favorite operates?"

"Right. It's actually a corporation that owns it. The name's the Miami Club. Ed Favorite—we call him 'Pony'—he runs it."

"This Ed Favorite, Pony, you say, he any relation to Frank?" asked Haines.

Knoop nodded as he answered. "I think they're cousins."

"If I understand it right, the five of you were the last ones to leave the club that night—that is, except for Ed Favorite—and that you all left at about the same time and started to walk back toward town together…"

"More or less together," Knoop interjected. "We were kinda strung out. I'd left last and caught up with Starry and Heitman. Then when they stopped to take a leak against the ticket house, I went on and caught up with Ellicker and Favorite."

"And then, the story goes, you and Favorite got into an argument over some damn thing or other. Upshot of it is, you're supposed to have hit him over the head with a bottle, and busted both his head and the bottle…."

Slicker Knoop tried to interrupt Haines' narrative, but the lawyer cut him off. "I said that's what's supposed to have happened. Trouble with that story is that I challenged the prosecutor, Frank Goodrich, to go up there this afternoon and show me all the broken glass that should've been there. There wasn't any. No bottle. Nothing. We took the sheriff along too. He hadn't been there before either, so today's trip was part of his official investigation.

"What all that means is, their bottle theory just went out the window. So if they're going to try to show that you brained him with some kind of weapon, they'll have to come up with something else."

Slicker Knoop paid close attention to his counsel, processing the information provided. In a trice his earlier volubility changed to reticence. "There wasn't anything else," he protested.

"You can bet they're going to try to put some kind of instrument in your hand," Haines continued. "It's their whole case. A blackjack, a billy-club, maybe a piece of pipe? Was there anything like that?" he asked.

"No sir. Nothing like that."

"Then I guess you can assure me that you didn't hit him on top of the head with any kind of weapon. Am I correct?" Haines demanded.

"Yes sir."

"Sounds to me like he must have hit his head on the cement highway. That's where he was, wasn't it? Near the highway?"

"Yes sir."

"Tell me what the argument was about?" probed Haines.

"Nothing much. We were all pretty drunk and Frank was kinda feisty. He'd lost some money in the card game, then some more at dice. I think he was just out of sorts. He seemed to be trying to pick a fight with me. He'd spent some time Saturday night with a girl from Piqua and wanted me to know all about it. Her name's Mamie Bergin. Everybody calls her 'Peerless Mame.' I'd dated her myself a coupla times and I guess Frank thought I'd laid some kind of claim to her. Anyway, he kept hinting he'd been real cozy with her Saturday night, like he thought I'd get all hot about it. When I told him I didn't care about Mame, he started to goad me.

"He kept insisting she was worth fighting for and if I wouldn't fight for her, I wasn't much of a man. Then, when I still didn't rise to the bait, he took off his coat and handed it to Ellicker. It finally became obvious we were going to have a fight, so I hit him with my fist and he fell down. He hadn't got back up when Heitman and Starry caught up with us, so we all tried to get him to his feet. We thought he'd just fallen asleep. Remember, he was pretty drunk. We all were.

"I recollect that Charlie Heitman was pretty sore at me. I thought I was gonna have to fight him too. Charlie's married to Frank's cousin Anna. She'd be Pony's sister. When we couldn't rouse Frank, Charlie told us to go on to town and send a taxi back for him. Said he'd stay with him. The rest of us, Starry, Ellicker and I, we came on into town, stopped by the restaurant for some soup. Then I went on home to bed."

"Did you call for a taxi?"

"I didn't, but I think somebody did."

"One more thing, Slicker," Haines pressed. "When you hit Frank Favorite with your fist, you didn't hit him on the top of his head, did you?"

"No sir, I didn't."

"That would have required an overhand blow, wouldn't it?"

"Yes sir."

"Where did you hit him? What part of his anatomy?"

"I think I hit his shoulder, or maybe his chest."

"You didn't hit him hard, did you?"

"No sir. I don't think he'd have fallen down if he hadn't been so drunk."

Bill Haines and Slicker Knoop spent some three hours together that evening, hashing and rehashing the events of the previous day. They kept at it until Haines was confident that they had it—both of them—well in hand. Then, after they were finished, Slicker Knoop told his attorney that his friend Clyde Starry, also facing charges for his own part in the affair, wanted to retain Haines to represent him as well.

After an hour's interview with Starry, Haines was satisfied that there was no possible or potential conflict of interest in his undertaking to represent each of the two co-defendants simultaneously, and he therefore agreed to do so.

Chapter Five

The following morning, at 10:30, the defendants were arraigned in Mayor Milton Dilts' court. Bill Haines appeared for Slicker Knoop and entered a plea of "Not Guilty" to a charge—surprisingly—of *manslaughter*. He also appeared for Clyde Starry and entered the same plea, on his behalf, to the charge of assault with intent to rob. Bob Ellicker and Charlie Heitman were charged with the same offense and entered similar pleas. Knoop's bond was set at $3000 and that of each of the other defendants was set at $1000. The bonds were required to insure that the defendants would appear in the same court at 9:00 A.M. Thursday for preliminary hearing. Slicker Knoop's uncle, Louis Knoop, the Miami County Surveyor, scrambled about most of the morning garnering the signatures of Slicker's grandfather, D.B. Knoop, and his uncle, Charlie Martin, on the surety bond necessary to procure his release. By noon, all of the defendants had posted their respective bonds and were released.

As soon as the arraignments were completed, the Coroner's Inquest resumed. This time Bill Haines participated as counsel for defendants Knoop and Starry. Only eight witnesses were called to testify, i.e. Clyde Starry, Charlie Heitman, Bob Ellicker, two physicians, an undertaker, a taxi driver and a Chris Sherman, who had passed by after the fight, spoken with Heitman, examined Favorite, concluded he

Troy Daily News, June 28, 1915

was simply drunk and agreed to call a taxi. There was no mention of a beer bottle and no one identified a weapon of any kind. The session was adjourned immediately after Sherman's testimony and no findings were issued.

THURSDAY'S PRELIMINARY HEARING was a brief affair. Bill Haines again appeared as counsel for defendants Knoop and Starry, and Asbury Kerr, an able attorney from nearby Tipp City, appeared on behalf of defendants Ellicker and Heitman. The prosecution was represented by Troy City Solicitor G.T. Thomas, County Prosecuting Attorney Frank Goodrich and, as if further representation were necessary, by Leonard Shipman, who had been privately retained by the victim's father, Daniel Favorite. Predictably, all of the defendants waived hearing and consented to be bound over to the Miami County Grand Jury. The bonds of Starry, Ellicker and Heitman were continued at $1000, but that of Slicker Knoop was increased from $3000 to $5000 because of the perception that the evidence against him might eventually result in an indictment for murder.

FUNERAL SERVICES FOR FRANK FAVORITE were conducted that same afternoon at his parents' residence on West Water Street. The attendance was one of the largest anyone could remember, with automobiles, carriages and other vehicles parked along the street for several blocks in every direction. At the time of her son's death, Mrs. Favorite had been in Denver, on her way home from a trip to the 1915 Panama Exposition presented that summer in San Francisco. The services had been delayed just long enough to allow her time to return to town. Mr. and Mrs. Favorite, along with their daughter, Frank's sister, Mary Rudy, were seated directly in front of the casket. Both father and daughter were so much overcome with shock and grief that they promptly and totally collapsed. Dan Favorite was so greatly affected that he had to be removed from the room and taken to the porch. The services were necessarily interrupted until Drs. Warren Coleman and W.R. Thompson, two of the same physicians who had tried to save his son's life three days earlier, could attend him. Mary Rudy revived and accompanied her mother to the cemetery. Dan Favorite remained on the porch. He was simply unable to go.

THE CORONER'S INQUEST, which had been adjourned again after the testimony of just eight witnesses, was reconvened and that proceeding bumbled along spasmodically throughout most of the summer. An additional twenty-six witnesses were called to testify, not only concerning their knowledge of the circumstances surrounding the death of Frank Favorite, but also as to their observations of his movements and activities during the last weekend of his life. The cumulative effect of their testimony yielded a fairly detailed account of his activities over that crucial time.

Because Frank Favorite couldn't have known it was to be his last two days on earth, he'd passed the time in much the same manner as he did any other weekend. Thirty-one years old and still unmarried, he was already considered to be a confirmed bachelor. Although he most certainly had a healthy interest in girls, it seemed unlikely that he would ever settle on any one of them in particular. He liked them all too well for that. Besides, he was perfectly happy living alone and not having to answer to anyone concerning his activities, his coming and goings. Life was fine just as it was.

Frank had made his home on a family-owned farm near Eldean, a crossroads town just three or four miles north of Troy. The morning of June 26, 1915 began in the usual way. Up at first light, he dressed quickly, fed the stock, filled the watering troughs and scraped together a cold and unpretentious breakfast for himself. That accomplished, he spent the rest of the morning making some overdue repairs to his farming equipment, his buildings and his fences. Then, because it was Saturday, he spruced himself up a bit, wolfed down a sandwich, hitched the black mare he'd bought just yesterday to his buggy, and made for town. Town, at least for present purposes, meant Piqua, another Miami river town yet another four miles upstream from Eldean.

On the way to Piqua, Frank picked up George Hart, a black liveryman and farmhand who had worked as a servant for the Favorite family, off and on, for some fifteen years. As the two men rode along together, Frank showed George an impressive wad of paper money.

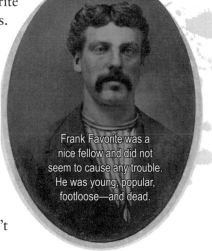

Frank Favorite was a nice fellow and did not seem to cause any trouble. He was young, popular, footloose—and dead.

"My dad settled with me for last year's crop," he said. "Plus, he gave me some money to buy that horse. Ain't she a beauty?"

Without waiting for an answer, he alluded again to the packet of bills, "Bought and paid for the mare yesterday and still got $179 left. You know I don't ever lock the house, but I was kinda skittish about all that cash, so I slept with it under the mattress last night." He put the wad back into his pocket and grinned. "That got the bed all scrunched up and made it lumpy. It wasn't real comfortable and I didn't sleep all that good. I may have to find a way to get rid of some of it, so I can sleep better tonight."

They went first to the Plock Saloon where Frank settled a long-standing account and then bought drinks for himself and for George Hart. They repeated the process at several other similar establishments and ended up at Behringer's Saloon, where Frank bought another couple of rounds. When George finally said he needed to go to Troy, Frank gave him forty-five cents. "That'll pay your fare on the traction car and buy you a drink when you get to Troy," he said. "It might turn out to be a dusty ride."

Frank's next trip was a short one. He left his rig at Behringer's and took a taxicab over to Market Street and called on one of his several girlfriends. Evalynn Waymire said she'd be glad to do the town with him, but four o'clock was much too early. She agreed to meet him at the Lorimer Bridge at eight o'clock that evening and Frank took the taxi back downtown, retrieved his buggy and continued on his round of the Piqua saloons.

By early evening, Frank had purchased a fifth of whiskey from Plock's and migrated the eight miles downriver to Troy. Here, in the very center of town, on the public square, he'd managed to link up with two more of his many girlfriends, Margaret Miller and Martha Van Hoven. The three of them traveled in Frank's buggy to the carnival grounds on the outskirts of the city. By the time they arrived there, the carnival was in full swing. They met another male friend there, an awkward-looking young man whose name was George Seeh, but he told the girls that everybody called him "Jack" and he'd be pleased if they would do so also. Seeh paired off with Margaret Miller and Frank attached himself to Martha Van Hoven. Together, they toured the carnival, dined on fish and chips, rode on the merry-go-round and took chances on raffles and other contests. Frank was free and easy with his money and paid for everybody's amusements. He was still working, he'd said, on getting a decent night's rest on a smooth mattress.

It was only a few minutes past ten when Frank raised his whiskey bottle high in the air and up-ended it to demonstrate its emptiness. "Well, Marty," he'd said to Martha Van Hoven. "Seems like you've run clear out of booze. And—since Troy is still a 'dry' town—I guess we'll have to run back to Piqua for another bottle." He grinned at her impishly. "While we're about it I can show you a couple of places you haven't seen before."

"No, I don't think you will," she retorted. "I'm not going anywhere with you. That black mare of yours is too fast and too frisky. Besides," she added, "you've had way too much to drink. You'll get us both killed."

Frank Favorite's only response to Martha's rebuff was to shrug his shoulders and go off in search of other companions. He'd never had much difficulty in that department and when Martha, in company again with Margaret Miller, next saw him, he was with Bob Ellicker and Tot Spain. The three friends had won a full set of dishes from one of the concession stands and were carefully loading the individual pieces into Frank's buggy.

"How wonderful!" she exclaimed. "You can drop them off at my house when you take me home tonight. It's just what I've been needing."

"Don't see how I can do that," Frank answered wryly. "I seem to remember you're kinda chary about riding with me this evening."

"We came to the carnival together," she pouted. "And you said if we won anything, I could have it."

"True enough," he replied. "But *we*—that is, you and me—we didn't win this set of dishes. Me and Bob and Tot, we won it together. And since there's six full place settings, that means there's two of everything for each of us."

If Frank had ever had anything going with Martha Van Hoven, it ended abruptly at that moment. She and Margaret moved away in a state of high dudgeon, found other companions and finally motored to Richmond, Indiana, where they all spent the night together. Frank, Bob Ellicker and Tot Spain gathered George Seeh off the street and the four of them drifted back up the road to Piqua where Frank bought them all a round of drinks at Plock's. Then, shortly after eleven o'clock, Frank set up another round, promised to return in an hour or so, and left the establishment. He had needs, he'd said, and they required immediate and urgent attention.

Frank Favorite's needs were carnal in nature and they were swiftly and efficiently accommodated by an unscheduled late-evening visit to the Piqua residence of Mamie Bergin. Mamie's natural bawdy charms, and her reputation, were such that she was often sought after by a great many of the randy young men who found themselves at liberty on a Saturday night. She herself was not only well aware of her reputation for promiscuity, she actually encouraged it. When one of the local rakes had lewdly referred to her as "Peerless Mame," she reveled in the compliment and wore the sobriquet proudly as though it were a badge of exceptional merit.

Mamie Bergin was a relatively recent acquaintance of Frank's. He had met her several months earlier while in company with Slicker Knoop and Clyde Starry. They had gotten to know one another soon thereafter and he had gotten in the habit of visiting her frequently and at odd hours. She had always made him feel welcome and this Saturday night was no exception.

Considerably more than the promised hour or so had elapsed before Frank returned to Plock's, but another round of drinks proved to be a sufficient act of contrition. That penance paid, and armed with a fresh supply of whiskey, the four friends commuted back to Troy again and spent the balance of the evening riding around the town in Frank's buggy. It was nearly two o'clock Sunday morning before their collective supply of booze and their separate stores of energy ran dry and they called it a day. Frank dropped his companions at their respective homes, drove back to Eldean and went directly to bed. He had apparently forgotten his commitment to meet Evalynn Waymire at the Lorimer Bridge. She had kept the appointment and waited for him for nearly an hour. She did not see or hear of him again until Monday, when she learned that he had died that morning.

FRANK FAVORITE HAD BEEN IN BED less than four hours when a heavy pounding at his front door roused him at six o'clock Sunday morning. It was George "Jack" Seeh, who had had no more sleep than Frank. He too was a farmer and this morning he had an injured calf and needed some antiseptic powders. Frank invited him in, put on a pot of coffee and some toast in the oven, and returned to his bedroom to dress. Jack Seeh found a skillet and fixed bacon and eggs while Frank made ready to face the day.

The two friends relived their respective Saturday night adventures over a leisurely breakfast. Frank admitted to having lost count of the number of drinks he'd had, but allowed as how it had all been worthwhile. He'd had a fine evening. He reflected a moment, then pushed himself away from the table. "Let's us just see how much fun I had," he said, and signaled Seeh to follow him into his bedroom. There, he pulled back the corner of his mattress and withdrew a shabby leather pocketbook, examined its contents and breathed a sigh of satisfied relief.

"Well, now," he remarked easily. "Looks like I didn't do so bad. I spent a little change at the carnival, bought a whole lot of whiskey and gave some money to a woman in Piqua—that was well spent, I can tell you—and I still got $147 left in that baby."

Seeh shook his head with disapproval. "Frank, you shouldn't carry that kind of money around. Or even keep it in the house. It ain't safe. Or smart, either, for that matter."

Frank pointed to a heavy hand-hewn club leaning against the bedstead. "It's safe enough here," he assured. "I got protection."

Seeh helped Frank feed his hogs and they agreed to go to Piqua that afternoon. "I'll come by here on the way," said Seeh. "I don't find you here, I'll see you in town."

Frank produced the needed antiseptic powders, provided a bit of unsolicited advice on their use, and Seeh returned to his neighboring farm to tend to his calf. The entire visit had lasted no more than an hour.

Shortly after eleven o'clock that same Sunday morning, at a time when Frank was merely sitting on his back step, a taxicab arrived. A plain, strongly built young man got out and introduced himself, "Morning sir. I'm Clifford Lease. Me and my wife live over by Covington. This here taxi-driver told me he bought a shepherd pup from you the other day, for a dollar, and said he thought you might sell me one too."

"I might," Frank drawled. "Depends."

"On what?" asked Lease.

"On what you want him for. And whether you're gonna care for him proper," replied Frank.

"Well, sir. That's fair enough," replied Lease. "What I'd like him for is my baby girl. She don't care much for dolls, but she loves dogs. I do, too, for that matter, so he'll get real good care."

"That's the case, I'll give him to you. I've just got two left. You and your girl can take one and I'll keep the other," Frank offered.

"That's mighty nice of you, Mister. Is there anything I can do for you?"

"Maybe," answered Frank. "You and that taxi going towards Piqua?"

"Matter of fact, we are," said Lease.

Frank stood up. "If you can wait while I change clothes, I'd like to ride along."

Minutes later, Frank and Clifford Lease were seated in the rear of the taxi, the puppy nuzzling comfortably between them. "Nice place you got back there," said Lease. "Looks like a good life."

"Would you like to work on a farm?" Frank asked.

"I would," came the answer quickly. "I do day labor now. It's a living, but I prefer farming."

"Tell you what," said Frank. "I'll hire you to work on my farm at $25 a month and you can have a house and all the firewood you need—that's till corn-shucking's over. After that I'll pay $15 for feeding over the winter."

"I'll do it," said Lease.

"One thing, though," cautioned Frank. "I want your wife to see the house before we make a deal. I'm gonna spend some time in Piqua, then I'll get a taxi and pick you and her up. We can go back to the farm and the two of you can look it over. If it suits you both, then we got a deal."

WHEN FRANK CALLED TO PICK UP CLIFFORD LEASE, his wife and little girl, it was late in the afternoon. It was also plain enough how he had spent the day. His face was flushed and his speech more than a little slurred. After the Leases had surveyed the house and expressed their satisfaction with it, Frank invited them to move in the following day.

"I can't be ready to move tomorrow," Lease rejoined. "I'll do that later in the week. Got some packing to do and some arrangements to make. But I will be here for work first thing in the morning."

"That's fine with me," said Frank, and the two men shook hands on their deal. The Leases climbed back into the waiting taxicab, homeward bound, and made to bid Frank goodbye. "Wait a minute," said Frank. "I think I'll just ride along with you and get off at the clubhouse."

"Ain't none of my affair, Mr. Favorite, but it seems to me you might better stay around home for now," counseled Lease deferentially.

Frank took no offense at Lease's veiled suggestion that he might have already had more to drink than was prudent. "No, no," he replied, crawling into the front seat of the taxi, beside the driver. "I'll be all right. It's lonesome here all by myself on a Sunday evening. I expect I could stand a little company."

Five minutes later, the taxicab came to a stop at the edge of the cement highway that followed the river and connected Troy, Eldean, Piqua and a number of other small towns that had sprung up along its course. They were just opposite a rude, iron, suspension-type footbridge that provided access across the now-abandoned Miami-Erie Canal to the clubhouse that was located on a narrow strip of land separating the canal and the riverbank. Pony Favorite's Miami Club was the largest and most popular of a series of small, privately owned clubhouses strung along the strip. The strip itself ran the entire distance between Troy, an officially "dry" town, and Piqua, eight miles to the north and officially "wet." The clubhouses were located between and beyond the corporate boundaries, of the two communities. They were actually situated within the rural area of Concord Township, which, by reason of the most recent local option election, was a dry township. And, while it was common knowledge that alcoholic beverages were routinely bought, sold and consumed at all of the riverbank clubs, the local law enforcement agencies caused them no trouble.

Frank Favorite gave the little Lease girl a dime, paid the cabdriver a dollar for the fare, and bid the family goodbye. "Don't worry about me," he assured Clifford Lease. "I'll see you at first light."

Chapter Six

There hadn't been much doing at the clubhouse when Frank arrived that Sunday afternoon. His cousin, Pony Favorite, was asleep on a mattress in the middle room and Pony's 10-year-old son, Russell, was in charge of the beer and liquor sales to the handful of young men who lounged about the several rooms. Although there had been a poker game earlier, a recess had been called and there were no card or dice games then in progress.

Frank took a chair at the poker table and drank a beer with Clyde Starry and John Arnold. Then he wandered out onto the porch overlooking the river, where he found Harry Morton and "Horseradish" Charlie Wright seated side by side on a swing. They were engaged in a desultory conversation and were watching a fond mallard hen lead her meager clutch into the water for a lazy afternoon swim. It had been a cold, damp spring and this was a typical late hatch. The ducklings still had the size and coloration of small, yellow tennis balls.

Horseradish Charlie Wright was a thick, heavyset man with a full, scraggly beard and an equally full head of untamed, salt and pepper hair. A jovial, eccentric man in his mid-forties, he was easily the oldest person in the clubhouse. He had come by his nickname because of his trade. Each day of the work-week, Monday through Friday, Charlie would wheel his pushcart downtown and set up shop in the sheltered alcove created by the wrought iron outdoor stairway alongside the old Joseph Brown Building on the so-called "Bee Hive" corner of the public square. Here, working in the open air and using the tools and supplies he had carried on his pushcart, he would grate, grind and chop horseradish roots into a tart, pungent horseradish sauce which he peddled, in paper containers, to passers-by. He sold very little of his product, however, to the locals, because of their awareness of the fact that Charlie's rather persistent nasal drippings frequently became part of the mix.

Despite his several unconventionalities, Horseradish Charlie was nonetheless good company. He invited Frank to join them on the wide porch swing and ordered another round of beer. The three men rocked back and forth, trading stories and working at their drinks.

Then, perhaps half an hour later, Bob Ellicker turned up and he and Frank became restless and the two of them decided to go on to Troy on Ellicker's motorcycle. They each bought a bottle of beer from Russell to sustain them on the trip.

Because they had no real destination, and because their principal objective was simply to waste a stretch of time until the club activities livened up, they went first to the corner of Main and Elm, near Otto Smith's grocery, then to the local poolrooms, Beehner's and Horace Smith's. They knocked around for a couple of hours, then stashed the motorcycle, caught a taxicab at Smith's poolroom and rode back up the cement highway to the clubhouse again, arriving at about seven o'clock. There were not yet very many people on hand, but Pony Favorite had finished his nap and was in the kitchen, cooking up a kettle of turtle soup. A poker game was in progress in the cardroom with Slicker Knoop in charge. Frank Favorite didn't play poker, but he staked Bob Ellicker to two dollars worth of chips, took a seat near the table, nursed his beer, and watched the game. The chips were a nickel apiece, twenty for a dollar, and there was no limit on the bets. Knoop dragged a single chip out of each pot for the house and the winners were assessed for the beer as necessary.

As the evening wore on the crowd increased and the poker players came and went. Slicker Knoop, Clyde Starry and Charlie Heitman remained in the game all evening. Bob Ellicker soon ran out of chips and relinquished his seat. A craps game began in the small outbuilding Clyde Starry had built earlier in the spring. Everyone in attendance, whether in a game or not, partook of Pony Favorite's turtle soup and drank ample quantities of beer and whiskey, most of which was served up by little Russell. After Ellicker withdrew from the poker game, he and Frank Favorite went outside and sat on yet another swing overlooking the river. They reminisced about the Great Flood which had occurred just two years earlier when the river overflowed its banks and inundated all the towns and farmlands within the watershed. Now that everything was back to normal, and the river flowed peacefully, well within its banks, it was hard to conceive of the turmoil and chaos that had reigned throughout the area such a short time ago.

The games wound down and the crowd began to leave shortly before eleven o'clock. Frank Favorite, Bob Ellicker, Clyde Starry and Charlie Heitman were among the last to leave. Slicker Knoop remained behind to settle up with Pony Favorite for the moneys taken in. Starry and Heitman left first, then Favorite and Ellicker followed. They had all intended to catch the southbound traction car at Stop 39, located alongside the cement highway near the ticket office for the county fairgrounds. Although Frank Favorite's home was located to the north, at Eldean, he had meant to accompany the others back to Troy for a bowl of soup at Harmon and Edmunds' restaurant. None of the men seemed to be in any hurry and they sauntered along leisurely towards the car stop, drinking from the beer bottles they carried with them. When Charlie Heitman and Clyde Starry stopped to relieve themselves against the ticket office, Frank Favorite and Bob Ellicker overtook them and passed on by. Then Slicker Knoop moved past them also and caught up with Favorite and Ellicker.

At that point, and for some reason never to be fully understood, things began to go sour. Slicker Knoop started to chafe Frank about his unwillingness to play poker. "Seems to me," he needled, "a man ought to want to engage in a little competitive action with his friends. Kinda match wits with one another—and with ole Lady Luck, too."

"I suppose," acknowledged Frank. "But I don't really much care to play. Like to watch sometimes, but don't care to play."

"Chicken, maybe?" demanded Slicker. "Maybe gambling's too much a man's calling for you, that it?"

"Oh, I guess I'm man enough, if that's what this is about," answered Frank tightly. Then, after a rankling pause, he took the offensive. "And, speaking of a man's calling, you'll be interested to know I've been seein' your old girlfriend lately. Actually, I 'spect she's my girlfriend now."

"Girlfriend?" exploded Slicker Knoop. "What the hell you talkin' about? I don't have a girlfriend."

"Not anymore you don't," replied Frank. "I do believe Peerless Mame belongs to me now."

"Peerless Mame! That who you've been pratin' about?" scoffed Slicker. "Who wants her? She ain't nothing but a ten-cent whore. Every man in the county's had her at least once. Take her, and welcome to the trash pile."

Slicker Knoop's last remark had its intended effect. Frank Favorite, already thoroughly inebriated from a hard day's drinking, rose up in umbrage. "Slicker, you crummy bastard! You can't talk that way about Mamie." He pulled off his jacket and tossed it to Bob Ellicker. "Take off your coat and let's settle this right here and now."

"Frank, I'm not gonna fight with you over that damn trollop. I just told you she ain't worth the trouble," Slicker's tone was pure condescension. "Put your jacket back on, go home and sleep it off."

Bob Ellicker forced Frank's coat between the two men in an attempt to create an uneasy truce. "Come on boys, let's go on to the restaurant and get something to eat. This is stupid."

But Frank wasn't having any of that either. His anger turned to rage, he thrust his jacket back onto Ellicker and fairly squawked at Slicker, "You don't think she's worth fighting for, do you? Well, goddamn it, I do. And I'm gonna do it now."

"Relax, Frank," Slicker disdained. "You're not in any kind of shape to fight me anyway. Go on home."

And before Frank Favorite knew anything further, Slicker struck him sharply and dropped him to the ground, where he lay unconscious and totally oblivious to the world and all that was in it. Starry and Heitman ran up to learn what the ruckus was about.

"Slicker, what the hell did you do that for?" demanded Heitman angrily. He hadn't heard the argument, but was nonetheless well satisfied that Frank had been sucker-punched.

Now Knoop seemed to lose control. "Back off, Heitman," he snarled. And when Heitman seemed about to press the matter, Slicker pointed to a seam in the road and taunted, "Cross that line, you son-of-a-bitch, and you'll get some of the same."

Before they came to blows, Clyde Starry and Bob Ellicker managed to get between them and restore order. As the would-be combatants parted, Heitman looked hard at Knoop. "That was a cheap trick, Slicker, and you shouldn't have done it. You're drunk now, but I'll talk to you in the morning."

TRY AS THEY MIGHT, THEY COULDN'T WAKE FRANK FAVORITE. His pupils were rolled upward and his breathing stertorous. The expressed consensus was that he was drunk, so they carried him away from the cement roadway, covered his chest with his jacket and his face with his straw boater-type hat. Heitman agreed to stay with him and the others said they'd go on to the restaurant and send for a taxi.

As it happened, they arrived at the restaurant, mentioned that there had been a fight, but neglected to call for a cab. Charlie Heitman, alone with his charge, finally enlisted help from Chris Sherman, a mutual friend who passed by on his way home from town. Sherman agreed to call a taxi as soon as he got to his house. When yet more time elapsed, Charlie despaired of help from any of them and set out for town, leaving Frank by the wayside. The taxicab sent by Chris Sherman passed him just as he reached the halfway mark.

Chapter Seven

Counsel for both the prosecution and the defense had been permitted to examine each of the thirty-four witnesses who testified at the Coroner's Inquest and it soon became obvious from their questions that each side had already evolved its game plan for the contest that would eventually follow.

County Prosecutor Frank Goodrich, together with attorney Leonard Shipman who had been privately retained by the Favorite family, inquired for the State. Their efforts were principally directed to the eliciting, from the various witnesses, of testimony which would support their claims that Frank Favorite had been flashing a considerable wad of money on the night of his death, that the motive of all the defendants had been to rob him, and that defendant Knoop had struck him an overhand blow to the head with a hard and lethal instrument of some kind or other. This latter consideration was crucial because the medical evidence, supplied by Drs. Thompson and Wright, was that the top of Favorite's skull had been shattered into three pieces by one or more downward strokes with a hard object. The prosecutors needed to jockey themselves into position to show that Slicker Knoop had used such a weapon.

Because Sheriff Barnett and his investigators had been unable to find any evidence of the mythical beer bottle that rumor held to have been broken over Favorite's head, that particular item was discarded as a possible weapon. Instead the questions dealt with other potentials. As a part of his examination, Clyde Starry was asked:

Q. Do you know what Slicker hit Favorite with?
A. I do not.
Q. Did you see anything in the road, any stick, club or anything?
A. Not a thing.
Q. What do you think he hit Favorite with?
A. If he hit him with anything, I think he hit him with his fist.

Robert Ellicker was the person closest to the action. He was questioned closely as to the events leading up to the fight and as to how much money Frank had had on his person. Included within a long series of questions were:

Q. Did Favorite have any money on him that you saw?
A. No sir. All I know is he said he had some winnings Saturday night.

And, as to a weapon:

Q. What did Slicker hit him with?
A. I don't know—I didn't see.
Q. You were standing right there.

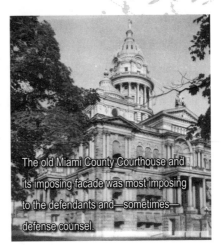
The old Miami County Courthouse and its imposing facade was most imposing to the defendants and—sometimes—defense counsel.

A. I didn't have any idea Slicker was going to hit him. He was standing there and just hit him. It was struck before I could see. I had my back to Slicker.

Q. Didn't you go between them at one time?

A. No sir.

Q. Did you tell anybody he pulled a blackjack out of his hip pocket and struck him with it?

A.No sir, I didn't tell that to anybody.

Q. Did you see Slicker have anything in his pocket that day?

A. No sir.

The only other person within the vicinity when the fatal blow was struck was Charlie Heitman and he said he had been too far behind to either hear the argument or see any part of whatever fight had occurred. Despite Heitman's denials of any real knowledge about the crucial issues, the coroner, along with the prosecutors, began to grasp at straws in their search for a possible weapon. Because of the nature of the proceedings, they were unhampered by the usual proscriptions against hearsay evidence. They were, quite literally, free to ask anybody anything provided only that the question had some scintilla of relevance to the subject of the inquiry. Troy Mayor Milt Dilts had presided over the initial proceeding in Mayor's Court and had heard Heitman's earlier statements. Now Dilts was called to the stand and was asked about his recollection of Heitman's prior testimony:

Q. Did Heitman see what he hit him with?

A. He said he did not see what he hit him with, had his right hand in his hip pocket, and struck down on him from his hip pocket.

Q. Did either one of those boys tell you they saw Forrest Knoop hit him over the head with a blackjack?

A. Never indicated what the weapon was.

An entire panoply of other persons, none of whom had any direct knowledge of the occurrence, were nonetheless questioned, however obliquely, concerning potential weapons. Johnnie Mouch had been involved in a conversation with a Mrs. Stanup the morning of Frank Favorite's death. He quoted her as having said, "It looks mighty bad. That little boy found the club—Russell—the one they hit him with; they throwed it in the canal."

And Anna Bayhour, with whom Pony Favorite and his two children, Bessie and Russell, boarded, was asked:

Q. What did Russell say to you about the affair?

A. I didn't see him Thursday.

Q. Didn't he say he found a club up there?

A. No, he didn't tell me anything like that.

Q. Did he tell anyone else that you know of?

A. No. I didn't hear anyone speak of a club.

Q. Did Ed Favorite ever tell you about Slicker carrying a blackjack in his pocket?

A. No, he never told me that.

Pony Favorite and his son Russell had slept at the clubhouse Sunday night. He was questioned about the phantom club:

Q. When did you bring that boy home?

A. Monday morning about seven o'clock.

Q. How did you come?

A. Walked down.

Q. Find anything along the road?

A. No sir.

Q. Did Russell pick up a club and show it to you, and throw it into the canal?

A. No sir.

Ten-year-old Russell had been well coached. He told the coroner that he had gotten out of bed early Sunday morning and followed his father to the clubhouse, then spent the entire day fishing in the river. He'd been in the clubhouse only long enough for meals and for a short nap in the afternoon. He had most certainly not served or delivered any beer or whiskey to anyone and he was wholly unaware of any card or dice games. He had gone to bed at the clubhouse at eight o'clock, slept the night there, and then accompanied his father back to town the next morning:

Q. What time was it Monday morning when you came home?

A. I got up at six o'clock and we started down the pike.

Q. How did you come down?

A. Walked down.

Q. Who was with you?

A. Father.

Q. Did you find anything along the road, Russell?

A. No sir.

Pony Favorite's son, "Little Russell", and his sister, Bessie. Although Russell was only 10, he was already working at the clubhouse.

Q. Did you pick up the club along the road?

A. I didn't find a club.

Q. Didn't you tell Mrs. Bayhour that you found a club up there?

A. No.

Q. Didn't she tell you that was probably the club they hit Frank Favorite with?

A. I didn't hear her.

Q. Did you pick up any club any place that Monday morning?

A. No sir.

Q. Did you ever tell anybody that you picked up a club?

A. No sir.

Albert Powers had not been involved, and had no knowledge whatever, concerning the events in question. He did offer that which the prosecutors deemed to be helpful insights into the character of their principal defendant:

Q. How long have you known Slicker Knoop?

A. I have known him for four or five years.

Q. What's Slicker's reputation for fighting?

A. I guess he will.

Q. Didn't he have a fight with you up in the Red Men's clubroom?

A. Yes sir.

Q. Didn't Slicker hit you over the head with a beer bottle that time?

A. Yes, Slicker hit me with a beer bottle. I guess you can see the mark on my face yet.

Q. Have you seen Slicker Knoop in any other fights?

A. Yes.

Q. Did he make any move to hit a fellow with something that he had in his hands at those times?

A. Yes, he tried to hit a fellow with a beer glass up in the clubroom.

Q. That is his general way of fighting, if he has anything in his hand?

A. That is the only way he will fight.

Eugene Hamman was a counter clerk at the Railroad Restaurant, colloquially known as the Triple R. He lived there too. Hamman had been at the clubhouse that Saturday afternoon and evening, bought a couple beers and played some poker. He had no knowledge of the homicide, but was asked about the defendant:

Q. You knew Slicker, didn't you?

A. Yes sir.

Q. Did you ever know of Slicker carrying a blackjack?

A. Not to my knowledge.

Q. You know it is said that he had one?

A. Heard it a lot of times.

Q. Ever see it?

A. No sir.

Ed Wilmington was a waiter at Harmon & Edmonds and had been behind the counter when Knoop, Starry and Ellicker came in that Sunday night:

Q. Now Ed, didn't Starry tell you, or tell in your hearing that he just saw a fellow blackjacked up on the cement road?

A. No, I heard John Landrey say he said something like that.

George Seeh, with whom Frank Favorite had spent most of Saturday night, was asked:

Q. Now, did you talk with any of these fellows after this thing occurred—Starry, Heitman, Ellicker or Knoop?

A. Heitman.

Q. Did he tell you how this thing happened?

A. He told me Slicker Knoop hit Favorite with a blackjack.

Q. When did he tell you that?

A. Tuesday night.

Fred Smith had watched the poker game for awhile that Sunday evening and was well acquainted with all the players. He knew that Slicker had owned a blackjack at one time:

Q. You said you saw the blackjack?

A. Yes sir.

Q. At the pool room?

A. Yes sir.

Q. How did you come to see it?

A. He displayed it.

Q. What kind of blackjack was it?

A. It was an ordinary billy.

Q. Did it have an open strap to put around his wrist and then buckle at one end?

A. Yes sir.

Q. The handle was made of black rubber, wasn't it?

A. I don't know.

Q. The handle was black?

A. The entire instrument was black.

Troy Police Officers A.W. Harris and John Sharits arrested Slicker Knoop early Monday morning. In the process, Harris had remarked, "Slicker, you hit that fellow a bitch of a lick." To which Knoop had replied, "Did I? I thought I did."

And then Harris had asked, "What did you hit him with, Slicker, a rock?"

John Sharits was questioned about the conversation:

Q. John, did Harris ask him what he hit him with?

A. He didn't answer at all.

Q. He didn't claim he hit him with his fist?

A. No, he simply didn't answer at all. He said he had not hit him with a stone.

Finally—and mercifully—the inquest ground tediously to a halt. On August 25th Doc Ullery issued his official finding:

After having heard the evidence, examined the body, and considered the facts and circumstances, I do find that the said deceased came to his death by a blow or blows on the top of his head inflicted by some blunt instrument in the hands of Forrest Knoop; that such blow or blows caused a depressing fracture of the skull and an injury to its coverings to such an extent that death ensued within a few hours after the assault.

Chapter Eight

"That's it?" Blanche Haines was incredulous. She had been kept abreast, by her husband, of the summer-long proceedings before the coroner and her interest had fed itself on his daily reports of the testimony. By that same route she had just learned of the verdict. Haines had recited it to her, nearly verbatim, as they sat together on the front porch of their home, sharing a pitcher of iced tea. It was late in the afternoon on the last Wednesday in August, and Haines had himself just seen the coroner's finding.

"That's all of it?" she demanded petulantly. "Doctor G.C. Ullery and four of the more 'distinguished' members of our local bar have just spent virtually the entire summer grilling more than forty witnesses in order to figure out that Frank Favorite died of a skull fracture? That's ridiculous!"

"Now, now, love, be fair," Haines cajoled. "We didn't grill more than forty witnesses—although I admit it did seem like it. Actually, there were only thirty-four of them and they weren't exactly grilled. They were simply questioned, appropriately and with civility."

"And about a great many things that had nothing whatever to do with how Mr. Favorite died," Blanche added.

"I acknowledge that much of what we heard, and inquired about, was seemingly irrelevant to the central issue," Haines conceded. "But we needed

to learn all that we could concerning the matter. Sometimes it happens that occurrences, observations, or even remarks which are not themselves precisely germane to an event will nonetheless lead us to other matters directly in point. Remember that a Coroner's Inquest is, by definition, an inquiry. It provides all of us with the opportunity to flush out whatever information is available without the evidentiary constraints we will later encounter in a courtroom setting."

"All right," she sighed. "I still say the verdict was stupid. It seems so meaningless."

"Well, yes and no," Haines responded thoughtfully. "Think about it a minute. The finding was really very carefully—and very efficiently—worded. To be fully understood it must be properly parsed."

"Oh?" She shot him a look of pure skepticism. "Parsed? How so?"

"Let's work through it, one step at a time," he began. "You've already pointed out that the verdict says that Frank Favorite died of a skull fracture. Please note that it also specifically articulates that the fracture was to the *top* of his head, that it was caused by one or more blows with a *blunt instrument*, and that the instrument was *in the hands* of Forrest Knoop. Each of those separate elements is significant, in and of itself, and the sum total equates to a charge of murder. Not manslaughter, which is the present charge, but murder."

"But you've always spoken as though it was a murder case," she remonstrated.

"That's true enough," answered Haines. "But the official charge, thus far, is that of manslaughter. That's bound to change. There's never been any doubt of that.

"But let's get back to the finding. I want to finish my analysis. The finding *presumes* the existence of a weapon. A fracture to the top of the head could only have been produced by a weapon. Is that fair?"

Blanche thought that one over for a moment. "Wasn't there some suggestion that he hit his head on the cement road when he fell?"

"Mmm-hmm," Haines conceded. "And that will necessarily be my defense when we get to trial. But you tell me, if you can, how a man can fall to the ground, from an erect position, and land on the *top* of his head. Now, if he had fallen out of one of Mr. Wright's aeroplanes, he just might have fractured the *top* of his head on the roadway, but I don't see how he could have done so otherwise."

"I hadn't thought of that," she mused.

"Well, you can bet that Doc Ullery and the prosecutors have. That's why the finding presumes a weapon—*a blunt instrument*, since the blow had to have been delivered with considerable force, and the medical testimony was that there was no break in the skin."

"And?"

"And they can't prove the existence of a weapon. God knows they've been poking around about it all summer, talking about rocks and clubs and blackjacks, but they haven't been able to develop any proof that Slicker—or any of the others—had any kind of weapon in possession that night. And that's crucial. No weapon, no conviction. That's the way I see it."

Blanche Haines spared a moment to digest all that her husband had said. Then she looked at him quizzically. "Then how did Mr. Favorite fracture the *top* of his head?"

"I don't know," answered Haines wryly. "That's the prosecution's problem. Maybe he hit his head on the roadway when he fell."

LATER THAT SAME EVENING, after supper, after Haines had returned from a twilight ride on his Colonel Pope and the girls were in bed, the subject came up again.

"So what comes of the coroner's verdict? What do they do with it?" she wanted to know.

"Nothing, really," Haines answered absently. "It's just one more piece of evidence for the grand jury to consider when it meets in October. Remember that these boys have all been bound over to the Common Pleas Court. They gave surety bonds to guarantee they'll appear in court to answer whatever charge the grand jury finds against them.

"Grand jury generally meets three times a year, considers those criminal cases that have arisen since their last session, hears whatever evidence the prosecutor cares to present, and makes its own charges—accusations actually—against people they believe to have committed criminal acts. If they make an accusation, it'll be called a 'true bill', an indictment. If they don't believe a crime was committed by the person charged, they'll return a 'no bill.' That means they've refused to indict and the defendant can go free. And the prosecutor is not going to let that happen if he can help it. So when this case comes up, you can bet Frank Goodrich will bring in all the same witnesses we've just seen, together with any other evidence he can find. One bit of new evidence will be the coroner and his verdict."

"And without the coroner's verdict?" Blanche inquired.

"Same answer. The verdict doesn't really add a damn thing to what they've already got. There'll be an indictment against all four. That'll follow just as surely as night, the day."

"For murder?"

"Against all four," Haines answered swiftly. "If one's guilty, they're probably all guilty. Slicker's the principal defendant, but if a jury finds against him they can also find the rest of them to have been *particeps criminis* and therefore equally guilty."

Blanche Haines digested her husband's remarks, then asked, "How do we know they'll still be around when the grand jury meets? October's a long way off. Might they not simply run away? Just disappear?"

"That's what the surety bonds are for," Haines answered glibly.

"A thousand dollars apiece, five thousand for Knoop? What's that against the chance of conviction? And maybe the electric chair?"

Bill Haines wrinkled his brow and smiled. "They were initially arraigned on charges of manslaughter and assault with intent to rob. Judge Jones thought the bonds were appropriate."

"Well, I don't," Blanche responded sternly. "If I were one of the defendants, I'd find some means to be somewhere far away from here long before October."

"That's the prosecutor's problem. I'm sure you know I can't advise them to run."

PERHAPS IT WAS BECAUSE OF HER PREGNANCY, but it seemed that Blanche's interest in the proceedings involving Frank Favorite and Slicker Knoop was very nearly obsessional. As they prepared for bed that evening she couldn't resist another rehash of the testimony described by her husband at the end of each day over the past weeks.

"By the way," she remarked casually, "You've not told me about this Piqua woman Mr. Favorite visited the night before he died. The one he and Mr. Knoop were arguing about?"

"What about her," asked Haines vacantly.

"Mamie something or other. Did you say *Peerless* Mame? Was that what they called her?"

"Mmm-hmm," Haines mumbled, unlacing his shoes. "That's what they called her."

"Was she exceptionally attractive?"

"I don't know, love. I've not laid eyes on her. She wasn't called to testify, you know." Now, Haines stole a sly look at his wife. "Why do you ask?"

"Well, I was only curious. If everyone considered her to be 'peerless,' I should imagine she must be very beautiful. And I wondered what you thought."

"Blanche," he said in a patronizing tone, "I haven't the slightest idea whether she is as beautiful as the Queen of Sheba or as ugly as Graymalkin—and I don't really give a damn. She wasn't called as a witness because everybody knew why Frank Favorite visited her that Saturday, and what surely transpired between them. It would doubtless have been indelicate to have called her.

"Besides," he added as he turned out the bedside lamp, "I doubt the name 'Peerless' has anything to do with her appearance."

"You do? Then, what?"

"I rather expect it's performance-related."

"I don't understand."

"Goodnight, Blanche." He turned on his side and was sound asleep in a moment.

Chapter Nine

The coroner's verdict, with all its implications and ramifications, was the subject of considerable scrutiny in yet another household that same evening.

Although the verdict had been issued and filed with the office of the county prosecutor, it had not been reported in the newspapers; however, attorney Leonard Shipman, in his capacity as a privately retained, special assistant to the prosecutor, had commissioned a deputy sheriff to deliver a copy of the verdict to his clients, Dan and Mary Favorite. He had sent along a short note, suggesting that they first review the document and then schedule an appointment to discuss the matter further.

And, at approximately the same time that Bill and Blanche Haines were having their dialogue concerning the significance of the coroner's findings, the Favorite family, less than a dozen blocks distant, were engaged in a similar exercise. Their perspectives, however, could not have been more different.

Dan Favorite was seated at the head of the maple table in the kitchen where his murdered son had taken his meals from early childhood until just a few years back when he had moved onto the farm at Eldean. Mary Favorite was seated at her accustomed place directly opposite her husband. At either side were their daughter Mary Rudy and her husband, Elta Rudy. The four of them were virtually huddled together about the table, in the manner of whipped puppies, distraught and utterly inconsolable in their pain. None of them had recovered from the initial shock and the deep-seated anguish occasioned by Frank's death, but each had been affected differently. Dan Favorite seemed mortally stricken. He was essentially disoriented and barely communicative. He was staring, sightless, at the darkness outside the window to his left, glancing only occasionally at whomever happened to be speaking, then quickly returning his attention to the dark vista beyond the windowpane. It would have been difficult to say how much he comprehended of their conversation.

Mary Favorite's grief had made her angry. More than anything else, she was resentful at what she perceived to be the law's delay in bringing her son's murderers to justice. "I just don't understand it," she railed at no one in particular. "Everybody in town knows that Slicker Knoop bludgeoned Frank to death with a bottle—or a club—or something or other, and that the rest of them were either in on it in the first place or they're covering it up now to protect Knoop. Either way, they're just as guilty as he is."

"I know, mother," agreed Mary Rudy evenly. "And I think that's what the coroner's verdict says."

Mary Favorite demurred crisply. "Not really," she snapped. Her daughter was not at all offended by the sharpness of the retort. She fully understood the source of her mother's rancor.

"The coroner simply says that Frank 'came to his death' by reason of a fractured skull—and that that injury was caused by one or more blows to the head with 'some blunt instrument in the hands of Forrest Knoop.'" Mary Favorite grimaced as she read the operative wording from the document supplied by Mr. Shipman.

"It does *not* say that he was intentionally beaten to death—murdered—for the few paltry dollars he had in his pocket. The way this 'verdict' thing is written, a body might almost conclude it was an accidental occurrence, rather than a brutal, deliberate killing."

Mary Rudy tried to defuse her mother's ire. "I'm sure that's what was intended, Ma. This paper is just written in legalese—it's lawyer-talk. Doc Ullery probably wrote what the lawyers told him to write, and nothing more."

"Maybe," conceded Mary Favorite, "but lawyers, just like everybody else, ought to say what they mean. This is just plain mealy-mouthed.

"What's more," she huffed, "you'll notice there's no mention of Starry, Ellicker or Heitman anywhere in the verdict. This whole thing looks more like a whitewash than a verdict."

"You're absolutely right, Mother Favorite," said Elta Rudy, "on all counts. This thing is no more a verdict than yesterday's newspaper. I don't think it even charges a crime against Knoop. There's no suggestion he struck Frank on purpose, let alone whether it was for the money, or in a fight, or whatever. And it sure doesn't say a word about the other three."

Mary Favorite had a high regard for her son-in-law's judgment and his generally stable common sense. "So what do we do about it?" she asked plainly.

"Nothing, I'd say," replied Rudy. "We can't change it, make it say what it ought to say. Besides, I don't think it means anything anyway. That paper and a nickel wouldn't buy you a cup of coffee anywhere in town. We didn't write it and we don't have to like it, but I don't think it amounts to a hill of beans anyway. Those guys have already been charged and if I understand it right, the grand jury will probably indict all of them no matter what the coroner's verdict says."

"But Slicker's been charged only with manslaughter, and the others with simple assault," Mary Favorite complained.

Elta Rudy was ready for that one. "I think those are just preliminary charges. You know, just something to hold them with till they get it all sorted out. Everyone I've talked with expects the grand jury to charge all four of them with first degree murder."

"I should certainly hope so!" exclaimed Mary Favorite, somewhat mollified by her son-in-law's opinion.

Then, in a more subdued tone, she remarked, "I guess what really rankles me is the fact that none of this seems to have affected anyone except Frank, who's dead and buried, and us, his family; we're devastated. For everyone else, life seems to be going on as usual. The river clubs are still open, the beer and booze still run like water, and the gambling operations continue to flourish.

"I know, I know," she conceded before she could be interrupted. "Frank was a regular at the clubs. He drank their beer and their whiskey—far too much, I'm afraid, and he played in their card games. He was no angel. But he didn't do anything to deserve what happened to him either, and if it hadn't been for those damned clubs, he might still be alive.

"Most of all, it bothers me that Slicker Knoop and those other hoodlums are still walking the streets, free as birds, proud as peacocks, and spending their time at the clubs just like always. It's like nothing has really happened, nothing's changed."

"They're out on bond, Ma," Mary Rudy reminded. "Just till the trial."

"Bond?" snorted Mary Favorite. "Bond, indeed! Five thousand dollars for Slicker Knoop and a thousand apiece for the others. That's no kind of assurance of anything. They call them 'appearance bonds.' 'Disappearance' bonds might be closer to reality. The Knoop family would pay that in a heartbeat just to avoid a trial. You mark my words, none of those boys will be within five hundred miles of the courthouse when the trial's set to begin."

Elta Rudy nodded in agreement. "You're right about that. They'd be foolish to hang around these parts against the probability—or even the bare possibility—of a conviction."

Now Mary Rudy was concerned as well. "Shouldn't the prosecutor have thought of that? The likelihood they'll all simply vanish before the trial?"

"Probably," Rudy mused. Then, to Mary Favorite, "Mother Favorite, I think you said Mr. Shipman invited you to discuss this thing further, after you'd reviewed the coroner's verdict?"

"That was part of his message."

"I think you should arrange to see him as soon as possible and acquaint him with our concerns, all of them," said Elta Rudy. "He may have some answers—or maybe even some suggestions."

"I will," declared Mary Favorite resolutely. She looked at her husband as if for affirmation. "I'll do it first thing. Is that all right with you, Dan?"

For a long moment it seemed as though Dan Favorite had not heard the question, or even realized he had been spoken to. Then, slowly and reluctantly, he returned to them and answered softly, "Why, yes, Mary, I think that's what you should do."

ON TUESDAY, SEPTEMBER 7TH, the day after Labor Day, the same four people were ushered into the spacious conference room at Leonard Shipman's Main Street law office. The room was primly decorated and was essentially dominated by a massive table of solid oak, around which were arrayed no less than eight directors' chairs of matching white oak. Seated at the far end of the table, at its head, was Leonard Shipman. Middle-aged, with a full head of graying hair and chipmunk-like jowls, Shipman was a distinguished, somewhat pompous, yet nonetheless intimidating presence. A younger, somewhat larger man, with a round genial face and a subtly receding hairline, occupied the chair to Shipman's immediate right.

Leonard Shipman performed perfunctory introductions and invited his visitors to be seated. That much accomplished, he quickly took command of the interview and guided the discussion in accordance with what seemed a planned agenda. His manner was overly formal, almost stilted. He seemed to take refuge in his corporate counsel persona.

"Good afternoon, folks," he began. "I'm glad everyone could make it in today. I rather expect you all know the purpose of this meeting—and how it came about—but just let me take a minute to sum it up.

"I think everybody is aware that Mr. and Mrs. Favorite have retained my services in order to render such assistance as I might in the endeavor to bring their son's murderers to justice. And, in that regard, Mr. Goodrich, the county prosecutor, has accorded me every courtesy and has permitted me to participate fully in the proceedings directed to that end. We have just concluded nearly two months of testimony taken before the coroner and that officer has now entered his official findings.

"Perhaps a week or two ago, I provided Mr. and Mrs. Favorite with a copy of the coroner's verdict, invited them to review it and then to arrange an appointment so we could discuss it in all its ramifications. They have done exactly as I had asked and we did have a chance to discuss it last week, just Mrs. Favorite and I."

He looked meaningfully at Mary Favorite, then continued. "I must say she had some interesting observations to make, and she expressed a number of very significant concerns. Those concerns are quite valid and they have led to some exceptionally challenging questions.

"In attempting to properly respond to Mrs. Favorite's questions, I was constrained to point out to her that while my own practice is somewhat extensive, it is nonetheless principally devoted to the civil—as distinguished from the criminal—aspects of the law." Shipman drew himself up tightly, cleared his throat for effect, and continued. "I do, of course, handle a few criminal cases, and I am most certainly quite comfortable in all of the courtrooms of this state.

"Nevertheless," he acknowledged, "I must remind you that my experience in criminal cases is confined to the defense rather than the prosecutorial side of the bar."

Leonard Shipman seemed almost to grow in importance as he confessed, for all practical purposes, that he was in over his head and needed some first class assistance. His clients had asked questions and sought guidance concerning matters that neither he, nor the new and inexperienced prosecutor, Frank Goodrich, could readily address. Now, he surveyed the room as if to assure himself that he had everyone's attention, sat yet higher in his padded chair, and cleared his throat for the second time in as many sentences.

"And," he added with that degree of gravity which he deemed to be appropriate to the circumstance, "in view of the complex nature of the proceedings thus far, it has occurred to me that it might be helpful if we were to bring on board a lawyer whose expertise lies principally in the criminal side of the practice, someone who is intimately familiar with all the nuances, the ins and outs, so to speak, of the prosecutorial arts.

"In short, and with Mrs. Favorite's permission, I have engaged this gentleman, Mr. Alvah B. Campbell, whom I have already introduced, to assist Mr. Goodrich and myself in the prosecution of these four defendants. Mr. Goodrich has heartily endorsed that engagement and has promised that he will welcome Mr. Campbell's participation."

It was true that Shipman had introduced Campbell at the beginning of the session, but the introduction had been by name only. Now, he nodded deferentially to the amiable-looking, avuncular man seated to his right, and explained, "Mr. Campbell here was the county prosecutor back in '02. He served two terms. That would be four years. The remarkable thing is, that in all that time, he never lost a single case. Not one. No other prosecutor in the history of the county has made such a mark, and I seriously doubt that such an achievement will ever be accomplished again."

Alvah B. Campbell was only a few days shy of his thirty-ninth birthday. He had, indeed, enjoyed an exceptionally successful tenure as county prosecutor before crossing over to the defense side of the bar. There was nothing about him to summon an image of the vengeful, fire-breathing prosecutor he was reputed to have been. By contrast, he seemed a pleasant, comfortable man, with soft features and a friendly mien, very much like an overgrown teddy bear. Understanding that Shipman, by his remarks, had intended to pass the mantle of authority to him, he leaned forward, rested his forearms on the conference table, and took charge.

"I'm not that good," he deprecated easily. "No one is. I was very lucky for a period of four years. Thought I'd quit before my streak ran out.

"Enough about all that. First thing, I want all of you to know how terribly sorry I am about your son," he looked to Dan and Mary Favorite, then to Mary and Elta Rudy, "and your brother. It shouldn't have happened. But it did, and nothing we can say or do will ever change that. 'The moving finger writes....'" He let it go unfinished, and got down to business.

"I'm fairly well acquainted with what's happened thus far in the proceedings. I've read the newspaper accounts of the event itself, and the coroner's inquest; then, since Leonard asked me to become involved, I've examined the court papers and the actual transcripts of testimony. Finally, of course, I've discussed the case with Mr. Goodrich and with Mr. Shipman. Result is, I think I'm pretty much up to ground level."

Campbell directed his attention to Mary Favorite. "Leonard tells me that you've expressed some concerns about the way matters stand. Let's see if I can help. First and foremost, I think, is that you want to see these men convicted in a court of law for what they did to your son."

Mary Favorite nodded affirmatively, swallowed hard, and interjected,

"Yes, Mr. Campbell, I do. We all do." Her eyes took in her husband, who stared stoically at the wall at the far end of the room, and her daughter and son-in-law, as if to include them in the expression of her sentiments.

"I know—we know—that convicting those men won't bring Frank back, but we think we're entitled to simple justice. All of us, Frank included. We just want justice to be done. These men have done a terrible thing and they should pay the price for it."

And when the Rudys murmured their agreement, she added, "I know it's wrong for us to be asking for revenge, an eye for an eye, just to somehow get even with these men for what they did, but I don't really care. I can't stand the thought that they might get away with it, that having taken Frank's life, they might simply get on with their own lives with total impunity."

Alvah Campbell reached across the table and took Mary Favorite's hand in his own two paws. He spoke to her gently, "Mary—may I call you Mary? You need not apologize for your emotions. You speak of getting even, revenge, as though they were evil, unnatural concepts. That's wrong, entirely wrong. There is nothing wrong about your demanding vengeance. You're entitled to it. Society as a whole is entitled to it and must, if we are to survive as a civilization, demand it also. The principle of vengeance— call it retribution—is as old as the world itself. Even the bible admonishes us to forfeit an eye for an eye, a life for a life. So please, do not apologize for your natural desire for vengeance. And I do pledge, by all that is sacred, that I will do all that is in my power to secure for you that justice which is so rightfully due."

Campbell was silent until Mary Favorite returned his gaze and signaled her acquiescence. He gave her hand a final pat before releasing it and leaning back in his chair. "Leonard also tells me that you are concerned that the defendants are free on insufficient bail—that they might flee the jurisdiction and be unavailable for trial."

He looked to her for confirmation, and upon its receipt, he assured her, "I think we can solve that problem swiftly and directly. We shall have them all safely in jail by the end of the week. Is that all right?"

She nodded tentatively. "But how...?" she began to inquire.

"Never mind for now. There are ways," he assured. "And finally, I understand that you are distressed over the fact that these so-called river clubs are still operating, openly and notoriously, in spite of all that they represent and their patent illegality?"

"That too," Mary Favorite admitted. "I know Frank was a part of that scene, but if they hadn't been there, maybe he would still be alive. They're wrong, they're illegal and they're unrepentant. So, yes, I very much resent the fact that they continue to thrive and to thumb their noses at the law."

For all that he was more than twenty years her junior, Alvah Campbell smiled at Mary Favorite like a kindly, older uncle. "We may not solve that problem entirely," he consoled, "but I think we can make a difference."

Chapter Ten

No one in the county could have been more surprised than Slicker Knoop when he was re-arrested for the murder of Frank Favorite. Just before midnight on Tuesday, September the 14th, Town Constable Hi Bumbli and Police Officer Al Landrey appeared at the Burton residence, took Knoop into custody and placed him in the county jail.

"Get offa me, Bumbli," Knoop remonstrated just as the heavy iron gate slammed shut on the cellblock. "You can't just come in and drag me off to jail every time the mood strikes you. I've already been arrested on that charge and you damn well know it. I've been arraigned and I'm currently out on bail till the grand jury meets next month. There's no big mystery about that. The whole goddamn county knows it."

"That may be so," said the constable with an easy equanimity. "But I've got this here warrant, has your name on it, says I'm supposed to take your body, keep it warm, and have it before Squire McCurdy in the morning." Bumbli tested the key in lock, prepared to leave, and added, "I'm just doin' my job."

Bob Ellicker and Charlie Heitman were arrested that same evening and Clyde Starry was taken into custody early Wednesday morning. All four were arraigned before Squire Cyrus McCurdy on charges of murder in the first degree. They were thereupon remanded into the custody of the sheriff, without bail, to await the preliminary hearing which was set for Friday morning.

Alvah Campbell had been as good as his promises to the Favorite family. Not more than ten hours before Slicker Knoop's re-arrest, the operators of all five of the local river clubs were arrested on charges of bootlegging and selling liquor illegally. Then, upon arraignment before Mayor Dilts, with representatives of the State's Attorney General and the State Liquor Control Board in attendance, each of the operators entered a plea of guilty and agreed to pay a fine of $100 and court costs.

And, just for good measure, Edward Furrow, who sold only modest quantities of liquor out of the back of his wagon on Sundays and on other infrequent occasions, was arrested along with the club operators and fined the same amount.

Ed Favorite was the first of the defendants to enter a plea of guilty. He admitted having sold intoxicants during the period April 1 through August 1, 1915. He told the court that he managed the club for his brother and for two local lodges. Then, when City Solicitor G.T. Thomas pointed out that this was the very club the principals of the Favorite murder case had visited on the day of the killing, Assistant Attorney General C.R. Bell, of Columbus, insisted that the club should be abated as a public nuisance and all liquor and "wet goods" should be confiscated as contraband. Favorite said the club had not been open since July 28th and there was no liquor or wet goods on hand. He also agreed to pay his fine and costs in monthly installments of $7.50 and to refrain from further sales in the future.

BLANCHE HAINES' INQUIRIES OF HER HUSBAND mimicked those of his clients. "How can they do that?" she asked querulously. "They've already been arrested; they've been charged—bound over, I think you said—to the grand jury, and they've posted bail to secure their release until the next stage of the proceedings. Isn't that what you've explained to me?"

"Mmm-hmm," answered Bill Haines absently. He was rereading the newspaper accounts of the events of the past few days. Blanche had just been through the same articles and was trying to make sense out of what she had read.

"Then how can they do it all over again? Isn't there a thing called double jeopardy, or some such, that prevents them from re-enacting the whole process time and again?"

Bill Haines lowered his newspaper, adjusted his reading glasses so he could look over the top of them, and smiled at his wife. "Yes, love. There is a thing known as double jeopardy. It's a constitutional protection, a guarantee against prosecutorial harassment. It means that a person may not be twice placed in jeopardy for the same crime; however, the prohibition does not apply until—or unless—the defendant has been placed once in jeopardy."

Then, when Blanche began to protest, he interrupted with a single raised finger. He hadn't finished his answer. "And most significantly," he continued pedantically, "the courts have consistently held that jeopardy— the concept of having been in jeopardy—does not attach until the accused has actually been brought to trial. Trial, in fact, must actually have begun. It need not have been completed, but it must have at least started, if jeopardy is to attach."

Bill Haines waggled his raised finger in a plea for another moment's forbearance. "Your question really isn't too far off the mark. If Slicker Knoop and company had been brought to trial, that is, if trial had begun, a second charge arising out of the same offense could not be maintained because of the prohibition against double jeopardy. However, since no trial has been started, the defendants have not yet been placed 'once in jeopardy' and the protection does not apply. They can be *charged* a half dozen times, but they may be *tried* only once."

Blanche turned her attention back to her mending. "It just doesn't seem right, that's all," she minced.

"You're right there," he acknowledged. "It doesn't seem right. But it is. If the State—the prosecution, that is—had done it correctly the first time around, the defendants would have been properly charged in the first instance, and there would have been no reason for these second arrests. Messrs. Knoop and company would have been safely ensconced in the county hoosegow from the beginning, and we wouldn't be having this conversation."

"I'm afraid I still don't understand," she persisted. "You'll have to help me see it."

"All right," he agreed. "I'll try."

"In words of one syllable."

"Yes, dear," he conceded. Bill Haines had been a school teacher before he became a lawyer. He recognized his tendency to be didactic to the point that what he had intended as explanations often became lectures. "I'll try to do better."

Laying aside his newspaper and assuming a conversational tone, he took her through a short reprise of the more salient features of the case against the four defendants. A man had been killed, perhaps robbed, in the presence of his companions; the death had been caused by blunt trauma to the head; there had been an argument just before the trauma occurred.

"So," he continued, "what happens next?" Rubbing his hands together in conspiratorial fashion, he answered his own question. "Our local peace-keepers charge Knoop with manslaughter and let him out on $5000 bond; the other three are charged with assault and released for a thousand apiece. Think about it, Blanche, it's like a one-cent soap sale. Four thugs who are charged with murder one could have walked—or fled—for a sum total of $8000! You and I discussed that possibility a few weeks ago. But you'll remember that whatever crime they may have committed, they were never actually charged with murder—in any degree. There's the rub; the failure to actually charge them with murder is what made the whole thing possible. If they'd been charged with murder one in the first place, they wouldn't have been eligible for bail, and they'd have been in jail all this while awaiting grand jury action. Everyone just assumed that the grand jury would eventually indict for murder one, so nobody thought it might be necessary to charge them beforehand. I've been halfway expecting them all to jump bail before now—or, at least, before the grand jury meets next month. And don't think for one moment that Slicker Knoop—with his connections—couldn't have raised the entire amount in a twinkling."

"But they haven't fled," demurred Blanche.

"Haven't needed to," retorted Bill Haines. "Not yet, anyway. The prosecutors, along with the coroner, have dilly-dallied around all summer taking testimony from everyone and his brother. Testimony that could just as easily have been produced with the defendants safely behind bars. And while the coroner's verdict, carefully parsed—and we did that, you and I—essentially charges the elements of first degree murder, it did not result in a formal charge and no arrests were made. Net result was that the defendants could remain free on bond until the grand jury indicted them on murder charges."

"Then what's changed? How did it happen that they were arrested again?" Blanche reiterated her original question.

"What's changed, my love, is the *dramatis personae* for the prosecution. You'll have to remember that while Frank Goodrich is an experienced prosecutor, he's never handled a murder case. That's why they've involved Leonard Shipman—only Shipman hasn't been through a murder prosecution either. He's a good trial lawyer, but his experience is mostly limited to the civil side. What I'm thinking is that between the two of them, they just figured the defendants would hang around till the grand jury charged them properly; then, of course, they'd all come in like perfect gentlemen and surrender themselves to the sheriff.

"And, in all fairness, they might have done so. I'd have been surprised if it had worked out that way, but it might have."

"You still haven't told me what happened," Blanche persisted.

"I know," he replied. "I'm gettin' there. What happened is that someone, probably Shipman, involved Alvah Campbell and he recognized the very real risk that Messrs. Knoop and company would not be around for trial."

"Alvah Campbell?" asked Blanche Haines.

"Mmm-hmm," answered Haines. "Best prosecutor in the history of the county. Served two terms. Remember the DiUlio trial? Donato DiUlio, the Italian boy I defended back in '07?" And after she had nodded, "Well,

48 *Shards, Pellets & Knives, Oh My!*

Alvah Campbell was the prosecutor. He did a damn fine job in that case and got a conviction.

"Anyway, Campbell had sense enough to walk Mrs. Favorite, Frank's mother, over to Squire McCurdy's office and have her swear out an affidavit that the defendants had deliberately, and with premeditated malice, killed her son. Murder in the first degree. First time anyone has formally filed that charge and enough to hold the four of them without bond until the preliminary hearing."

"When's that?" she wanted to know.

"Nine o'clock tomorrow morning."

"And then they'll be released?"

"No, no, love. At this point, the preliminary hearing is nothing more than a charade. Only question is whether there exists probable cause to believe that murder has been done and that these four men did it. With the evidence that's already available, that's a shoo-in. Asbury Kerr and I will necessarily refuse to waive the defendants' right to preliminary hearing and consent that they be bound over to the grand jury. What will happen is that we will appear with our clients and require the prosecution to rehash all that we've heard before, together with whatever else they can come up with, specifically including the coroner's verdict, and the court will quite predictably find the existence of the requisite probable cause, bind the defendants to the grand jury on charges of murder in the first degree, and remand them to the custody of the sheriff. There will be no bond. The whole process is virtually automatic."

"Then there is no longer any risk of flight?"

"None whatever," came the response.

Blanche Haines considered all that her husband had said, signified that she understood it, and ventured, "It sounds to me as though your job of defending Slicker Knoop and this Starry person just became considerably more difficult."

"It has indeed," acknowledged Haines. "Alvah Campbell is a formidable adversary. It will be a severe challenge."

Later, as they were preparing for bed, Haines added a postscript to their earlier conversation. "Tell you something else Campbell has accomplished. He got the state authorities involved, the liquor control people and the attorney general, and they arrested all of the river club operators. Closed them all down last Tuesday—in a stroke. They'll probably sneak back open again, but he's made his point. I expect he did that at Mary Favorite's behest. She's been pretty upset about the clubs' continuing on all this time."

"But wasn't her son—Frank Favorite—a frequenter of the river clubs?"

"Yes, he was," answered Bill Haines deliberately. "And Mary Favorite acknowledges that fact. She actually deplores it. Says her son would be alive today were it not for the clubs and the traffic they attract. She wants them gone."

"And the club he'd just visited, before he was killed," Blanche persisted, "wasn't that one actually managed by someone named Favorite? A relative?"

"Mmm-hmm," came the reply. That's Ed Favorite. Everyone calls him Pony, don't ask me why. He and Frank were cousins."

"Cousins? Do you mean remote cousins? Shirttail cousins?"

"No, love," he answered. "I mean they were *first* cousins. Dan Favorite, Frank's father and Mary's husband, was the brother of Pony Favorite's father—John, I think his name was. That means that Dan and Mary are Pony Favorite's aunt and uncle, and their son Frank, the victim, was Pony's first cousin. Does that help?"

"Seems as though they're all inter-related somehow," she sniffed. "Isn't that Heitman fellow married to another Favorite?"

"Charlie Heitman is married to Pony Favorite's sister, Anna," he told her. "It's a small town, honey. There's lots of that going around."

Blanche wouldn't let it go. "I hadn't realized that this whole thing was something of a family matter. I suppose, then, that this Pony Favorite was actually a kind of ring-leader. It seems as if all of these people, miscreants actually, must have gathered about him; as though he were the center of all that's wicked and evil."

"Now Blanche," he reproved, "Don't start with that sort of nonsense. You don't know anything about any of this, least of all about Ed Favorite. He's not some sort of monster. He really isn't."

And when she seemed unconvinced, Bill Haines continued in a more thoughtful manner. "Actually, I think if you were to meet him under ordinary circumstances, you'd like him. He's an exceptionally handsome man, tall, strongly built, good facial bones. He's what you might call a man's man. And he does have a magnetism about him. People are just naturally attracted to him. He's a good, solid man; trying to raise a couple of kids. Ed and his brother Bill were employed at the wagon works for a lot of years. Lately he's worked as a cement contractor; I'm told he's pretty good at what he does. Then, by way of a part-time job, weekends mostly, he's run this river club for a couple of the local lodges. Sells some liquor. I know that's illegal in this township, but the officials don't really much care, unless someone complains. What he does do, is cook up some soup for the boys, make sure the games are run clean, and keep order. There's nothing intrinsically evil or nefarious about any of it. It gives these young fellows a place to hang about, play cards and stay out of real trouble."

"Till now," she reminded.

"Until now," he agreed. "But I don't really think any of this—this killing—is Pony's fault. It didn't happen on his premises, the clubhouse. It happened after closing. On the way home. Hell, Blanche, it could have happened on their way home from church."

"How many people, do you know, go home from church drunk," she asked sarcastically, "in the middle of the night?"

"All right," he admitted. "That's a *touché*. Perhaps I've overstated the case a bit. And I won't try to tell you that there isn't a bit of adventure in Ed Favorite either. But, all in all, he's not an evil man.

"Do you remember the Troy Belle?" he asked, in an apparent change of direction.

"The Troy Belle?" she mused. "You mean that old canal boat?"

"Wasn't really a canal boat," he answered. "It was a houseboat. An old carpenter, fellow named Herman, lived around the corner from the Favorites; he built it, had it hauled up to St. Marys Lake, and used it for a vacation home. That would have been fifteen, sixteen years ago. Well, it seemed like one summer was enough of that, so he sold it. And who do you suppose bought it? Ed Favorite and Billy Young. They were just a couple of kids then, early twenties, I'd guess, and I don't suppose they had to pay much for it because the Hermans had had about all of it they wanted. Anyway, Ed and Billy had it moved over to Dawson Lake, just above Lockington; figured to use it to go muskrat hunting. Then, after no more than a day or so, that operation wore out and they hauled the damn thing back to Troy, put it into the canal, and tied it off on the west bank up by the lock. That's just a stone's throw from where Pony's clubhouse is located now, and I'm sure you'll remember that that worn-out old houseboat soon became a popular place for drinking and card-playing. Actually, it was probably the first clubhouse of its sort in the area."

"I remember the boat, whatever it was, but I'd forgotten what happened to it. It's not

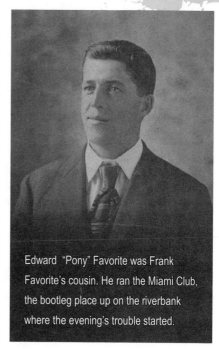

Edward "Pony" Favorite was Frank Favorite's cousin. He ran the Miami Club, the bootleg place up on the riverbank where the evening's trouble started.

still there, is it?" asked Blanche, searching her memory.

"No, it's gone now. Someone, likely a sore loser, shot a hole in it and it sank. The boys sold it where it lay on the bottom. It changed hands a few times, got raised and repaired, then it was used as a photographic studio for awhile. I think it's back up on Dawson Lake now.

"Point of that story is that Ed Favorite's always been something of an entrepreneur, and that's probably what recommended him to the lodges to run their clubhouse."

"Yes, I should certainly think so," she remarked stiffly. "Since he seems to have pioneered the local gambling industry, he is undoubtedly well-qualified to keep it going."

Recognizing that his own perceptions had been lost on his wife, Bill Haines opted to retire from the field of controversy. "Mmmm," he murmured as he turned off the lamp and closed his eyes.

IT VERY SOON BECAME APPARENT that Squire McCurdy's modest courtroom would be less than adequate to accommodate the needs of those in attendance at Friday's preliminary hearing. There were, after all, the Squire himself, his bailiff, clerk and court reporter, the four principal defendants, five lawyers, sixteen witnesses under subpoena, a generous handful of newspaper reporters, and the surprisingly large number of spectators who turned out for what promised to be a three-ring circus. Small clusters of the latter group began to mill about the courtroom and outside the building along the intersection of Main and Plum Streets—Courthouse Corner—nearly an hour before the session's 9 a.m. beginning time. In recognition of the difficulty, Squire McCurdy swiftly arranged to hold the proceedings at the local grange hall, a considerably more commodious facility, and all of the participants and observers adjourned to the new location in time for court to open at the scheduled hour.

Bill Haines had interviewed his clients at the jailhouse conference room earlier that morning in final preparation for the hearing. They should understand, he told them, that this would be the prosecutors' show. All of the evidence would be presented by the State of Ohio. For today, anyway, the defendants had nothing to prove. They would not call any witnesses, nor take the stand themselves; nor would they offer any evidence. They would simply attend, sit by his side at the counsel table, and remain mute. He might ask a question or two of the state's witnesses, as on cross-examination, but that would only be for the purpose of clarifying their testimony and not for any other purpose.

Today, he reiterated, would be the state's turn at bat, and all the

52 *Shards, Pellets & Knives, Oh My!*

prosecution had to do was to show the existence of probable cause to believe that a crime had been committed and that the defendants had committed it. That result, he said, was a foregone conclusion. The squire would hear the testimony, enter a finding of probable cause, and bind them over to the grand jury.

Their innings, he reminded, would come later—at trial.

THEN, JUST BEFORE THE DEPUTIES CAME to escort the prisoners to the impromptu grange hall courtroom, word came to Bill Haines that defendant Charles Heitman wanted to speak with him. It seemed that Heitman and his erstwhile attorney, Asbury Kerr, had had some sort of falling out— probably over the matter of attorney fees—and Kerr had withdrawn as his counsel. Would Mr. Haines undertake his defense as well as that of Knoop and Starry?

A brief conference ensued and Bill Haines was engaged as counsel for Charlie Heitman. Heitman reported that Bob Ellicker had had the same problem, but he had already retained Gilmer Thomas, who was the Troy City Solicitor, to represent him. It was probably a poor choice, considering the relative abilities of the lawyers involved, and everyone recognized it but Ellicker. It was also a clear conflict of interest for Thomas to accept the retainer. He had been acting, through the early stages, as assistant counsel for the state. Surprisingly, however, no one thought to object, and Thomas became a part of the defense team.

"No matter," remarked Haines affably. "I can work with Gil. We'll get along fine. Besides that, anything I can do for Knoop, Starry and Heitman has to redound to Ellicker's benefit—and vice-versa."

IN ALL ITS ESSENTIAL ELEMENTS, the preliminary hearing progressed exactly as predicted. The anticipated sixteen witnesses appeared and, in response to the anticipated questioning by Frank Goodrich, Leonard Shipman and Alvah Campbell, provided the anticipated testimony. Defense counsel Bill Haines, and to a limited extent, Gilmer Thomas, cross-examined some of the witnesses, solely for clarification Haines reminded, and offered no evidence of his own. And finally, at the end of the day, Squire McCurdy overruled the anticipated, but perfunctory, defense motions for dismissal, announced his expected finding of probable cause, and bound the four defendants to the grand jury.

If there was any subtle difference in the testimony taken in the prior proceedings and that taken on this occasion, it consisted only in the greater detail of the medical evidence provided by two of the three physicians who had seen and treated Frank Favorite just before he died of his injuries. Dr. W.R. Thompson was the first of the medical witnesses. He testified that he had been summoned to the home of Daniel Favorite on West Water Street at approximately 2:00 o'clock on Monday morning, June 28th. He had found Frank Favorite lying on a lounge, totally unconscious. Although he could find no wound, and very little blood, he diagnosed a serious injury to the skull. He immediately sent for Dr. T. M. Wright and caused Favorite to be removed to Dr. Warren Coleman's hospital. A thorough examination was conducted at that place and it was discovered that there had been an extensive fracture, three inches in length, with a depression of a sixteenth of an inch, and from that fracture ran a second fracture, perhaps an inch long, also depressed. He said it looked as though there had been two blows delivered. It was Dr. Thompson's opinion that the fractures had been produced by some sort of blunt instrument, such as a blackjack, and that they had caused the death of Mr. Favorite.

Dr. Wright testified that he had noted a "concussion of blood," which caused the decedent's head to appear to be elongated. He said he could feel a depression in the skull and that the depression was about a quarter-inch deep. After Favorite's head had been shaved, and the skull "lifted," an effusive jet of bright red blood shot out a foot and a half into the room. Dr. Wright opined that the fractures he observed had been caused by a heavy instrument and caused Favorite's death. And yes, he acknowledged the injuries could have been made with a blackjack.

Bill Haines had been especially attentive to the testimony of the two physicians. He insisted that they not only describe the fractures in every detail, but that they locate their precise situs as well. Had an autopsy been performed to confirm their findings? No, there had been no autopsy. "Why not?" Haines wanted to know. The doctors agreed that the cause of death had been obvious. Perhaps so, Haines acknowledged, but an autopsy might have been helpful to a description of the precise location, the precise contour and the precise angle of the fractures, might it not? Well, perhaps, it might have been of some assistance, the doctors allowed.

SEVENTEEN DAYS LATER, on October 4th, the grand jury convened in the capacious third floor courtroom of the new Miami County courthouse. Although it had been completed and placed in service more than a quarter century ago, in 1887, the imposing stone structure was still generally referred to as the "new" courthouse. It was, quite properly, the source of considerable civic pride and had been widely pronounced to be one of the most impressive such structures in the nation.

Fourteen shackled prisoners were led into the courtroom by Sheriff Joe Barnett and three of his deputies. Included within their number were the "Favorite" defendants, Slicker Knoop, Charlie Heitman, Clyde Starry and Bob Ellicker.

Judge Walter D. Jones opened the special session of court and presided over the selection of a panel of the fifteen men who would comprise the grand jury. That matter having been expeditiously accomplished, and the jurors sworn to do their duty, he directed the sheriff to return the prisoners to the jailhouse, yielded the floor to the prosecuting attorney, and excused himself. The proceedings of the grand jury were to be entirely secret, even from the judge. Only their report would be entered of record and made public.

The absence of newspaper coverage concerning the grand jury's proceedings was no great loss, however—at least as far as the Favorite defendants were concerned—because the evidence presented by the prosecutors was precisely the same as that previously adduced at the preliminary hearing before Squire McCurdy. The only difference was that this time there was no cross-examination, because defense counsel had not been permitted to attend the session.

LATE FRIDAY AFTERNOON, after five days of testimony and deliberation, the grand jury report, signed by its foreman Walter LeFevre, was filed with the court. Of the thirty-four cases which had been submitted on transcript or information, twenty-three resulted in "true bills" and eleven were ignored. Among the true bills found by the grand jury were indictments against the four Favorite defendants, each of whom was indicted for first degree murder. The manslaughter charges against the same four defendants were ignored.

The indictments charging the four defendants with the murder of Frank Favorite were phrased in that same stilted, arcane language that the law once deemed so necessary to the process. Perhaps it was the rhythm of the words, or the resonance with which they were pronounced, or their cadence, that seemed to impart a greater solemnity to the charges asserted against the malefactors than that which might have been achieved by the use of direct and ordinary English phraseology. Whatever the rationale, the perception that the use of an inordinate verbosity in the framing of the indictments lent a greater dignity to the offense charged seems to have originated in antiquity, and to have persevered to the present time.

The indictment against Knoop set forth that:

The Jurors of the Grand Jury of the State of Ohio, within and for the body of the County of Miami, impaneled, sworn and charged to inquire of crimes and offenses committed within said County of Miami, in the name and by authority of the State of Ohio, upon their oaths do find and present that Forrest Knoop, late of said county, on the 27th day of June, in the year of our Lord one thousand nine hundred and fifteen, with force and arms, in said County of Miami and State of Ohio, in and upon one Frank Favorite then and there being, unlawfully and forcibly did make an assault, with intent then and there forcibly and by violence, and by putting him, the said Frank Favorite, in fear, to take from the person and against the will of him, the said Frank Favorite, the money and personal property of great value of him, the said Frank Favorite, and thereby, then and there the said Frank Favorite to rob, and the money and personal property aforesaid to steal, take, and carry away; and that the said Forrest Knoop, then and there, did attempt unlawfully, forcibly, and by violence, and by putting the said Frank Favorite in fear, to take from the person and against the will of the said Frank Favorite the money and personal property of great value of him, the said Frank Favorite, with the intent thereby, then and there, the said Frank Favorite to rob, and the moneys and personal property aforesaid to take, steal and carry away; and the said Forrest Knoop with a certain black-jack or other blunt instrument, which he, the said Forrest Knoop, in his right hand then and there had and held, then and there unlawfully, purposely, and whilst engaged in said attempt to perpetrate a robbery in and upon the said Frank Favorite, as aforesaid, him, the said Frank Favorite, in and upon the left side of the head of him, and upon the back part of the head of him, the said Frank Favorite, then and there, did beat, bruise and strike, with the intent the said Frank Favorite unlawfully and purposely to kill and murder; and the said Forrest Knoop with the black-jack or other blunt instrument aforesaid, so as aforesaid, by him, the said Forrest Knoop then and there unlawfully, purposely, and while engaged in said attempt to perpetrate a robbery in and upon the said Frank Favorite as aforesaid, did him, the said Frank Favorite, beat, bruise and strike with intent him, the said Frank Favorite, unlawfully and purposely to kill and murder, thereby then and there giving to him, the said Frank Favorite, in and upon the left side of the head of him, and upon the back part of the head of him, the said Frank Favorite, one mortal wound of the length of four inches and of the depth of one-eighth of an inch, of which said mortal wound the said Frank Favorite then and there died. And so the jurors aforesaid, upon their oaths and affirmations aforesaid, do say, that the said Forrest Knoop him, the said Frank Favorite, in the manner and by the means aforesaid, unlawfully purposely, and in the attempt to perpetrate a robbery, did kill and murder, *contrary to the form of the statute in such case made and provided, and against the peace and dignity of the State of Ohio.*

For all its frills and foofarraw, the indictment effectively charged Knoop with felony-murder. In a case where a person's death results from the commission, or attempted commission of a felony, such as robbery, the charge converts, by operation of the so-called felony-murder rule, to one of murder in the first degree. The elements of premeditation, malice or intent to kill, ordinarily necessary to sustain a first degree charge, need not be proved.

And, as it happened, the indictments against the other three defendants were, except for the names, worded precisely the same. Each of the defendants was charged with striking the lethal blow.

The only real surprise in the grand jury report was the return of an indictment for perjury against Ed Favorite. A warrant was issued immediately and Favorite was in jail that same evening in time for supper.

Chapter Twelve

The following day was a Saturday and Bill Haines had closed his office at noon. He had come home to help Blanche with the children and to perform the vast accumulation of household chores that needed his attention. Blanche was nearing the end of her second trimester and found her own energies to be at a low ebb. Although the girls were old enough to be moderately helpful, they also required considerable attention, and Blanche wanted some assistance from her husband in tending to their needs and in just getting her through the week. Because they had both been thus occupied during the day, the opportunity to read the newspapers and to discuss the week's events did not present itself until the dinner dishes had been cleared and the children put to bed. It was shortly before their own bedtime when Blanche, seated in her favorite easy chair opposite her husband, found the *Troy Daily News* reportage of the grand jury's activities.

"What on earth is the meaning of this?" she inquired petulantly as she waved the front page article at her husband.

"The meaning of what?" asked Bill Haines innocently, although he had no doubt about what had caught her attention.

"You know perfectly well what I mean," she rejoined. "This article about the grand jury indictments. You've told me that they would unquestionably indict Slicker Knoop and his friends for murder, and

I see that that has happened, but what's this about charging Ed Favorite with perjury?"

Bill Haines snorted. "Yes, love. I knew that's what you meant. What that 'is' is a cheapjack stunt on the part of the prosecutor. He did that out of pure spite."

"I don't understand," she queried.

"Well, it seems that Mr. Goodrich was a bit miffed about Ed Favorite's testimony concerning the activities of his little boy. Russell's his name. It's pretty obvious that the boy spent most of that Sunday helping his dad at the clubhouse, serving beer and tending to business, but he said he was up there fishing all day. Then his dad backed him up under oath, and everybody knew it was a lie. Didn't matter a bit to anyone; had nothing to do with the killing. Ed Favorite was just trying to protect himself and his kid, but our Mr. Goodrich got his back up about it and made the grand jury indict him."

"Frank *made* the grand jury indict?" asked Blanche with surprise. "I thought the grand jury was fully independent. How could he make them do anything?"

Bill Haines snorted for the second time. "You need to understand, love, that the so-called independence of the grand jury is a myth. Pure myth. They're entirely under the control of the prosecutor. If he *recommends* an indictment, he'll get it."

"Really? Is that really true?"

"Hell, Blanche, any prosecutor worth his salt could get a grand jury to indict the Pope for heresy, if he really wanted to. These people have little or no concept of what they're supposed to be doing. They just sit there, listen to the witnesses, nod wisely at each nuance, and ultimately do just what the prosecutor tells them to do. The system has outlived its usefulness and ought to be abandoned. It will be one day," he reflected, "but not in our lifetime."

"So what comes of this thing with Ed Favorite?

"Nothing much," he assured her. "He was arrested, spent the night in jail and will have made bond by now. They'll never bring him to trial. They'll just let it pend for a while, then quietly dismiss it. I'm just disappointed in Frank Goodrich; I'd thought he was above that sort of pettiness."

Apparently satisfied on the score, Blanche Haines resumed her reading of the newspaper. Then, a moment later, she lowered it again and asked her husband, "What about the murder indictments? Were they pretty much what you had expected?"

Bill Haines flashed a crafty smile. "Well, yes and no. They were clearly all that I had expected. And, in spite of all the superfluous, obfuscatory language, they very plainly charge the defendants with felony murder. Which, of course, is exactly what we had expected. But," he paused for emphasis, "there was a surprise of sorts. A nugget, in fact."

"A nugget?" she inquired. "What kind of nugget? Explain it to me."

"Pure gold, my love, pure gold." He rose from his chair. "As an act of quintessential mercy to its readership, the newspaper has refrained from printing the painfully trite and repetitive language of the indictment, so you won't have seen it. But I have a copy in my briefcase and I want to show it to you." He left the room and promptly returned with two sheets of foolscap on which the language of the indictment against Slicker Knoop had been copied, laboriously and verbatim. He handed it to his wife and she worked at it for as much as five minutes before throwing it down in disgust.

"I can't read this," she complained. "It's so full of 'then and theres' and 'aforesaids' and other such tripe that its utterly unintelligible. I can't figure out what it says at all, let alone seek out a nugget. And I don't have either the energy or the inclination to look any further. You'll have to help me."

Haines laughed sympathetically. "You're quite right. It *is* virtually unintelligible. And it's certainly not worth your trouble trying to make sense of it. But let me show you my nugget." He took the papers from her, knelt beside her chair and pointed out the salient parts of the indictment. "See here," he said. "Where it says that 'the said Knoop' dahdah dahdah dahdah 'in and upon the left side of the head of him, and upon the back part of the head of him, the said Frank Favorite, then and there, did beat, bruise and strike, etc., etc.' See where I am?" he asked, pointing at the paper. "And, further down the page, is virtually the same language, 'upon the left side of the head' and 'upon the back part of the head....'"

Blanche followed her husband's finger along the page and protested querulously, "But I thought they said he'd been hit on top of his head? With an overhand blow? Isn't that what they've been saying all along?"

"Precisely, my love, precisely. That's what they've been saying all along. That's what the evidence has been. All of the evidence. The testimony of the so-called eyewitnesses and the testimony of the physicians. That testimony represented a strong refutation to our argument that Favorite actually fractured his skull on the cement highway when he fell."

"It's surely just a mistake, isn't it?" she wondered.

"Probably," conceded Haines. "It's probably just carelessness, but the indictment charges a lethal blow to the left side and back of the head, and that's what the State has to prove."

"But surely they can show it to be an inadvertent mistake, can't they?"

Haines nodded. "They can, but it's going to cause a lot of confusion and a lot of doubt. And remember, my dear, all I really need is a reasonable doubt."

"So, what will you do now? How do you use it? Your nugget, that is."

Bill Haines affected a benignant smile for her benefit and mused thoughtfully, "Well, I suppose we'll just have to dig him up and have another look at his skull."

Chapter Thirteen

On Monday morning, October 18th, just ten days after the grand jury had returned felony-murder indictments against the four defendants, they were escorted into Judge Jones' courtroom for arraignment. That procedure was rapidly getting to be old hat for the prosecution team as well as for the defendants. They had already been arraigned twice before, once in Mayor's Court on charges of manslaughter and assault and once before Squire McCurdy on Mary Favorite's affidavit charging first degree murder. This time they were called upon to answer to the grand jury's indictments for felony-murder.

Judge Jones began the session by appointing Bill Haines and Asbury Kerr as counsel for the defendants. That action seemed to have resolved any difficulties concerning the matter of attorney fees. As court-appointed counsel, at least a portion of their fees would be paid by the county. As a result of that order, Asbury Kerr was on board again as counsel for defendants Ellicker and Heitman. It was understood that Gilmer Thomas would remain in the case as privately retained counsel.

The next item of business was the entry of not guilty pleas on behalf of all four defendants, and upon acceptance of their pleas, the court announced that the four of them would be tried separately, beginning with Forrest Knoop. The specific starting dates would be set by subsequent order and after consultation with counsel.

The whole business, the arraignment, lasted less than ten minutes, after which time the defendants were remanded to custody. There would be no bail.

ALSO ARRAIGNED THAT MORNING was Ed Favorite. He appeared without counsel and pled not guilty to the perjury charge included within the grand

jury report. He was promptly released on nominal bail, with trial to be scheduled later.

As soon as his business at the arraignments was concluded, Bill Haines passed through the swinging door which connected the courtroom with the offices of Brooks Johnson, Clerk of the Common Pleas Court. He was virtually accompanied by Johnson, whose presence in the courtroom for arraignments had also been required, and who was returning to his office.

"I've got a present for you this morning, Brooks," Haines remarked cryptically. "What do you suppose it is?"

"Damned if I know, Bill," came the congenial response. "It's much too early for Christmas—or Thanksgiving either, for that matter. So, I'll have to suppose you're about to file something or other that'll cause me a whole lot of grief."

"No, no," Haines assured quickly. "It won't cause you any trouble. But I'd be willing to bet it'll cause a considerable commotion in a lot of other quarters. What I've got here is a motion to dig up poor Frank Favorite and have another look at his injuries."

"Seriously?" queried Johnson.

"Seriously," responded Haines. "We've got some important discrepancies in the evidence and the charges against my clients, and I don't know any other way to resolve them."

Johnson shook his head in mock bewilderment. "First time I've seen that kind of pleading," he said. "Let's take a look at it."

Bill Haines had already removed the three-page document from his worn and battered leather briefcase. He laid it out on the tall counter between the two men so that both could read it together.

In its essence, the motion recited that Forrest Knoop had been indicted by the grand jury for murder in the first degree; that the indictment charged that Knoop had struck the decedent with a blunt instrument upon the left and back side of the head; that, in order to protect himself, Knoop had shoved Favorite with his hand and that the latter, being drunk, lost his balance and fell heavily on the cement road, thereby causing his injuries; that the only examination ever made of the decedent's skull was "hurried and casual"; that the testimony of the examining physicians was uninformed, imprecise and inconsistent; and, finally, that a proper autopsy, including a thorough examination of the decedent's skull and neck, would exonerate all the defendants.

Then, upon the basis of those recitations, the motion requested the court to appoint a commission of competent and reputable physicians, that such commission be authorized to cause the disinterment of Frank Favorite's body and that a thorough examination of his injuries be conducted.

Brooks Johnson was considerably reserved in his reaction to the motion. In point of fact, he was at a total loss as to how, or whether, he should react at all. The prospect of exhuming a man who'd been buried in the earth nearly four months ago disturbed him.

"Do you anticipate the judge will grant your motion?" he asked equivocally.

"I'm sure he will," answered Haines affably. "How could he not do so? Who could object? After all, we all want to know the truth of the matter, and I see no other way to learn what that truth is. Do you?"

Johnson had no answer to that one. "I guess that'll be up to the judge," he evaded.

Chapter Fourteen

As it turned out, there were a great many objections to Bill Haines' proposal to exhume Frank Favorite's body for the purposes of a complete autopsy and, most specifically, an examination concerning the situs and course of the fractures to his skull.

The mere prospect of their son's exhumation horrified Dan and Mary Favorite. Bill Haines' plea to the court was an abomination, they considered, an inexpressible indecency. Most of all, it was a shameless and despicable invasion of their privacy and their grief. Frank Favorite's sister, Mary Rudy, was outraged at Haines' unfeeling temerity. And it helped not one whit that the plea had been made on behalf of Frank's murderer. The family and most of the community felt that Slicker Knoop had already inflicted quite enough pain; it was monstrous that he and his representatives now sought to compound their anguish in such an ignoble cause.

Judge Jones was also having difficulty with the prospect, though on a more intellectual level. He was fully sympathetic to the family's feelings, but he also knew that if there were a realistic chance that exhumation and re-examination would provide proper evidentiary support for the defendant's arguments, he was constrained to grant the motion, however distasteful it might be to do so. He had to balance the equities, so to speak, between the rights of the victims and the rights of the accused. It was a close call, and he avoided the decision for as long as he could. Maybe, he thought despairingly, the question would simply go away.

Finally, just before Christmas, the matter came on for a pre-trial conference with Judge Jones, the prosecution team of Frank Goodrich, Leonard Shipman and Alvah Campbell, and Messrs. Haines and Kerr for the defendant. As a first item of business, it was mutually agreed that Slicker Knoop would be tried to a jury beginning on Monday, January 24, 1916. Other technical matters pertaining to the manner of proceeding, the order of witnesses and the presentation of the evidence and arguments were discussed and either agreed upon by the participants or ordered by the court. Then, after all such matters had been disposed of, Judge Jones asked the attorneys to make their oral arguments on the defendants' motion for disinterment and examination.

Bill Haines and Asbury Kerr contended long and hard that it was crucial to their theory of defense to be able to show precisely where and how the decedent's skull had been fractured. They pointed out the obvious fact that the testimony of the doctors was wholly inconsistent with the plain language of the indictment, and that the plain language of the indictment was equally inconsistent with the testimony of the eyewitnesses to the event. It was essential, they argued, that the jury be placed in possession of all the facts, and particularly all those facts from which they could fairly determine whether the decedent's injuries were produced by an overhead blow or by contact with the highway upon the event of falling down.

Alvah Campbell argued the state's position that the original examination had been quite adequate, that the examining physicians' testimony was wholly consistent, and that if the evidence at trial differed in an entirely harmless particular from the charge contained in the indictment, the indictment itself could be amended at trial in order to conform to the evidence. And, Campbell added, if the court were to rule against exhumation the victim's family might be spared the indignity and anguish of seeing their son's cadaver resurrected, exposed to the light of day, and then further mutilated, for no good reason, only to be re-buried, in fragments, in the cold, winter ground.

Judge Jones heard both sides respectfully, agreed to render a decision promptly, and adjourned the session.

THE PRE-TRIAL CONFERENCE had occurred on Tuesday, December 21st. The following day all counsel received a copy of the anticipated order setting trial for January 24th. Then, one day later, came the order overruling, without explanation, the defendant's motion for exhumation and examination.

BILL HAINES DID NOT SURRENDER EASILY. Eight days later, on the last day of the year, he filed a similar application for disinterment and examination with the county coroner. This application set forth that it had been the coroner's duty to precisely determine, in the first instance, the cause of Frank Favorite's death and because he had failed to do so, the application ran, it was incumbent upon him to order the body to be exhumed and examined in order to rectify the omission. Much to everyone's surprise Drs. Wright and Coleman joined in this latest application by means of a separate document filed concurrently. Simple and straightforward, it recited that:

We, the undersigned physicians who made the examination of the body of said Frank Favorite join with the defendant Forrest Knoop and his attorneys in the request that this application be granted for the following reasons:

First: The interests of justice will be subserved and the truth and the whole truth will be revealed by such an examination.

Second: Because there is an uncertainty and difference of opinion as to the character, nature, extent and location of the wounds by the undersigned physicians who examined the body.

We therefore deem it fair to the State of Ohio and the defendant that you should grant the foregoing application and immediately order the disinterment of the body of Frank Favorite and cause to be held an autopsy thereon in accordance with said application.

BLANCHE HAINES WAS INCREDULOUS. "How on earth," she demanded over their New Year's Eve cocktails, "did you ever manage to induce the doctors to sign that thing?"

"It was easier than you might think, "Bill Haines replied blandly. "I appealed to their sense of fairness—and to their professional pride. 'Surely,' I told them, 'you're not worried that an autopsy might prove your findings to be in error.' And, thus challenged, they were virtually shamed into joining in the application in the interests of justice."

"You bullied them," she accused.

"I did no such thing," he rejoined with mock indignation. "I *persuaded* them."

"A distinction," she mused, "without a significant difference." A sip of her drink, an annoyed glance at her husband, and "I notice that Doc Thompson didn't join in the application along with his colleagues. Does that mean you were unable to persuade *him* to do so?"

Bill Haines returned his wife's glance. "Something like that," he conceded. "You just can't persuade all of the people all of the time."

They had declined the customary invitations to the traditional New Year's Eve receptions, ostensibly because of Blanche's maturing pregnancy, but actually because they preferred to spend the evening together in the uncomplicated quietude of their own home. And, as is usually the case, their observance of the holiday proved to be less a celebration of the new year than a final benediction of the old.

As they watched the Seth Thomas clock on the mantel tick off the final moments before midnight, they reminisced together about all that had occurred during the year. There had been much that was regrettable, much that was admirable, and a great deal that was merely trite. 1915 had been the year in which the wanton sinking of the British steamship *Lusitania* by a German U-boat, with enormous loss of life, set the stage for America's eventual entry into World War I. It had also been the year in which the wrongly convicted Leo Frank had been broken out of a Marietta, Georgia, jail and lynched by an out-of-control mob of rednecks and anti-Semites.

On the other hand it had been a year of unprecedented domestic prosperity, productivity and achievement. Earlier in the year the Victor Talking Machine Company had introduced a spring-operated phonograph called a Victrola, Alexander Graham Bell made the world's first transcontinental telephone call, and just three weeks ago the one-millionth Model T had rolled off Ford's Detroit assembly line.

Because Bill Haines was an enthusiastic sports fan, he considered the more memorable events of the year to include Jess Willard's 23-round victory over Jack Johnson for the world heavyweight boxing championship in April, Jerry Travers' capture of the U.S. Open golf tournament in June and, most especially, the 12th annual World Series in October. After losing the opener to the Philadelphia Phillies, the Boston Red Sox, led by center-fielder Tris Speaker, won the next four games to claim the championship. The first game had been close, but Boston's last batter, a twenty-year-old pitcher named George Herman Ruth, was unable to get a game-saving pinch-hit off Philadelphia's Grover Cleveland Alexander.

Also remarkable was the fact that during the regular season that year a 30-year-old Detroit player, Tyrus Raymond Cobb, had managed to steal 96 bases, a major league record that would stand for nearly fifty years.

And while Cornell University won the national college football championship with a perfect 9-0 record, the local sports fans identified more closely with the Troy High School eleven who, behind the hard running of a couple of young stalwarts, Perlema Sewell and Jake Nesbitt, had afforded their followers a great deal of excitement.

On balance, Bill and Blanche Haines reflected, 1915 had been a decent year. Their hopes for 1916 included a new baby within the first month, perhaps a boy, an avoidance of America's involvement in the escalating firestorm in Europe, continued prosperity and productivity at home—and perhaps, just for good measure, an acquittal for Slicker Knoop.

Chapter Fifteen

For Slicker Knoop—and for Bill Haines—the new year began pretty much as the old year had ended. The struggle for exhumation continued unabated and the defense attorney's efforts were persistently frustrated. On Friday, January 7th, Coroner Ullery rejected the defendant's request that he cause the body of Frank Favorite to be disinterred in order that he, the coroner, might inquire further about the decedent's injuries and cause of death. Although a strong argument had been made—and was supported by two of the treating physicians—the coroner nonetheless refused to grant the application because, according to his order, he could "find no authority" which might authorize him to do so.

Bill Haines was undaunted by the coroner's rebuff. On Monday the 10th, he went back to Judge Jones with a renewal of his earlier motion. This time, he recited all that had gone before, his previous motion to the court, his application to the coroner, the joinder in that application by the two physicians, and the irrational refusal by the coroner to properly do his job. Because there had never been a proper autopsy on the decedent's body, he insisted, there was both a continuing uncertainty and an irreconcilable difference of opinion as to the precise character, nature, extent, and location of the fractures which had produced Frank Favorite's death. On behalf of his client, the enterprising defense attorney offered to give an indemnity bond for the payment of all costs and expenses connected with the disinterment and the conduct of a proper autopsy by two or more disinterested physicians to be appointed by the court.

Two days later, on the 12th, Dan and Mary Favorite, who were, of course, strongly averse to the proposal to dig up and further mutilate their son's body, filed with the court their own formal written objection to the defendant's latest application for violation of the grave in which Frank Favorite had rested for more than half a year.

And, on the 15th, in an inexplicable turn-around, all three of the original physicians filed a statement describing their ministrations to the mortally wounded Frank Favorite and their findings. Their examinations had been thorough, they asserted, and there was practically no difference of opinion

among them as to the nature and extent of the decedent's injuries.

"How could they have done such a thing?" demanded Blanche Haines when her husband arrived home that same evening. Word of the physicians' surprising about-face had made the rounds that day and she had heard it at the local dry-goods store.

"What's that, Blanche?" Bill Haines asked innocuously. "What 'such a thing' are you referring to?"

"You know very well what I'm talking about. Don't play that game with me," she retorted. "Everyone's talking about the three musketeers, the doctors, having closed ranks and joining with the Favorites in opposing your application for exhumation. Aren't these the same doctors you persuaded to join in your application to the coroner? Didn't they certify that there was a difference of opinion among them?"

"Oh, that," Bill Haines remarked blandly. "Is that on the street already? Actually, only two of them changed color. Dr. Thompson wouldn't go along with us the first time. He, at least, has been consistent."

"Well, what about Drs. Wright and Coleman? They certainly haven't been very consistent have they?"

Bill Haines seemed strangely unperturbed over what his wife had considered a major setback to his efforts to establish a credible defense for his client. "No, love," he conceded languidly, "I guess they haven't been. People change their minds sometimes."

"Is that it?" she demanded. "People change their minds? Don't you care any more than that? What effect do you think this will have on your chances for a proper postmortem? Is there any real chance that Judge Jones will order disinterment now?"

"Gee," Bill Haines sighed, almost facetiously. "I hope not."

Blanche Haines looked at her husband quizzically. "What do you mean by that? Have you changed your mind now? Have you decided you don't want an autopsy after all?"

Bill Haines flashed her a cryptic smile. "Actually, love, I've never really wanted an autopsy."

"You what?" Blanche was scandalized. "You're not making any sense. You filed a motion with the court, argued it long and hard. Then, when the judge turned you down, you enlisted the help of two of the doctors, went back to the coroner, and insisted that he order an exhumation, and when he refused, you renewed your application to Judge Jones. And after all that, you now tell me you've never really wanted a postmortem? Am I missing something here?"

"Yes, love, you are," answered her husband patiently. "And I'm truly glad of it. It means my little ploy was not too obvious. If you haven't seen through my stratagem, I doubt if anyone else has either. You see, I had anticipated that no one would be especially eager to dig up poor Frank—and pick through his putrefying remains—and that there would be tremendous resistance to my importunities to do so. Understand, if you can, that it wouldn't have mattered all that much if the court *had* ordered an exhumation and a re-assessment of his injuries; I could have abided that, if necessary. But I really prefer the present scenario."

"How's that?" Blanche was skeptical. She couldn't believe he was serious.

"You need to remember, hon, that a defense attorney's most effective weapons are *confusion* and *inconsistency*. When I undertake to defend a client against a criminal charge, I don't really have to prove anything. That's the state's obligation; the prosecution has the burden of proving its version of the facts. All I have to do is to create a reasonable doubt as to the validity of their proofs. And the more doubts I can create, the better are my chances to secure an acquittal." Blanche had long understood that Bill Haines' early training as a schoolteacher would not allow him to overcome his tendencies to lecture.

"Look at what we have now," he continued. "There has always been a question about the so-called murder weapon. The prosecution has no idea what it was. There are reports out on the street that it was a beer bottle, a rock, an iron pipe, a blackjack, a billy-club...you name it, but the stories are all at odds with one another. No one can really say with any degree of certainty what it was that Slicker is supposed to have used to bash in Frank Favorite's head. And they can't produce any evidence as to what it really was—if it was anything. Now that's *confusion*.

"The next thing we have is the very salient fact that these three doctors, all of whom examined the body while it was still warm, still can't seem to agree about the nature and extent of the injuries—and even if they could agree, their testimony will necessarily be inconsistent, one with the other, and with the plain language of the indictment."

Bill Haines was fairly chortling. "Can you imagine the fun I'll have on cross-examination? The doctors are already on record as to their own uncertainty and differences of opinion—and as to the fact that they subsequently changed their minds about those very same issues. No matter what tack they take at trial, they simply cannot avoid becoming mired in the morass of their own inconsistencies. And that, my dear, will create yet more *confusion*—which will, in turn, further undermine the prosecution's case.

"Best of all," he added, "I can remind the jury that I'm the guy who tried as hard as he could to resolve the issue, but the state opposed me and the court overruled me. I did all that I could to help with their dilemma, but it wasn't enough. It's as though I've been the only one who wanted to learn the truth of the matter."

"Do you mean to tell me you've deliberately orchestrated this entire thing?"

"Perhaps it could be better said that I have encouraged events to unfold as they have," he allowed. He was almost smug with satisfaction. "But, remember, love, that it's a small advantage at best, and it's a long way to pay dirt."

Chapter Sixteen

During the last week of December, Clerk of Courts Brooks Johnson, in accordance with ancient tradition, had caused the names of thirty-six prospective jurors to be drawn from the large wooden jury wheel which resided within the inner recesses of his office. The persons whose names were thus selected were called veniremen and they were then summoned by the sheriff to appear for jury duty, as needed, during the next ensuing term of court. In this instance, all thirty-six of them were specifically directed to appear on Monday, January 24th, for trial of the cause entitled *The State of Ohio vs. Forrest Knoop*, No. 4598 on the docket. Then, in early January, it had occurred to Johnson that because of the widespread interest the case had engendered throughout the county, an initial panel of thirty-six might not be sufficient, and he therefore caused an additional ten names to be drawn from the wheel and summoned to court for the 24th, just in case they might be needed. As it happened, the clerk's apprehensions were more than justified because the panel, even thus enhanced, would prove to be woefully inadequate. Before noon on the first day of trial, it would prove necessary for him to select, and summon, an additional one hundred veniremen in order that the trial might proceed.

THAT FIRST DAY OF TRIAL HAD DAWNED much as any other January day in southwestern Ohio, bleak and stark, with colder temperatures and increasing cloudiness predicted. Better that, thought Bill Haines, than the unseasonably heavy rains and the dangerous flooding that had characterized the middle part of the continent these past several weeks. His own attire, carefully selected for the occasion, matched the ambient somber weather. His dark blue, three-piece suit had been freshly pressed and was relieved only by a high-collared, stiffly starched white shirt and his customary checkered bow-tie. It had become a tradition for him to dress in that fashion for all of his major court appearances. It was his way of communicating to the jury that he meant business, that his business with them was serious, and that he intended to command their full attention. It was also, in no small measure, the product of an inborn superstition.

Although the trial was not scheduled to begin until 9 a.m., the spectators' section was completely filled, all seats taken within moments after the wide, double doors of the courtroom were opened by the bailiff, Perry Moyer, at 8 a.m. By 8:30, the defense team of Bill Haines, as lead counsel, Asbury Kerr and Gilmer Thomas was assembled at the wide counsel table on the far side of the room. Their file jackets, briefs and notepads were neatly arrayed on the table in front of them. A fourth chair awaited the arrival of their client, Forrest Knoop. Across the room, nearer the jury box, was the prosecutors' counsel table. The prosecution team of Frank Goodrich, Leonard Shipman and Alvah Campbell was just then in process of setting up shop, arranging their materials and tools so as to best suit their own needs.

Moments later, at a nod from Bill Haines, Brooks Johnson escorted Eva Burton to the defense counsel table. Haines arose with alacrity, introduced her to the other members of his team, and drew yet another chair up to the table. The defendant's mother intended to sit at her son's elbow for the duration, however long that might prove to be.

There was a minor stir in the arena when Slicker Knoop was brought into the courtroom from the single door which led from the clerk's office. He was manacled to Chief Deputy Sheriff Mont Spillman, a great bear of a man. Spillman led his prisoner to the seat which had been reserved for him at the counsel table, released his shackles and seated him between his mother and lead counsel Bill Haines. Sheriff Joe Barnett and Deputy Spillman took up station by the rail, just behind the defendant.

Then, at the stroke of 9 a.m., Bailiff Perry Moyer commanded "All rise," and made way for Judge Jones, who swiftly entered through the clerk's door, mounted the dais and took his seat at the bench. Perry Moyer declared the Court of Common Pleas for Miami County, Ohio to be in session, invited all those persons having business with the court to "draw near and be heard," and granted the assemblage permission to be seated.

Judge Jones nodded to counsel, then addressed the spectators who thronged the gallery, aisleways and window seats. He welcomed their interest in the proceedings, and issued a stern, but tempered admonition that he would brook no outbursts or other displays of either pleasure or displeasure with the

testimony of the witnesses or the remarks of counsel. Then he announced that the defendant's motion for disinterment was overruled. Exceptions by defense counsel were duly noted, and Judge Jones directed the bailiff to bring in the jury.

Of the forty-six veniremen summoned for duty that morning, four had been excused prior to the time for trial; another two did not appear. A waning epidemic of the grippe had closed many of the manufactories and schoolrooms that winter and was believed to account for the no-shows. The remaining panel of forty veniremen was exhausted by 10:30. Eleven were excused because they separately acknowledged having formed an opinion concerning the guilt or innocence of the accused; another thirteen avowed their unwillingness to return a verdict that might entail the death penalty; three more would not return such a verdict based on circumstantial evidence; others were related to the accused or one or more of the material witnesses, and so on until Judge Jones called a recess and ordered the clerk to select and summon another panel of 100 veniremen for immediate service. Finally, just after noon on Tuesday, the second day of trial, twelve men had survived critical examinations by the court and by the attorneys, were pronounced acceptable to all, and were sworn by Brooks Johnson to "well and truly try, and a true deliverance make" of the issues presented between the State of Ohio and the defendant, Forrest Knoop. There were but five prospective jurors left out of the second venire of 100.

No one was terribly surprised that an entire day and a half was consumed in the process of selecting a jury, nor that it had been necessary to select and summon nearly 150 veniremen for the purpose. Although it was certainly true that considerably less time and personnel were necessary, as a rule, for civil cases, or even lesser felony cases, this case was neither. In the ordinary run-of-the-mill civil trial, there was no second venire; the bailiff simply went outside the courthouse and conscripted a likely-looking citizen or two. As soon as the parties had examined and accepted these volunteers, they were summarily pressed into service for the duration.

But this was no ordinary case. It involved a charge of first degree murder and its potential for the death penalty in a small rural community where such cases were exceptionally rare. The victim had been a well-liked young farmer, a friend to everyone, and the scion of a substantial businessman. The defendant was the bastard offspring of a locally prominent family, himself considered to be a charismatic, if not particularly admirable, young man-about-town, and the media (the local newspapers) had already pandered shamelessly to the widespread interest shown by virtually everyone in the county.

A final item of business was necessary before the noon recess. In the traditional pre-trial charge to the jury, Judge Jones explained the process that was about to begin and their role in the process. He admonished the jurors in severely somber terms all that would be expected of them. They would, from that moment forward, be segregated from the rest of the world, kept together in a body. They would, in fact, be housed within the 12' by 30' jury room just across the corridor from the courtroom. There was a single bathroom; cots and blankets would be provided; meals would be prepared by the jailhouse matron and served by the bailiff. (None of this regimen seemed particularly onerous. It was, after all, 1916. Women were not yet eligible for jury service, and the type of communal living arrangements described by the judge was more or less a customary incident to jury duty.) Judge Jones also instructed that the jurors were to avoid contact with outsiders, to forbid anyone from addressing them on the subject of the trial, to refrain from discussing it among themselves or from forming an opinion concerning the ultimate issues until all the evidence had been adduced, the arguments concluded, and the final charge delivered. Then, in a more genial manner, he assured them that they would not be put to any unnecessary hardship and that each would be permitted to telephone his respective family members to advise of his detention, provided only that all such communications would be under the surveillance of the bailiff.

"With those admonitions," he pronounced, "you are now excused for lunch. Please report back to the jury room at 1:30. The bailiff will then arrange for you to be taken by the sheriff and his deputies to the scene of the occurrence which is central to these proceedings. The purpose of that expedition is not to permit you to gather evidence for yourselves, but merely to acquaint you with the landscape, the location of things such as buildings, roadways, fences and the like, in order that you may better understand the evidence as it is presented in the courtroom. All of the lawyers in the case, and the defendant himself, are entitled to attend this jury view, but you may not speak with any of them. It may be that the bailiff, Mr. Perry, will be requested by one or more of the attorneys to direct your attention to different things, landmarks or structures, which they may deem to be significant. And if such be the case you should, of course, heed the bailiff's directions. If you have any questions concerning that which you are shown, those questions may be addressed to the bailiff—and to no one else."

Judge Jones rapped his gavel sharply. "Court's adjourned."

Walter D. Jones had been Judge of the Common Pleas Court for Miami County since before the turn of the new century. He had been appointed to the office by Governor Bushnell in 1899 to complete the unexpired term of his immediate predecessor, Judge Theodore Sullivan, who had himself been elevated to the Circuit Court of Appeals.

In January of 1916, he was in the sixtieth year of his life and the seventeenth year of his judgeship. He had already been re-elected four times by the voters and later this same year would stand unopposed for an unprecedented fifth term. In the entire history of the county, only two other jurists, Ebenezer Parsons and Calvin D. Wright, at ten years apiece, had occupied the position for significantly long periods of time. Judge Jones would ultimately serve as Common Pleas Judge until 1937, an incumbency far surpassing that of any other person to hold the office.

Above all else, Walter D. Jones was the consummate jurist. He was the son of Mathias H. Jones, one of the pre-eminent lawyers in southwestern Ohio. Matt Jones had been involved in many of the high-profile cases of his day and had been the lead prosecutor in the widely publicized murder trial of Elizabeth Jane Ragan back in 1856. He had practiced law in the county for more than sixty years.

Walter D. Jones had fallen in love with the law at an early age and the resultant affair had flourished and matured under his father's tutelage. The two men, father and son, had practiced together in partnership for more than twenty years before the governor's appointment of the younger Jones. That event had come at an opportune time for both. Matt Jones was well past his seventieth birthday and was already in process of winding down his practice. And, by reason of that circumstance, Walter found himself ready to accept the challenge of becoming a member of the judiciary. Both father and son were saddened to mark the end of their long-term partnership, but they were consoled by the fact that their professional association had been culminated by Walter's summons to the bench.

Judge Walter Jones—four times elected and more to come—was distinguished by both time and service. Fair and practical, he was the consummate jurist.

The judgeship of Walter D. Jones was distinguished not only by the length of its tenure, but by the quality of its jurisprudence. A learned and compassionate man, Judge Jones was considered to be fair-minded, practical, and approachable. He had swiftly won and long since enjoyed the respect and admiration of not only the lawyers who appeared before him but also the county personnel whose official duties and activities meshed with his own. He was, in sum, a highly regarded and most excellent judge of the Court of Common Pleas.

Had he been a judge of lower caliber, or lesser sensitivity, the decision concerning Bill Haines' earnest and persistent importunities to unearth the body of Frank Favorite would not have occasioned him the intellectual anguish that it did. He could not ignore the cogency of Haines' arguments that a trial was, after all, a search for the truth and that the very best answer to the questions concerning the mechanism of Frank Favorite's injuries could only be achieved by means of a postmortem examination of his skull under the auspices of a judicial officer. And he clearly recognized the elementary principle that a defendant in a criminal case, clothed in the protective presumption of innocence, is entitled to every opportunity to examine and produce any and all of the evidence available, or potentially available, in his own quest for the truth. On the other hand, Judge Jones was wholly unconvinced that there was the slightest chance that a postmortem examination would add anything new to the reports of the three examining physicians, and thus he considered that exhumation and re-examination would be nothing more than an exercise in futility. He also suspected that Bill Haines' fervent pleas were more in the nature of a tactical ploy than a genuine reconnaissance for truth. Finally, of course, he was not unmoved by the fervent pleas of the Favorite family, and that single, unarticulated consideration may have tipped the scales against the defendant's arguments. It had not been an easy decision, but Judge Jones believed it to have been correct.

THE JURY VIEW HAD BEEN AN OCCASION almost festive in nature. The individual jurors had initially followed the bailiff and the lawyers on what greatly resembled a guided tour of the local landscape, then attended carefully to the bailiff's invitations to take note of a myriad other points, places and things deemed to be of significance. Afterwards, when released from their scripted itinerary, they fairly crawled about the riverbank, the clubhouse, the canal and its suspension bridge, the fairgrounds and its ticket office, and the environs in general, like a plague of locusts in search of fresh vegetation. When that enterprise had run its course, the entire cast, the lawyers, the bailiff, the sheriff and his deputies, and all twelve jurors, posed solemnly for photographs commissioned by the local newspaper.

Slicker Knoop, who had attended the jury view manacled to Chief Deputy Sheriff Spillman, had remained at a discrete distance from the other participants. He declined Spillman's invitation to enter the clubhouse, sulked moodily, and finally insisted that he be returned to his jail cell to await the jury's return.

THE TWELVE MEMBERS OF THE JURY did not return to the courtroom with the same degree of alacrity with which they had appeared on the crime scene. Those who had been escorted to the scene by the bailiff and the sheriff's deputies, in official cruisers, were promptly returned by the officers in the same fashion. Unhappily there had not been a sufficient number of official vehicles to ferry all of the court personnel, lawyers, deputies and jurors to the same place at the same time and it had been determined that some of the jurors might be taken by taxicab. After their view had been completed, these several jurors simply opted to walk—saunter, rather—back to the courthouse. As it happened it was nearly four o'clock before the bailiff sent word to Judge Jones that the jury had finally re-assembled and was ready to proceed.

Under the circumstances, absolutely no one was surprised—least of all the lawyers—to learn that His Honor had no thought of releasing the jury for the day. Judge Jones was a firm believer in judicial economy and he had every intention that this trial would proceed both smoothly and efficiently. And because everyone in the county and its environs had expected that the trial would proceed directly upon the return of the jury, the spectators' gallery was already overflowing. Local residents and visitors alike had seized every available seat and occupied every other vacant space in the courtroom, the aisleways, free areas alongside the perimeter walls, the doorways, and even the window seats and wells. The local populace was well aware that the real trial was about to begin, that all that had gone before had been prologue. The selection, impaneling, swearing of the jury, the admonition by the court, and the view of the scene had simply

Troy Daily News, January 24, 1916.

prepared the field for the struggle which was now fairly joined and ready to commence.

No sooner had the members of the jury settled themselves in the walnut-paneled jury box on the right side of the courtroom than Judge Jones rapped his gavel for order, stared down the clamor from the gallery, and nodded a tacit signal in the direction of the prosecutors' table. It was time for opening statements, the first opportunity for each of the protagonists to address the jury, to describe the issues for trial, and to present their respective expectations as to what the evidence would show as it was unfolded to them from the testimony of the witnesses and from the exhibits admitted by the court. The prosecution would lead, and the defense would have its innings directly afterward.

Frank Goodrich consulted briefly with his colleagues, gathered his notes and papers, and rose to face the jury. "Good afternoon, gentlemen. It's already been a long day, so I'll be as brief as possible."

And he was. Unfortunately, however, it was not *possible* for him to be terribly brief because of the procedural requirement, then current, but now long since abandoned, of actually reading to the jury the indictment returned by the grand jury against the accused. Verbatim. In all its stilted, prolix, arcane and essentially unintelligible grandeur, the indictment was read by the prosecuting attorney in measured sonorous tones, and most wondrous of all was the fact that he held the rapt attention of every ear in the courtroom. There was no cough, whisper or shuffling of the feet to detract from the formal expression of the grand jury's charge against the four men accused of snuffing out the light of Frank Favorite's life.

Then, having completed the formal aspect of his address, Frank Goodrich told the jury precisely what it was the state expected the evidence to show.

"I'm sorry I had to put you through all that," he began, with reference to his having read the formal charge, "but it's one of those things we need to do so that you'll all be fully conversant with the issues presented to you for decision.

"Simply stated, we expect the evidence to show that on June 27th of last year, a Sunday, Forrest Knoop and his friend Clyde Starry went to one of the so-called river clubhouses located along the west bank of the Miami River just north of Troy. This particular clubhouse was located about two miles out of town and was operated by an Ed Favorite; you'll hear him referred to as Pony Favorite. Knoop and Starry arrived in the early morning, spent the entire day at the clubhouse and remained until late in the evening. While those two men were on the premises, they conducted

a poker game, with Knoop acting as the banker. The game continued throughout the day with various other patrons sitting in or dropping out at pleasure. Virtually everyone there was either playing cards, shooting dice, drinking, or all of the above.

"Frank Favorite, the victim in this case, just happens to have been a cousin of sorts to Pony Favorite. Frank arrived at the clubhouse in the late afternoon, had a few beers, then left with his friend Robert Ellicker on Ellicker's motorcycle. The two returned to the clubhouse shortly afterward, this time by taxicab. Later in the evening, Forrest Knoop, whom everyone knew as 'Slicker', attempted to induce Frank Favorite to join in the poker game. Favorite declined to participate, but lent his friend Ellicker enough money to play and spent the rest of the evening drinking and watching the game.

"The poker game ended near eleven o'clock and all of the patrons left except for Knoop, Starry, Frank Favorite, Pony Favorite, Ellicker and Charles Heitman. Then Knoop attempted to draw Frank into a dice game, but was again unsuccessful. After a short consultation between Knoop, Starry, Ellicker and Heitman, Frank Favorite left the clubhouse in company with Ellicker, Heitman and Starry. A few moments later Forrest Knoop left and caught up with the others at the county fairgrounds, near the south end of the fence, between the cement road and the D.& T. Traction line.

"Your attention, gentlemen of the jury, was called to that precise location by the bailiff during your visit to the environs of the crime this afternoon. It was on that exact spot that the defendant Slicker Knoop assaulted Frank Favorite, struck him one or more mortal blows to the head, and fled the scene. When he was found several hours later, Frank Favorite was wholly unconscious, lying flat on his back, with his hat over his face and his coat laid across his chest. He was swiftly removed to the home of his father, Dan Favorite, and examined by three of the best and most eminent physicians in the county, Drs. T. M. Wright, W. R. Thompson and Warren Coleman. He was ultimately removed to the Coleman hospital, where the three physicians operated on him. Their ministrations, however ably performed, were unequal to the occasion and Frank Favorite died shortly after eight o'clock Monday morning. He had never regained consciousness.

"Frank Favorite had been carrying a great deal of money when he visited the clubhouse that Sunday evening, and the defendants—Knoop, Starry, Ellicker and Heitman—were well aware of it. When he was found at the location shown you this afternoon, he had no money about him. His pocketbook, containing only a nickel, was discovered under his inert body.

"For whatever reason, presumably his money, Frank Favorite was assaulted by the defendant Forrest Knoop, and by reason of the injuries sustained thereby, he died just a few hours later. As you know from the indictment, the grand jury has charged all four men, Knoop, Starry, Ellicker and Heitman, with the murder of Frank Favorite. These men will be tried separately, each to a different jury. Because it was he who actually struck the fatal blows, the state has elected to try Slicker Knoop first. As a part of that first trial, we will present you with such compelling evidence as will virtually mandate your verdict of murder in the first degree."

Frank Goodrich had been standing directly in front of the jury box. Now that he had concluded his opening statement, he remained in place, looked into the eyes of each of the twelve men in the box as though to gauge the extent to which they had attended and comprehended his remarks. It was, in effect, an unspoken admonition to the jury that this was serious business and he expected them to do their duty. Apparently satisfied, he nodded his thanks for their attention and resumed his seat at the counsel table.

Chapter Eighteen

Bill Haines had projected an attitude of studied nonchalance throughout the entirety of Frank Goodrich's opening statement to the jury. After Goodrich had concluded his remarks, looked his admonition to the individual jurors, and resumed his seat at the prosecutors' counsel table, an overlong pause in the courtroom activities ensued. No one moved, no one spoke, and no sound was heard. The preternatural silence was not quite reverent, but most certainly sepulchral. Bill Haines had both fomented and encouraged the effect. It created a palpable hiatus in the course of the proceedings, and that was precisely what he had intended. Like the interruption of play between the visitors' innings and those of the home team, the pregnant pause between the opening statements of the contending parties, which he had created and nourished, signaled a change in the direction of the flow of the trial and tended to underscore the difference in the viewpoints of the contenders.

Then, just a calculated instant before Judge Jones could be expected to call upon him to proceed, Bill Haines swung lithely to his feet, formally acknowledged the court and opposing counsel, moved to the front and center of the jury box and began his own opening. His manner was deliberately homey, almost colloquial.

"Evening, gentlemen. We've been at this business since early this morning and we're already well past our usual quitting time. I think it's fair to say, we'd all like to call it a day and go home to dinner. But we just can't do that. The court has instructed us to complete our opening statements today so we can proceed to the evidence tomorrow. And I think that's appropriate. You've just heard Mr. Goodrich tell you what he expects the evidence will show, and I don't want you to go to bed with his expectations—unwarranted and unanswered—still fresh in your minds."

"I listened closely to all that Mr. Goodrich promised, and I'd have to acknowledge that if he can actually prove all that he's promised to prove, you'll have no choice other than to find Mr. Knoop guilty as charged. But there, of course, is the rub. As it happens, the facts in this case will simply not support Mr. Goodrich's expectations—the promises he just this moment made to you.

"As you listen to the evidence over the next few days, I want you to regard Mr. Goodrich's promises in the same way you'd consider any other promises. It's as though he has presented you with his own personal promissory note, except that instead of his promising to pay the note in cash, he has promised to make good on his note by proving the occurrence of a sinister chain of events, conceived out of malevolent intentions and resulting in the wrongful killing of one Frank Favorite. When this trial has ended, and the evidence is all in, I'll remind you to call Mr. Goodrich's note, to see whether he has made good on his promises. If, at that time, you find that he has defaulted, it will be your sworn duty to acquit the defendant and to set him free.

"Now, don't misunderstand. Much of what Mr. Goodrich has promised to show is undisputed. We can all agree that most of the events described by the prosecution actually happened just as Mr. Goodrich says they did. In point of fact, the defense will not only present its own evidence concerning these events, but we'll elaborate on that produced by the prosecution. That's so you'll have the entire story and will be better able to sort the wheat from the chaff. Rest assured, there's considerably more chaff in this case than there is wheat. The chaff we can agree upon, but it's the wheat that needs to be examined. Mr. Goodrich will attempt to pay his note with chaff; but that's not legal tender in this courtroom and it's wholly unacceptable. Mr. Goodrich can produce no wheat—or any other proper tender—and he must necessarily default on those very promises we just heard him make."

Bill Haines had been leaning toward, if not actually into, the jury box as he blithely mixed his several metaphors, promissory notes, wheat, chaff and legal tender. Now, as if he had suddenly become aware that he might be perceived to be intruding into their space, he consciously withdrew himself from the jurors, pulled himself to his full height of five and a half feet, and retreated to the counsel table reserved for the defense team. It was, of course, a calculated theatrical artifice, but it had the desired effect. He had the full attention of everyone in the courtroom as he contrived to examine his notes preparatory to making his own exposition of what he expected the evidence to show.

Apparently satisfied that he was ready to continue, Bill Haines returned to the center of the courtroom and faced the jury.

"By the time the evidence is all in, gentlemen, you will know everything relevant to this case that happened on Sunday, the 27th of June, 1915. You will come by that knowledge by the testimony of all the people involved, whether those persons were involved directly or only peripherally.

"You will learn, from the testimony, that sometime between nine and ten o'clock that Sunday morning, Forrest Knoop and his good friend Clyde Starry went to Pony Favorite's clubhouse. They invited no one to accompany them, but went alone, just the two of them. Although Pony acted as proprietor of the clubhouse, it was actually better known as the rendezvous of a social club known colloquially as the 'Eagles.' All the young men of the club were accustomed to visiting the clubhouse of an evening, especially Sunday evenings, in order to play cards, shoot craps, and drink beer and whiskey.

"Along about seven o'clock on this particular evening the principal players began to arrive. The first of these arrivals was Charlie Heitman. Charlie is married to Pony Favorite's sister Anna, and both she and Pony are cousins of the deceased, Frank Favorite. Heitman had spent most of the day at a picnic at a location generally referred to as 'Davis's Place.' Frank Favorite and another of his friends, Bob Ellicker, arrived just moments after Heitman. They had hooked up that afternoon near Smith's Grocery at the corner of Main and Elm Streets, went from there to Beehner's poolroom, and then to Horace Smith's place to catch a taxi to the clubhouse. When they arrived, there were only a few people there, the two of them, Knoop, Starry, Heitman, Pony Favorite and Pony's little boy, Russell. A small crowd had been there earlier, and another small group of people wandered in and out during the evening. Some of these visitors played cards, others helped themselves to the turtle soup prepared by Pony, and yet others gathered on the porch overlooking the river, enjoying the view, telling stories and drinking beer.

"The crowd began to thin out sometime between nine and ten o'clock

and the card game ended shortly before eleven o'clock. A final beer or two later, our principals began to leave. Starry and Heitman went first, followed directly by Ellicker and Favorite. None of them were in a hurry and they simply sauntered down the pike towards Troy in leisurely fashion. Knoop and Pony Favorite remained at the clubhouse awhile longer, finishing their drinks and chatting about the day. Pony's little boy was asleep on a mattress in the middle room and he and Pony would stay the night. Knoop intended to catch the eleven o'clock southbound car at Stop 39 opposite the ticket booth for the fairgrounds. And because it was nearly that time, he took leave of Pony Favorite and hurried across the suspension footbridge over the canal and down the cement road towards the car stop. As he moved along, he heard the group of men ahead and recognized Starry's voice. He picked up his pace a bit and caught up with the four men who had preceded him; then, when Heitman and Starry paused long enough to relieve themselves against the ticket office, Knoop, Favorite and Ellicker went on ahead of them.

"Now, gentlemen, it's important for you to know that Frank Favorite had been drinking heavily all day Saturday and all day Sunday. He'd purchased two quarts of whiskey Saturday night and had consumed both of them, along with a number of other shots he'd paid for by the glass. By this time of a Sunday night, he was thoroughly inebriated. And because of his condition, he was also intensely quarrelsome. When their conversation turned to the subject of a woman who called herself 'Peerless Mame' and Knoop made a derogatory remark about her, Favorite became angry with a fury peculiar to those who become aggressive when drunk. He attempted, on three separate occasions, to assault Knoop. He repeatedly challenged him to fight and Knoop repeatedly declined. 'You're in no condition to fight anyone,' he said. Finally, after Favorite had taken off his coat, handed it to Ellicker, and advanced on Knoop, Knoop shoved him away with just enough force to repel the attack. Favorite, because of his condition, fell heavily to the cement road. And because he was known to have been drunk at the time, he was allowed to lie there. None of the people involved believed him to have been seriously hurt. He was drunk, they knew that. And it was probable that he'd hit his head when he fell; they figured that too. But he was very much alive. There was no blood, nor any other evidence of injury. Even the prosecution will agree that he was alive and without any sign of serious injury when the boys went home. And they didn't just run off into the night and leave him there like road kill either. They'd discussed things among themselves and it was decided that Knoop, Starry and Ellicker would go on ahead and send a taxi back to take him home; Charlie Heitman, because he was family, would stay with Favorite until the taxi came for him.

"And he was alive when the three doctors, our eminent local physicians, began their ministrations to him. The prosecution will agree with that also. Now, what did the doctors do for him? You'll hear testimony about that too. What they did, gentlemen of the jury, was to remove him to Dr. Coleman's hospital over on Water Street and cut transverse and longitudinal sections out of his scalp, diagnose two fractures to his skull, one on the side of his head, and one near the occipital bone. The evidence will show that those two fractures, by themselves, could not possibly have caused the man's death within a period of eight hours. The next thing the doctors did, presumably in the name of science, was to drill four separate holes into Frank Favorite's head. They'll call it 'trepanning.' That's a fancy medical term for boring holes through solid bone. And their drilling paid off, too. They hit a gusher. A stream of blood spurted from the man's head clear across the room and spattered against the far wall. And Frank Favorite died shortly thereafter. Not from anything Forrest Knoop or any of the others did, but from having four separate holes drilled through his head and into his brain.

"Now, gentlemen, it's important to note that these 'eminent physicians' made no examination of any other part of Frank Favorite's body, nor any attempt to diagnose any other injury. Not then, not ever. To this day there has been no further examination, no autopsy, no attempt to discover the true cause of this man's death. And for that reason, none of us will ever really know the answer."

Bill Haines had, in effect, just accused the three doctors of killing Frank Favorite, and if many of the spectators were aghast at his effrontery, that fact had little apparent effect on Haines. He barely paused in his opening as he shifted the focus of his remarks.

"Now the prosecution would have you believe that Mr. Knoop and his cohorts brutally and maliciously beat their friend, Mr. Favorite, to death—for his money. And in an attempt to make that case they're going to try to show that Frank Favorite had had a great deal of money on his person that night and that everybody at the clubhouse knew it.

"What you will really learn from the evidence, however, is that while Mr. Favorite had begun the weekend with a considerable amount of cash, he had spent virtually all of it on Saturday and Sunday—on beer, whiskey and women—and everybody involved knew that fact very well. The evidence will show that earlier that Sunday evening he had tried to borrow a dollar so that he could visit a woman in Piqua, that same woman I mentioned earlier in my remarks, Peerless Mame. That dollar was her price and Frank Favorite didn't have it. It turned out he couldn't borrow it either, so he didn't go to Piqua. He was simply going to go home. And that evidence, you will find, is entirely consistent with the fact that there was but a single nickel found about his person after his injury. It is not consistent with the prosecutor's theory that he was killed for his money. He didn't have any money and everybody knew it."

Bill Haines spent another twenty minutes or so detailing what he expected the principal witnesses to say, placed it all in context with his version of the facts, and wound it up. "His Honor, Judge Jones, will tell you, gentlemen of the jury, that nothing the prosecutor has told you about this case is *evidence*, and you may not consider it as such. Mr. Goodrich has represented to you only that which he expects the evidence will show. I will ask you, once again, to remember that those representations are nothing more than empty promises. The only evidence in the case will come to you from the sworn testimony of the witnesses and from any physical exhibits that are actually admitted into evidence by the court."

Chapter Nineteen

Blanche Haines was utterly scandalized that evening when her husband completed his reprise of the day's activities and his own remarks to the jury. Her eyes had widened and her attention heightened as he reached the end of his summary. Now she flashed.

"I can't believe you did that!" she snapped at him with more than a little rancor.

Bill Haines didn't quite get it. "Eh?" he asked guilelessly. "Did what? I haven't done anything, except begun a trial. We picked a jury, took them out to the clubhouse, came back to the courtroom and made our opening statements. That's what I do for a living. I try cases, Blanche. Criminal cases, for the most part. And they're not always pretty. They're not fairy tales, and that means we have to deal with a lot of reality. Real people, real crimes, real life. And there are times when that reality gets ugly. But we still have to deal with it. You know all that."

And when she did not seem mollified, he threw in the towel. "All right, then. I give up. What is it that's set you up this way? Something I said?"

Now she was steaming. "Oh, yes," she snapped. "It's something you said all right. But not to me. It's what you just told me—blithely and smugly, it seems to me—you said to that jury. I can't believe you accused the three doctors of killing Frank Favorite. Why, in God's name, would you do a thing like that?"

"Oh, is that all?" He allowed himself a small smile. "I thought I'd done something really egregious. That's just a matter of trial tactics; there's no substance to it. Of course they didn't kill Frank Favorite—at least not intentionally. Their treatment may, or may not, have contributed to his death, but that's a mere happenstance. Physicians lose their patients everyday; it's a part of their calling."

"If there's no substance to it, then why..." she began a retort.

Bill Haines didn't let her finish. He held up his left hand in the traditional stop signal. His right hand was wrapped loosely around a cocktail glass. "*Confusion*, love. Remember, we talked about this earlier. *Confusion and inconsistency*, the two most effective weapons of a defense attorney. If, by confusing the issue, I can plant a single seed in the mind of a single juror, of the idea that Frank Favorite may have died from some cause other than that contended by the prosecutor, that seed may well mature into the *reasonable doubt* that will entitle us to an acquittal. And if I can convey to any single juror the concept that the evidence in the case is no more consistent with Slicker Knoop's guilt than with any other potential scenario, I will have accomplished the same objective. *Confusion and inconsistency*, Blanche; that's what it's all about. It's the more true with a client who's guilty than with one who's pure as the driven snow, but it's a valuable tactic in either case. Whatever tends to undermine or even weaken the prosecution's case redounds to the benefit of the accused."

Blanche wasn't having any of it. "Is that all that matters to you? Winning by any means? Is there no honor in your profession? *Confusion* and *inconsistency*, indeed! What ever happened to the time-worn aphorism that a jury trial 'is, in its essence, a search for the truth'? It seems to me that those tools which you so blandly refer to as *confusion* and *inconsistency* might better be styled *artifice* and *stratagem*. You're not looking for truth; you're trying to deceive."

"Now, now, love. Let's not get over-excited. You're in no condition to be agitated. Besides, you know very well the nature of my obligation to my client—and to my profession. My duty is to do all that is possible to protect his interests—within, of course, the confines of the law."

"My condition!" she almost snorted. "You might well think of my condition. I'm due to deliver almost any day and you think nothing of attacking the very same doctor we expect to deliver our baby. I hope you've not forgotten that Dr. Thompson delivered both of the girls and will deliver this child too. That is, of course, if he's still willing to do so."

"It's all right, Blanche. Wilbur Thompson knows I've got a job to do. He'll not take it personally."

"When this is over, I'll have to speak to Laura. I'll apologize to her for your remarks. And you should too. She's one of the finest people I know. Actually, all three of the doctors, and their wives, are this town's leading citizens. In every sense of the word."

"All right, love. When it's over," he placated, "I'll speak with all three. But remember, please, that I will still have to cross-examine them before that time."

When she made an ill-tempered moué, he added, "In the meanwhile, I'm sure Wilbur will be there when your time comes."

THE PRESENTATION OF EVIDENCE began the following morning before an overcrowded courtroom. The legions of spectators and would-be spectators on hand had multiplied exponentially from the previous day's numbers. The usual seating areas of the gallery section were grossly inadequate to accommodate all those who had risen well before daybreak in the hope of securing a station from which to monitor the proceedings. It seemed that each passing day heightened the public interest in both the trial and the several personalities involved. The appearance, that morning, of the decedent's mother, Mary Favorite, produced a major stir among all those who recognized her and pointed her out to those others who had not known who she was. There was, of course, no evidence of her husband. He was in no condition to withstand the emotional ordeal.

It began slowly and blandly enough. J. W. Dowler, a civil engineer and a former county surveyor, was the first witness called by the prosecution. At the behest of Frank Goodrich, Mr. Dowler produced an armload of plats, maps and sketches depicting the clubhouse, the cement highway, the canal, the suspension footbridge, the fence between the D&T track and the road, the county fairgrounds and the ticket booth. After leading the witness through an exposition concerning what it was that each item showed, and requiring him to explain the precise measurements he had taken to show the relative position of the various structures, one with another, Frank Goodrich offered all of the plats, maps and sketches in evidence. There was neither any objection nor any cross-examination of Mr. Dowler. His evidence, however necessary, was entirely perfunctory and indisputable. It was, however, deemed to be of some help to both sides in the placing in context of the anticipated testimony of the ensuing witnesses.

Frank Goodrich had also caused a local photographer to take pictures of these same landmarks and structures. Then, on the event of his being called to the stand to authenticate and substantiate his photographs, the photographer was cross-examined by Bill Haines.

"When did you say these pictures were taken?" he asked the witness.

"They were all taken last October. On the 11th," came the answer.

"Do you contend, sir, that your photos, taken in mid-October, will fairly and accurately depict the scene as it existed in the early summer of last year?" pressed Haines.

"Yes sir, I believe they do. Except, of course, for the differences in the foliage, the leaves on the trees and shrubs. And maybe some of the detritus and discarded items on the ground. They may or may not have been there in June. I don't know about that; I wasn't there last June."

"Precisely," snapped Bill Haines. "You cannot possibly tell this jury that these photographs fairly and accurately depict the condition of the landscape and improvements as they were at the time of the event, and, for that reason," he turned to Judge Jones, "the defense objects to the introduction of all such photographs in evidence."

Judge Jones scowled at the prosecutors. "The objection will be sustained. The photos will not be admitted. If it should happen that the state becomes able to supply the deficiency we can reconsider the matter later. In the meanwhile, Mr. Goodrich, please call your next witness."

Dr. W. R. Thompson was the third witness called to the stand by Frank Goodrich. He testified that he had been a physician and surgeon for some forty years, and had, on occasion, attended the various members of the Favorite family. At approximately one o'clock on the night of June 27th, he was called on the telephone and summoned to the residence of Daniel Favorite. He responded immediately and upon his arrival he found Frank Favorite lying on a lounge, breathing heavily. He noted a "sunken place" in Frank's anterior skull and a slight rise in the posterior skull. There was no apparent scalp wound and no sign of any blood or bleeding. He was satisfied that there was a distinct fracture in the frontal region.

"What did you do then?" prodded Frank Goodrich.

"I called Dr. Wright and Dr. Coleman to the Favorite residence. After their respective examinations, we agreed to remove the injured man to Dr. Coleman's hospital."

"You said it was about one o'clock when you were summoned to the Favorite residence," interjected Goodrich. "Just to refresh your recollection, Doctor, was not the time..."

"Objection!" ejaculated Bill Haines caustically. "Counsel knows better than to challenge his own witness."

And Judge Jones promptly settled the matter.

"Ask your question properly," he admonished.

Frank Goodrich tried to do as he had been instructed. "Did you not hear the courthouse clock striking three?"

"Objection," cried Bill Haines. "Same reason."

"Sustained," ordered Judge Jones. "Same reason. Move on, Counselor."

Then, after he had led his witness to a discussion of the physicians' ministrations to their patient after transfer to the hospital, Frank Goodrich asked Dr. Thompson to describe for the jury the operation performed.

"Dr. Coleman had the head prepared for surgery. We did not administer chloroform because the man was already unconscious. We made an incision downward over the seat of the fracture, then towards the rear, following the fracture line. We noted a pronounced depression of the left anterior part of the skull. There was a fissure running back from the fracture a distance of some two inches and from that point it radiated in a V shape downward and backwards to the parietal bone.

"We next employed an elevator to raise the depression in the man's skull and ultimately trephined the skull to relieve the pressure of accumulated blood. When we did so, a considerable spurt of fresh blood was expelled. We also noted a second fracture behind the transverse suture, on the left parietal bone, which was open, but did not seemed to be depressed. There seemed to be a large clot of congealed blood at the site of this second fracture."

After further questions by the prosecutor concerning the probable effects on the decedent's brain of releasing the blood pressure, Dr. Thompson was asked what kind of weapon had likely caused the injuries which he had observed.

"Objection," sang out Bill Haines.

"Rephrase your question," instructed Judge Jones.

"Doctor, do you have an opinion as to what caused the fractures in the decedent's skull?"

"I do," replied the witness.

With a little help from the court, Frank Goodrich was beginning to get it right. "What is that opinion, sir?"

"Because there was no cut or break in the surface of the skin, I believe that the injury was produced by a smooth, dull instrument," replied Dr. Thompson.

"Like this?" asked Frank Goodrich pointedly, handing the witness a blackjack.

The question had no sooner been posed than all three defense counsel sprang to their feet to interpose their respective objections. And while the objections were sustained, and the prosecutor admonished, the witness was ultimately permitted, after a proper foundation had been laid, to answer the question in the affirmative.

Frank Goodrich next produced a plaster cast and asked the witness to tell the jury what it was and how it had come into existence. Dr. Thompson received the item from the prosecutor and displayed it to the jury. "This is a plaster model of the decedent's skull as we observed it at the time of our examination in the early hours of the morning of June 28th. Please note that we have recreated the fractures and depressions just as they appeared in Mr. Favorite's skull."

Further objections were registered by all defense counsel. Bill Haines was the first to protest. "Best evidence rule, your Honor," he cried. "The best evidence of the fractures and depressions is the decedent's skull. The prosecutors' 'plaster model' is nothing more than a fabrication after the fact. It's a poorly disguised attempt to create evidence out of whole cloth— or, more to the point, out of plaster of paris."

The defense objections were summarily overruled by the court, and the prosecution was directed to proceed.

Frank Goodrich plowed on, "Now Doctor, I think you still have at hand the blackjack given to you a moment ago. Please indicate whether or not you can detect any correlation between that instrument and the plaster cast of the decedent's skull taken subsequent to the decedent's death?"

Still more objections from defense counsel, all of which were summarily overruled. Bill Haines suppressed a grimace. He would have to content himself with dealing with the matter as a part of his cross-examination of the witness.

"Why, yes," answered the witness as he fitted the business end of the blackjack into the principal declivity in the plaster cast. "It is very obvious that the head of the blackjack fits quite neatly into the depression. They match perfectly." He held both objects up in order that the jurors might better see the union. "Like a ball and socket joint," he added gratuitously.

Bill Haines was on his feet before the answer had been completed. "Your Honor, the defense strenuously objects to this entire line of questioning. Neither of these two items, the blackjack and the plaster cast, has been properly authenticated, and the prosecution's reliance upon them as subjects for inquiry is both improper and inappropriate. We move the court to strike the testimony and instruct the jury to disregard."

Judge Jones considered the matter for a moment or two, then shook his head as though to arrange his thoughts, "The objection does have merit, counselor; however, the court will nonetheless overrule it. The motion to strike is also denied. The court considers that your objections go to the weight of the testimony and the probative value of the exhibits in question. You may address such matters on cross-examination."

Frank Goodrich seemed almost smug as he retrieved the two exhibits and drew Dr. Thompson's attention back to the wound itself. "Could such a wound as you observed have been caused by the decedent's having fallen on a cement road?"

"I think not," opined Dr. Thompson.

"Is it possible?" persisted Goodrich. "Please be explicit."

"No. It is not possible."

Perhaps an hour later, after some further questioning on matters purely peripheral to the central issues, and the introduction of the decedent's hat, which had come into the doctor's possession, the examination wound down and Frank Goodrich announced to the court that he had no more questions of Dr. Thompson.

AFTER THE INTERVENTION OF A SHORT RECESS, Judge Jones invited defense counsel to begin their cross-examination. Bill Haines, of course, would inquire for the defendant.

"Dr. Thompson, you've had occasion to treat the decedent, Frank Favorite, over the past several years, have you not?"

"I have," came the reply.

"And among the conditions or diseases for which you have treated him, may we not include the condition known as *delirium tremens*?"

"Yes sir, on occasion."

"Did Mr. Favorite suffer from *delirium tremens*?"

"He did, yes. From time to time."

"Please tell the jury what that condition is, and what it implies," asked Bill Haines.

Dr. Thompson ran his hand through his silver hair as if to refresh his memory. "The condition known as the DTs, *delirium tremens*, is essentially a mental condition, a psychosis which normally results from chronic alcoholism and causes tremors and hallucinations. It implies, of course, chronic alcoholism."

"And did Frank Favorite suffer from chronic alcoholism?"

"I haven't said so," came the reluctant answer.

Bill Haines persisted. "Did he, or did he not suffer from chronic alcoholism?"

"Yes, I suppose he did," conceded Dr. Thompson.

"It would be fair, then, Doctor, to say that Frank Favorite actually suffered from both conditions, *delirium tremens* and chronic alcoholism, would it not?" pressed Bill Haines.

"Yes sir, I suppose that's fair," answered the witness.

"Would it also be fair to conclude that a person thus afflicted might be severely compromised—emotionally, mentally and physically—and might therefore be more vulnerable than otherwise?"

Dr. Thompson looked to be bewildered by this line of inquiry. "I don't understand," he countered. "Could you restate the question, please?"

"Let me break it down for you, sir," offered Bill Haines. "Would you expect such a person to be argumentative or quarrelsome when under the influence of alcoholic beverage? Might he be quick to start a fight if crossed?"

"Perhaps," responded the doctor. "But common experience..."

Bill Haines finished it for him. "Common experience tells us that the effect of alcoholic drink frequently leads to fisticuffs, does it not, Doctor?"

And without waiting for the concession, the hardy defense lawyer pushed on. "And that same common experience tells us also that the condition known as *delirium tremens* frequently renders its victim uncoordinated and essentially unable to defend himself against the slightest assault or even to maintain his balance when jostled, isn't that true, Doctor?"

Frank Goodrich and Leonard Shipman leapt to their feet simultaneously. "Objection. There's no foundation for this line of inquiry"

And Judge Jones rapped his gavel sharply. "Sustained!"

Bill Haines was unabashed. "Your Honor, I should like to read certain passages from one or two authoritative medical texts, and ask the witness if he agrees with opinions expressed by the authors. I will limit my questions to matters involving both alcoholism and *delirium tremens*."

And again the prosecutors, three of them this time, rose and cried out their objections.

Judge Jones cast a stony look at Bill Haines. "You know better than that, Counselor. You will do no such thing. The objection is sustained. Move on to something else."

"Yes, Your Honor, of course." The point had been made. It could be revisited later in the trial.

IT WAS NEARLY LUNCH TIME and Judge Jones declared a recess. Cross-examination of Dr. Thompson would continue when court re-convened at one o'clock.

Bill Haines did not eat lunch that day. He was too much preoccupied with the task at hand. Instead, he conferred briefly with his co-counsel, then nursed his thoughts—and a single banana—at his office desk. He was the first of the participants to return to his station in the courtroom for the afternoon session.

"I THINK I UNDERSTOOD YOU TO SAY, DOCTOR, that when you first examined Mr. Favorite that night you found no cuts, bruises, contusions or other marks of injury about his head—or for that matter—anywhere else about his body. Is that correct?" asked Bill Haines as the proceedings got under way again.

"That's correct," answered Dr. Thompson guardedly.

"Is it possible, then, that he had not been injured at all? That he was quite simply drunk? In stupor?"

Dr. Thompson bristled at the question. "Of course not. I've already testified that all three of us noted a pronounced depression in the man's skull. It was fractured in two places, despite the lack of any obvious marks on the surface of the epidermis."

"And you concluded that from your empiric observation of the shape of the man's head, is that correct?"

"That's correct."

"And, based upon that observation, you performed an operation?"

"Yes."

"Which consisted of making an incision in the decedent's head, forcing a tool, an elevator, into his skull to pry the bones apart, and then drilling four separate holes into the skull cavity. Is that also correct?" asked Bill Haines.

"Essentially, yes," replied the witness. "We refer to the procedure as *trephining*. The instrument used is called a trephine. It's a small surgical saw sometimes referred to as a trepan and the procedure is sometimes called trepanning."

"And tell the jury, please, the purpose of this *trephining* operation."

"It's intended to relieve the pressure on the brain caused by hemorrhagic blood."

"And I think you said that upon the performance of that procedure a considerable amount of blood spurted from the openings which you had created?"

"Yes."

"So much blood, I believe, that it spurted clear across the operating room. Isn't that so?"

"Yes. That's true."

"Doctor Thompson, is it just possible that Frank Favorite may have died because the bones of his head had been pried apart and four holes had been drilled into his skull? Is that remotely possible?"

"Not very likely," answered the witness.

"But possible?" pressed Haines.

Dr. Thompson had become visibly upset over the insinuation that he and his colleagues might actually have killed their patient. "The operation was performed in a desperate attempt to save the man's life. He would most assuredly have died without our surgical intervention."

"Just as he died with your intervention, is that so?"

"Objection, Your Honor," cried Frank Goodrich. "This is intolerable."

"I'll allow it," remarked Judge Jones. "It's a fair question. The witness may answer."

Dr. Thompson was resigned to the matter. "I can't argue the issue. Regardless of the fact of our intervention, the man died."

"Do you believe, Doctor, that Frank Favorite died from hemorrhage?" asked Bill Haines.

"No. I think he died from shock. By that I mean a generalized injury to his nervous system, accompanied by hemorrhage."

"Dr. Thompson, tell the jury whether, in your opinion, a chronic alcoholic, afflicted with *delirium tremens*, would have been more— or less—susceptible to sustain a 'generalized injury to his nervous system, accompanied by hemorrhage' than would an otherwise healthy adult male."

And, predictably, the shouted objections of the prosecutors were sustained, and counsel for the defendant was admonished by the court.

Bill Haines then reversed his field, so to speak, and attempted to induce Dr. Thompson to concede that the top of a person's head is not the seat of his vital centers and might therefore sustain a severe injury without necessarily producing death. In response, the witness acknowledged that the so-called vital centers, connoting a medical nerve group, were not located in the cerebrum. The cerebrum, he noted, might even be said to be devoid of feeling, but there nonetheless existed certain nervous communications between that situs with other parts of the brain. So much so, he asserted, that if the cerebrum were injured, the nervous communications might be strong enough to produce death under certain circumstances.

A long and unnecessarily protracted dialogue ensued during which Bill Haines explored the mechanics by which a blow to the head might cause death, including considerations involving the existence of a pre-existing blood clot, a predisposition to serious injury by reason of chronic

alcoholism, *delirium tremens*, or vascular compromise. That discussion led to the question, "If the decedent were to have fallen on a cement road and ruptured a vein at the base of his skull, could such an event prove fatal?"

And the anticipated answer, "Of course."

"In the course of four to eight hours?"

"It could."

It soon became apparent that Bill Haines was not going to let Dr. Thompson off the witness stand easily. He next required the doctor to describe the distinctions between hematoma, subcutaneous hematoma, clot, and the dynamics of blood vessel rupture, skull fracture and resultant skull depressions.

"One more time, Doctor. Is it your opinion that Frank Favorite died from concussion?"

"I believe he died from rearrangement of the motor nervous centers, the vaso-nervous system, and shock to the entire system."

"Doctor, please answer my question directly."

And Judge Jones sustained the prosecutors' objections. "I think the witness's statements on this subject have been sufficiently comprehensive. Take the answer, and proceed."

"Dr. Thompson, during your direct examination you performed a little demonstration to show how a hypothetical blackjack could be fitted into a declivity in a plaster cast which you prepared for use in this case. Is that correct?"

"Yes sir."

"Has it been suggested to you that the blackjack with which you performed that exercise was the actual weapon utilized by the defendant—or by any other person—to work an injury on Frank Favorite?"

"No sir."

"Do you have any idea where this particular blackjack came from?"

"The prosecutor, Mr. Goodrich, produced it. I think he had a devil of a time locating one; they don't sell them in any of the local stores, you know."

Bill Haines was satisfied with the answer. Then he retrieved the plaster cast from the exhibit table and held it out for the witness' inspection. "And this plaster cast, sir, did you create it?"

"Yes sir."

"Was that done at the request of the prosecutor?"

"It was."

"When was that done?"

"I made it last week."

"How were you able to replicate the precise location and contour of the wounds which you noted on the skull of Frank Favorite three-quarters of a year earlier?"

"I did it from memory and by reference to the notes which I had made contemporaneous with my examination. It wasn't an easy task."

"Isn't it true, Doctor, that this cast was actually configured so as to mesh with the size and contour of the blackjack which had been provided by the prosecutor?"

"I suppose that was a consideration, yes."

"And the whole purpose of that artifice was to demonstrate to the jury that the object which produced the injury to Frank Favorite just *might* have been a blackjack?"

"Yes sir."

"Not this particular blackjack, but any blackjack?"

"Yes sir, that's true."

"To put it in context, Doctor, you testified earlier that it was possible that the injuries which you observed had been caused by a blackjack. Let me ask you now whether you consider a blackjack to have been the most probable instrument?"

"Judging from the nature of the injury, I would have to believe it to have been caused by a smooth object."

"Like a ball bat, or a lead pipe?"

"Equally probable."

"Well, Doctor, we've heard a lot of speculation about a beer bottle. Could such an injury have been caused by a beer bottle?"

"Absolutely."

Bill Haines was quick to put the cap on this particular aspect of his examination. "But we've seen no evidence of any of these potential instruments, have we? Has anyone disclosed to you that a blackjack was found either on the scene or on Slicker Knoop's person?"

"No sir."

"Or a ball bat?"

"No sir."

"A lead pipe?"

"No sir."

"A beer bottle?"

"No sir."

"Thank you, Doctor. Would you agree then that of all the potential 'instruments' we've considered, only one such was found to be at hand at the time of the incident?"

"One?" asked the witness innocently.

"Just one. The cement highway. That's the only potentially lethal instrument, among those suggested, that we know to have been on hand. Isn't that so?"

It was a question, but Bill Haines had not expected an answer. He switched direction again. "Doctor Thompson, you've been testifying here for several hours concerning the cause of death of Frank Favorite, and in the course of your testimony you've rendered a series of medical opinions. Is that fair?"

"That's fair."

"And you've based those opinions on your physical examinations of the decedent. Is that correct?"

"Yes."

"Please tell the jury whether you are entirely comfortable with those opinions and with your medical findings concerning the cause of death of Frank Favorite?"

Dr. Thompson couldn't see where this was going. "Comfortable?" he asked.

"Yes sir. Are you satisfied that your opinions and findings are correct?"

"I am."

"And the others, Dr. Wright and Dr. Coleman—are you all in agreement?

"We are. Yes sir."

Bill Haines, having laid the groundwork, sprang the trap. "Truly, Doctor, 'all in agreement'?"

"Yes sir."

Bill Haines made a great show of shuffling through the papers spread haphazardly before him on the counsel table until he seemed to have found that which he wanted. Holding a single sheet of paper in his hand as though it were the Holy Grail, he proceeded in the manner of a Spanish Inquisitor, "Dr. Thompson, I'm looking at a document that was filed with the Court in this very case on December 31st—just twenty-six days ago. The document purports to have been signed by Dr. Wright and by Dr. Coleman. Are you familiar with it?"

Dr. Thompson gritted his teeth as he answered, "I am."

"Let me show it to you so that there'll be no mistake. Do you recognize it?"

The peppery defense lawyer and the witness walked their way through the ritualistic motions of physical delivery, perfunctory perusal, and reluctant re-delivery of the document. And the examination continued in predictable fashion.

"Do you recognize the document?"

"Yes. I've seen it."

"Would it be fair to characterize this document—let's call it Defendant's Exhibit A—as a joint application, addressed to the court, for an order requiring the immediate disinterment of the body of Frank Favorite so that a proper autopsy might be performed?"

The answer came grudgingly, "That would be correct."

"And Doctor, does not the application, which purports to have been signed by Drs. Wright and Coleman, specifically recite that:

Because there is an uncertainty and difference of opinion as to the character, nature, extent and location of the wounds by the undersigned physicians who examined the body....

Did I read that correctly, sir?"

Now Dr. Thompson reddened. He was visibly angered at the turn of Bill Haines' examination. He seethed a long moment before answering, "Yes," he acknowledged tightly. "You read it correctly."

"Do you recognize the signatures as those of your colleagues, Dr. Wright and Dr. Coleman?"

"Yes, of course I do."

"Can we agree, Doctor, that the verbiage contained in this document, Exhibit A, is not really consistent with your testimony to the effect that all three of you were in total agreement concerning your opinions and findings?"

The answer was clipped and terse. "Apparently not."

Bill Haines pressed the point. "As I read this document, it seems that at least two of you admitted to 'an uncertainty and difference of opinion.' Is that fair?"

A grunt from the witness, "Yes."

"And that 'uncertainty and difference of opinion' concerned the 'character' of the decedent's wounds?"

Another grunt.

"And the 'nature' of his wounds?"

A nod.

"And the 'extent' of his wounds?"

A grimace.

"And even the 'location' of his wounds?"

And finally, an explosion. "All right, counselor, you've made your point! You prevailed upon my colleagues to join in your obscene attempts

to exhume the body. They agreed to help, and I refused. I still insist that no good purpose could have been served by digging up the bones of this unfortunate wretch. We all saw the damage that had been done to the man's skull."

Bill Haines waited for the storm to subside. Then he approached the witness and pronounced the benediction, "The point is, however, that there was no agreement among the three of you concerning the character, the nature, the extent, or even the precise location of the wounds. Is that correct?"

"As you like," conceded Dr. Thompson wearily.

"And, Doctor, to that extent, at least, do you now recant your prior testimony?"

Dr. Thompson had had enough, "My testimony is in; make of it what you like."

Judge Jones, also, had had enough. "The witness is excused. Court's adjourned until tomorrow morning. The jury will remember the usual admonitions." A solid rap of his gavel and it was over for the day.

Chapter Twenty

Blanche Haines was livid. "How could you have done such a thing?" she demanded of her husband that evening. "It's one thing to take issue with his medical opinions—and I can accept that its your duty to do so—but it's quite another to attack him personally. And that's precisely what you did. It's all over town. Absolutely everyone is talking about how you destroyed Dr. Thompson. I'm just glad I wasn't there to see it; I'd have been totally humiliated."

She continued on in that vein for some little time, and Bill Haines permitted her to do so as he pulled off his gloves, removed his hat, coat and scarf and carefully stowed all his winter gear in the hall closet. She was still at it all the while he patiently poured her glass of wine and mixed his own pre-prandial cocktail. She began to wind down as he eased himself into his overstuffed chair directly across the coffee table from the casual armchair which was her own customary station. She could scarcely avoid sitting down opposite as her tirade began to wane.

"Dr. Thompson is a fine man and an excellent physician. I cannot imagine that you found it necessary to savage him in that fashion—and to besmirch the both of us in the process," she finished.

"Please, Blanche," he beseeched her. "Try to understand. Whatever you may have heard on the street—or whatever the public perception may be—I did not 'savage' Wilbur Thompson. Nor did I 'destroy' him. And, by the way, I never had any desire or intention of accomplishing either end. I have the highest regard for the good doctor, his medical talents, his professionalism, and most importantly, his integrity."

"Then why..." Blanche attempted querulously.

"My intention, dear wife, has ever been to simply undermine his testimony—or, at least, to introduce some small doubt as to its reliability—and to thereby aid my client's cause. Nothing more, nothing less. There is certainly nothing personal about it."

"That's not the way I heard it," she snorted.

"Ah, love," he rejoined, almost humorously, "while I have no wish to give offense to you, I'm sure you know that I don't really give a tinker's dam about what you may have heard. What I do care about is how the jury heard the witness's testimony, whether they understood the contradictions and whether they picked up on all the nuances."

"What contradictions? What nuances?" she queried. Her pique beginning to dissipate, she was again interested in her husband's case.

"All right," he began, almost tediously, "Dr. Thompson's testimony on direct examination was precisely that which we had anticipated. He described the examination conducted by the three attending physicians, the nature and extent of the wounds they observed, their ministrations to the patient, their joint findings, and his own professional opinion as to the mechanism of the injury and as to the cause of death. However, he also assured the jury that all three of the examining physicians were in complete agreement as to all such matters."

"Well, weren't they? All in agreement?" she asked.

"Yes. Of course they were."

Blanche was totally perplexed. "Then...?"

Bill Haines rubbed his hands, smugly, it seemed to her. "Surely you remember that Drs. Wright and Coleman joined in my application to exhume Frank Favorite's body and, that as a part of their joinder, they asserted that there was an uncertainty and difference of opinion among the three of them concerning those same matters?"

"Well, yes, I remember that they did try to help, and that they joined in your application, but that was only done to accommodate your request. They signed that paper only because you 'persuaded' them. I think that's the way you expressed it. Besides, if I remember correctly, they later repudiated their assertion—at the request of the family, I'm sure, but they finally said there was a consensus."

"True enough," he conceded. "But the original application's a matter of record and it simply won't just go away." He gestured in the direction of her own swollen condition, smiled at her fondly, and added, "Anymore than you can suddenly become un-pregnant by the simple expedient of changing your mind."

"You forget," she replied, "that I expect to become 'un-pregnant' any day now, with the help of Dr. Thompson—if he doesn't refuse me."

Bill Haines dismissed her concerns about the doctor. "He'll be there, never fear. He may be a bit miffed at me, but we'll all get over it." He reflected a moment, then, "Besides, he promised me a boy and he'll deliver on it."

"I still think you tricked them," Blanche couldn't accept her husband's having presumed on the doctors' better instincts and then turning their attempt to be helpful against them. She considered the matter to have been an unfair stratagem and she didn't like it at all.

"I did no such thing," he countered. "I simply asked them if a postmortem might not be instructive and they agreed. At least, they agreed that it certainly couldn't hurt."

"And?" she pressed.

"And, they acknowledged that it might even confirm their findings, resolve any potential questions."

"Mmm-hmm, and you drew up the statement, with its reference to uncertainties and differences of opinion, and they signed it? To accommodate you? Did they even read it?"

"These are grown men, Blanche. Educated professionals. If they didn't read it carefully, they should have. And they should have realized its implications."

Unconvinced, she retorted, "I still think it was a rotten thing for you to have done. You asked them for their help, induced them to sign your stupid paper, and now you're beating them up with it."

"Well," he mused thoughtfully, "So far, I've only used it against Dr. Thompson—and he's the one who refused to sign it. I do, however, intend to use it against the others as well. I'd be a damn fool not to contradict them with their own statements—however much you may disapprove. You—and the good doctors—will just have to live with it, Blanche. None of them will be the first professional ever to have been 'hoist on his own petard'."

THE TESTIMONY OF DRS. WRIGHT and Coleman was entirely repetitive of that which had been offered by Dr. Thompson; and, for that reason, if for no other, it was essentially anti-climactic. Each of them separately acknowledged his signature to the request for exhumation of the body of the decedent and each agreed with Bill Haines that it would have been better for all concerned if the application had been granted.

"The only way you could be absolutely certain as to what caused the death of Frank Favorite was to have conducted a postmortem, wasn't it?" he asked Dr. Wright.

"Yes."

"And no such examination was ever conducted, is that correct?"

"Yes."

Neither of the doctors seemed particularly pleased by their having been confronted with the fact of their seeming vacillation concerning their belated request for a postmortem, or their sudden withdrawal of that request. And neither of them welcomed the opportunity to discuss the 'differences of opinion' alluded to in their initial request. Bill Haines reviewed with them, briefly, all of those same matters with which he had previously abraded Dr. Thompson, but ultimately dismissed them as though he considered their testimony to be of little value and wholly unreliable.

County Coroner G.C. Ullery got the same treatment. Called to the stand by prosecutor Frank Goodrich, he admitted that his examination of the body of Frank Favorite had been no more than cursory in nature. After all, he pleaded, three of the county's most eminent physicians had already viewed it and he was content to accept their findings. He, also, was forced to concede that a postmortem should have been performed.

"But, Doctor Ullery, in your capacity as Miami County Coroner, you nonetheless denied the defendant's application for just such an examination, did you not?"

"Yes sir. That's true."

"Why?"

"Well, I guess I thought, at the time, that is, that since Dr. Thompson and Dr. Wright and Dr. Coleman had all seen and treated the man, and since they all seemed to be in agreement, there didn't seem to be any real purpose in exhuming the body and doing another examination. Then, too, I'll admit, I knew the family didn't want the poor man dug up."

"Do you now agree, sir, that you should have granted the defendant's application?"

"If I had it to do over again..."

"Please, Doctor, yes or no?" insisted Bill Haines.

"I'm sorry. Yes, I agree."

Chapter Twenty-one

The principal thrust of the state's case against Slicker Knoop took on a different character over the next two days, Thursday and Friday, as the three prosecutors moved on from the presentation of the medical evidence and shifted their focus to the activities of the decedent over the final forty-eight hours of his life. In an effort to demonstrate that Frank Favorite had been carrying—and overtly flashing—a very considerable bankroll, and that he had also been drinking heavily over that period of time, the prosecutors called to the stand more than seventy witnesses. These were, presumably, all of those persons who had seen, spoken with, or otherwise encountered the decedent at any time or place on the Friday, Saturday or Sunday before his death.

The point contended by the prosecutors was that both circumstances, the decedent's patent, however ephemeral, affluence, coupled with his advanced state of inebriation, would have rendered him both prone and susceptible to robbery by assault. He was, in other words, ripe to be rolled, an obvious target.

From an evidentiary standpoint, there were no surprises. Frank Goodrich, Leonard Shipman and Alvah Campbell simply trotted out virtually all of those same witnesses who had already been heard from at last summer's Coroner's Inquest, and again at the preliminary hearing before Squire McCurdy in September, and yet again before the grand jury in October. The local newspapers had carried full, essentially verbatim, reportage of their prior testimony, and it had been widely discussed, dissected and critiqued by virtually everyone in the county. Now that same testimony, buttressed by the additional and purely cumulative testimony of an additional fifty-odd witnesses, made for a tedious and unexciting two days in the courtroom.

Troy Police Officers Harris, Landis and Sharits testified predictably that upon the event of his arrest Monday morning after the assault Slicker Knoop had admitted he had struck Favorite, but denied that he had killed him. Officer Harris told the jury that he had purposely taken Knoop past the Coleman hospital on his way to the city jail and that he pointed out the building to the defendant and said, "In there lies the body of the man you killed last night." Slicker Knoop, whom Harris described as "visibly shaken," responded that he didn't believe he had killed Favorite; he'd only hit him in order to protect himself. At a later time, he said, the defendant had conceded that he must have hit him too hard.

The final witness called by the state was Pony Favorite, the operator of the river club and the cousin of the decedent. He was also the brother-in-law of Charles Heitman, who had been indicted for the same offense as that presently levied against Knoop. His testimony related principally to a description of the club, its membership and purpose, and to the location and uses of the clubhouse itself. He also identified photographs of the clubhouse and its interior rooms. At the instance of Leonard Shipman, he pointed out the relative positions of the men present when Ellicker and Starry attempted to involve Frank Favorite in a craps or dice game and where Knoop and Ellicker had sat alone in the card room. Pony Favorite did say that at one time during the evening he had seen Bob Ellicker pick Frank Favorite's coat pocket, remove two bills and put them in his own pocket, and that he had overheard Starry and Elicker whispering together in one of the backrooms of the clubhouse, but that he was unaware of any plot directed against Frank Favorite. He also said that Heitman, Ellicker, Starry and Favorite had left the club at about eleven o'clock that night and that Knoop had left some ten minutes later. On cross-examination by Bill Haines, Favorite conceded that he might have been mistaken about Ellicker's having taken the two bills from Frank's pocket and that it was not unusual for two or more visitors at the club to go into a secluded room to converse privately.

For whatever reason, the prosecutors had expected far more from Pony Favorite's testimony than they got, and Leonard Shipman waived his chance for re-direct examination. Frank Goodrich announced that the state had concluded its presentation.

Surprisingly, because Frank Favorite was conceded to have visited her at least once that crucial weekend and because it was claimed by the defense that it was she who had been the root of the altercation between the defendant and the decedent, Peerless Mame was not called to tell what she knew about the decedent's activities, his bankroll and his relative sobriety. Her testimony was, of course, unnecessary. The several points had already been made. On the other hand, her appearance and her accounts might have added a bit of spice to the mix and thereby enlivened the otherwise tedious recitals provided by the phalanx of casual acquaintances and accidental observers summoned to the stand by the prosecutors.

The state rested its case against Slicker Knoop just after two o'clock Friday afternoon. They had presented the testimony of seventy-seven witnesses in their attempt to prove the defendant guilty of the wanton murder and robbery of Frank Favorite. They did not present any testimony from the three persons who were actually and physically present on the scene at the time and place of the alleged crime. Charlie Heitman, Clyde Starry and Robert Ellicker were scheduled to be tried separately for the same offense and the prosecutors had anticipated that their stories would tend to exculpate Slicker Knoop along with themselves.

Neither did the state introduce a murder weapon. Although the prosecutors had strived mightily to suggest that a rounded, blunt instrument, probably a blackjack, had been wielded by the defendant, there was no evidence sufficient to place any such object in the hands of Slicker Knoop.

IMMEDIATELY UPON THE EVENT of Frank Goodrich's announcement that the state had completed its evidence, the jury was excused in order that the anticipated defense motion might be presented and argued outside its presence. As soon as that had been accomplished, and the jury safely locked into its quarters, Asbury Kerr rose to his feet and presented, both orally and in written form, the defendant's motion for a directed verdict of acquittal. There was no evidence, he asserted, from which the jury could reasonably find that Slicker Knoop had committed any of the crimes with which he had been accused. He pointed out the obvious failure of the state to produce a murder weapon, any amount of cash or other property claimed to have been stolen from the decedent or a single eyewitness to the event. Absent such evidence, he contended a finding of guilty beyond a reasonable doubt would be not only legally untenable, but wholly absurd. The defendant was entitled to a directed verdict as a matter of law.

Alvah Campbell, as the most experienced of the prosecutorial team, responded for the state. Their inability to produce either a murder weapon or the spoils of the crime in the hands of the defendant was fully understandable; Slicker Knoop had every opportunity to dispose of both in the early morning hours before Favorite's death and he might certainly have been expected to do so. As to the claimed lack of an eye-witness to the crime, Campbell retorted that they had the best witness possible: the defendant himself had acknowledged to Officers Harris and Sharits that he had hit Favorite and that he thought it had been "a bitch of a lick."

Were that not enough, the testimony of the defendant's accomplices, Heitman, Starry and Ellicker, given at the Coroner's Inquest, was entirely consistent with Knoop's own admission. It was simple enough, Campbell concluded. Slicker Knoop struck Frank Favorite without provocation and Favorite died as a result of that blow. That simple postulate, coupled with the testimony of the witnesses, both expert and lay, would permit, if not positively mandate, the jury to find the defendant guilty of murder in the first degree.

Judge Jones had listened attentively to the arguments, but he wasted no time in reaching a conclusion. He found that the state had carried its burden of presenting evidence sufficient to sustain a verdict. The motion for directed verdict was overruled from the bench.

Chapter Twenty-two

It was nearly three o'clock on Friday afternoon; the state had completed its case and the customary defense motions had been resolved. If there was anyone within the overcrowded courtroom who expected Judge Jones to adjourn the proceedings, Bill Haines was not one of them. By reason of prior experience, he knew better. Walter Jones would live up to his longstanding reputation as a no-nonsense judge who moved his cases along as expeditiously and as efficiently as justice and fairness would permit.

As soon as the bailiff had returned the jury to its box, Judge Jones instructed counsel to proceed with the presentation of the case for the defense. Bill Haines was fully prepared. So, it seems, was the bailiff himself. At a signal from Haines, he escorted Charles Heitman into the courtroom as a first witness for the defense. There was a considerable stir among the spectators upon Heitman's appearance. A great deal of speculation had occurred concerning the current relationship between Heitman and Knoop and as to their present attitude towards one another. All questions on that score were resolved when Knoop greeted Heitman cordially and motioned for him to sit in an open chair beside him at the counsel table. The two men nodded, passed a whispered remark together and then returned their attention to the court proceedings.

When it ultimately developed—upon Haines' reconsideration—that Heitman was not to be the defendant's first witness, the prosecutors objected to his remaining in the courtroom and he voluntarily stepped into the adjoining clerk's office to await a further summons by the bailiff.

Leita Waddell was the first defense witness called to the stand. She had been one of the court reporters at the initial aborted Coroner's Inquest and was asked merely to confirm that the defendant had had no legal representation at those proceedings. Mrs. Waddell was a short witness and her testimony consumed no more than ten minutes. There was no cross-examination.

The second and third defense witnesses were also of the short variety. The defendant's uncle, L. P. Knoop, the county surveyor, was also the defendant's employer. He testified that his nephew was a man of excellent character and in good financial condition, and would not have been expected to rob anyone out of either malice or perceived necessity. He also told the jury that he had conducted a diligent search of the scene of Favorite's injury, including the adjacent canal, and was unable to find either a blackjack or any other potential weapon. Asked, upon cross-examination by Frank Goodrich as to when he had conducted that search, the answer came back, "The very next day, Monday afternoon."

The third defense witness was the shortest of all, and probably the most feckless. William Walters spent less than three minutes on the stand to tell of his having sold a black horse to Frank Favorite for $150 on June 16th and receiving payment in cash. Here again, there was no cross-examination.

Finally, Bill Haines signaled the bailiff to produce Charles Heitman again. The timing was right. The jurors, as well as the spectators, had begun to weary after nearly a week of trial and some eighty witnesses, many of whom had seemed merely superfluous.

Now, upon Heitman's second appearance in the courtroom, the entire assemblage, jurors and spectators alike, seemed to have been revitalized. Everyone in the county had read his prior testimony and knew that he had been on the scene, had confronted Slicker Knoop with what he'd done, and had remained with his stricken cousin until help arrived. Just as there had been much speculation concerning his present attitude towards the defendant, there was an even greater curiosity as to what his trial testimony might be. The local legal cognoscenti had already drawn inferences from the state's failure to call him as a part of its case in chief.

Charlie Heitman was an athletic-looking young man, solidly constructed. He appeared to be in his early thirties. He readily acknowledged himself to be a part of the free-wheeling river club group and had, indeed, operated such a club himself on more than one occasion. He was also a brother-in-law to Pony Favorite by virtue of his marriage to Pony's sister, Anna. Additionally, that same marriage tied him to his wife's cousin, the decedent Frank Favorite.

With minimal prodding from Bill Haines, Heitman gave a detailed account of his day, Sunday, June 27th. He had begun the day by attending a picnic with his family and a few friends. Late in the afternoon, and after the picnic, they had returned together on the northbound traction car. When the rest of his party debarked near their home he continued on as far as the Lytle place, near Pony Favorite's clubhouse. From there, he met up with a William Click and the two of them proceeded to the clubhouse, arriving at about seven o'clock. He sat around there, eating turtle soup and drinking beer until about nine-thirty when he went outside and sat on a bench, chatting with some of the other young men. At approximately ten o'clock Frank Favorite came out of the clubhouse and asked him for the loan of a dollar in order that he might go to Piqua to see his girl. Because he needed the dollar, Heitman assumed Frank meant to visit a Piqua girl known as Peerless Mame. Pony Favorite was standing in the doorway and made the same assumption. They both considered Mame to be a dollar-a-throw girl. Pony offered Frank some whiskey instead and Frank didn't renew his request for the dollar. He drank off a couple of shots of whiskey and later went back into the clubhouse, where he nursed another drink and watched a card game. So far as Heitman knew, Favorite did not play. Then, at about eleven o'clock, Heitman left the clubhouse, along with Clyde Starry; he believed that Frank Favorite and Bob Ellicker followed no more than a few minutes later. He had expected that Pony Favorite intended to stay the night at the clubhouse and that Slicker Knoop would have remained with him just long enough to tally the day's receipts before returning to his home in Troy.

The route taken by Heitman and Starry took them across the old canal by means of the suspension footbridge, then across the trolley tracks and the highway; from there, they walked south towards traction Stop 39 in order to catch a car into Troy. "We weren't in any great hurry," he said. "We were drinking some beer and having a good time on a nice summer evening. Clyde stopped to take a leak against the fairgrounds ticket office and I took a moment to tie my shoelace. While we were doin' that, along came Ellicker and Frank; they'd caught up with us. I was kinda surprised to see Frank because his home was up at Eldean—in the opposite direction. I made a remark about it and he said he'd decided to go on to Troy to get a bowl of soup at the H&E, the Harmon and Edmunds Restaurant, down at the corner of Main and Elm. So he and Ellicker went on while Starry and me were finishing our business, and pretty soon Slicker Knoop passed us, too. He didn't seem to be in a real hurry either, but he was movin' faster than we were and pretty soon he caught up with Ellicker and Frank. We were all going in the same direction, towards Troy, the three of them together and me and Clyde maybe fifteen yards behind. Couldn't see them very well, but heard them well enough to know they was havin' an argument. It got pretty loud and there was some strong language used. I heard some mention about Peerless Mame, but that's all I could make out."

Heitman interrupted his narrative and looked to Bill Haines as if seeking permission to continue.

"All right, Charlie. Tell the jury what happened next," said Haines.

And in accordance with the instruction, Heitman shifted in the witness chair and directed his attention to the jury. "Next thing I heard was something hit the ground, sounded like a sack of wet cement. Me and Clyde ran up and I saw Frank layin' on the ground. I grabbed Knoop by the arm and asked him what the hell he'd done. And he got real belligerent with me and said 'Damn you Heitman, mess outa' this or I'll do you too.' Then I let go of his arm and went to check on Frank. He was out cold, and snoring loud, like he was asleep. I tried to wake him up, shook him pretty good, but I couldn't rouse him. So then I hollered at Ellicker and Starry to come help me get him off the roadway before a machine came along and ran over him. The three of us half-lifted and half-dragged him over to the side of the road and covered him with his coat. We found that right nearby; we found his hat out in the roadway and I put that on over his face.

"We figured somebody ought to call a taxi and Starry said he'd do it. But first he and Ellicker went over to Knoop and he cussed them out real good. I went over to see what the trouble was and Knoop lit into me, called me one name after another till I got hot too. We were about to come to blows until Ellicker got between us, backed me off and told Slicker we'd all talk about it when he, Slicker that is, was sober. I told him he could damn well count on seein' me again after he'd sobered up.

"I told the rest of the boys to go into town and send a taxi back; I'd stay with Frank 'cause he's my kin. I waited quite a long time and no cab came. Then Chris Sherman came walkin' along on his way to his home on Lytle Road; he and I studied on it together and he promised to get on home and call for a taxi. I stayed with Frank for what seemed another long time, finally gave up and started to walk into town and call a taxi myself. Before I'd got over a few hundred yards a machine passed me; I could see by its lights that it stopped right by where Frank lay. I could see some commotion going on and then he turned around and headed into town. When he passed me I could see it was a taxi, so I figured he'd picked up Frank and was taking him home. There didn't seem to be anything else to do, so I went home too. Next thing I know, the police came to my house at six o'clock Monday morning and arrested me."

Bill Haines rose from his seat at the counsel table and approached the witness. "Charlie, tell the jury whether the four of you formed a plan, at any time, to rob Frank Favorite?"

"No sir."

"Did you rob him?"

"No sir."

"Did you see anyone strike him?"

"No sir."

"Did you strike him, either before or after he was down?"

"No sir."

"Did you feel his head with your hand?"

"Yes sir. I noticed a ridge on the top of his head, toward the back."

Bill Haines had one final question. "Charlie, I want to know if you can tell the jury whether Frank Favorite, when he passed you that evening, by the ticket house, was drunk or sober."

"Yes sir. He was kinda unsteady on his feet, seemed like he staggered just a little. I thought he was pretty drunk. We all did. That's why we thought he was O.K. We just needed to get him home so he could sleep it off."

LEONARD SHIPMAN CONDUCTED the cross-examination of Charles Heitman for the prosecution, but was unable to score any significant inroads on his direct testimony. If anything, the cross-examination served to buttress the effect of the witness's earlier description of the events.

Shipman's attempts to encourage contradictions were random and essentially ineffectual. When he asked, "Now Charlie, when Frank Favorite asked you for the loan of a dollar, was there some good reason you didn't lend it to him?"

"Yes sir."

"What was that good reason ?"

"I didn't have a dollar. I told him I only had thirty cents to my name, but he was welcome to it. Then I turned out my pockets to show him; I had two dimes, a nickel and five pennies. That's why I told him to have some whiskey and forget about goin' to Piqua."

And, with reference to the brief altercation, Shipman asked, "You heard a blow struck during the argument, did you not?"

"No sir."

"Do you mean to say that you took hold of Slicker and excoriated him without knowing that he had struck a blow?"

"Yes sir. I had an idea that he had, but I wasn't sure. I saw Frank lying there and I thought something serious had happened," answered Heitman. Then, as an afterthought, he added, "I guess I was right about that."

Judge Jones rapped his gavel to quell the laughter that erupted from the gallery at Heitman's response. He reminded the entire assemblage, spectators and jurors alike, that neither the trial nor the underlying events were laughing matters. Any further outbreaks would result in his clearing the courtroom.

Shipman persisted, "Didn't you tell Officer Harris that Slicker Knoop had hit Favorite with a blackjack?"

"No sir."

"Let me understand. You are aware that a blackjack, such as the one introduced here a few days ago, is usually filled with lead, are you not? That's what makes it so effective a weapon, right?"

"Yes sir."

"And when you were quarreling with Slicker, didn't he scratch a line alongside the road and tell you 'If you cross that line, I'll use the same lead on you'?"

"No sir. He drew the line alright, but what he said was that he'd fill me full of lead. I knew what he meant, but he didn't have a gun either."

Then, after exploring other seemingly unrelated matters, all without success, Shipman narrowed his eyes and quietly asked the witness, "How much of Favorite's money did you get, Charlie?"

Bill Haines barely reacted. He merely looked up from his notes and smiled at the witness; then he instructed, "Go ahead and answer it Charlie. It's not a fair question, but you can answer it anyway."

And Heitman complied, "Not a penny. Nor did anyone else."

Leonard Shipman's cross-examination of Charles Heitman had begun late Friday evening and continued on into the Saturday morning session. It was long, sometimes disjointed, and tedious, and ultimately served the state's case very poorly. For that reason, Bill Haines saw no need for re-direct and the witness was excused. Judge Jones declared a mid-morning recess.

Chapter Twenty-three

The presentation of evidence in the case of *The State of Ohio vs. Forrest Knoop* was taking somewhat more time than anyone had anticipated. For that reason, and because he had promised his medical experts that they might be released by week's end, Bill Haines now found it necessary to take them out of his intended sequence. In order to accommodate their schedules, and to fulfill his own promises, he interrupted his preconcerted flow of testimony long enough to call two physicians and a former coroner to the stand to refute the assertions made by the state's medical witnesses.

As soon as Judge Jones reconvened court after the morning recess, Dr. D. L. Trowbridge was summoned to the witness stand. He was a practicing physician with offices located in nearby Piqua and he controverted virtually all of the testimony offered by Drs. Thompson, Wright and Coleman.

It was most unlikely, said Dr. Trowbridge, that a wound such as that described by the examining physicians could have been caused by an overhand blow to the head. It was also unlikely that such an overhand blow to the top of the head would have proved fatal. Dr. Trowbridge believed it to be far more probable that an injury such as that described would have been produced by a backward fall to the pavement. Neither did he believe that the injury could have been the result of a blow delivered by a blackjack, a club or other round object. He scoffed at the prosecutor's suggestion that a blackjack precisely fitted the declivity as shown by the plaster cast fabricated by Dr. Thompson.

During the afternoon session Montgomery County Coroner J. W. McKenzie and former Dayton police surgeon H. T. Ryan agreed entirely with the testimony and opinions expressed by Dr. Trowbridge. Coroner McKenzie said that a depressed skull fracture could not have been produced by a direct blow to the top of the head without causing a visible laceration and/or contusion to the scalp at the point of contact. Since the examining doctors had reported no observable damage to the integument at that site, he believed that no such blow had been struck.

Leonard Shipman's cross-examination served only to strengthen the opinion testimony of the defense medical team. In response to Shipman's having pressed the point, Coroner McKenzie postulated that a normal skull could not be depressed to the extent reported by the examining physicians without an accompanying fracture of the "inner tables of the vault" and no such phenomenon had been reported. He added, gratuitously, that a fall to the pavement might have caused "an effusion at the lamboidal suture" and, in such an event, it was within the realm of reasonable probability that the skull would have been telescoped forward, fracturing the frontal and left parietal bones in a manner similar to that described. In point of fact, he said, over the course of his career he had seen cases where precisely that had occurred.

Then, on re-direct, each of the defense experts acknowledged that all the questions could have been resolved if an autopsy had been performed. Even at this date, they agreed, a post-mortem would be helpful.

Just before five o'clock Judge Jones inquired of the attorneys as to whether they had reached an appropriate point for recess, and upon being reassured by all counsel, he announced that court would be adjourned for the weekend. As a part of that process, however, he spent nearly half an hour charging the jurors concerning their conduct during the recess. They would not, of course, be permitted to go home on Sunday, but they might expect that every reasonable ministration would be made for their comfort. Finally, he admonished them to be meticulous in their avoidance of any mention of any of the evidence that had been adduced during the trial. With that, he thanked them for their service as jurors, bid them a felicitous weekend, apologized for their inconvenience, and gave them over to the custody of the bailiff.

Over cocktails and dinner that evening, Bill Haines described for Blanche's benefit the week's proceedings in court. He provided her with a thorough and in-depth reprise of the prosecution's medical testimony, his own cross-examination of the state's witnesses, and his perception of the effect of the defense rebuttal testimony. He was, he allowed, very well satisfied with the state of the record.

"Well," she said, "I am glad of that. But I think you know my own reaction to your rough handling of Dr. Thompson. I personally consider him to be a real gentleman. He's also the finest physician we know. I can't believe he much appreciated your niggling at him over matters which you, yourself, have acknowledged to be of little consequence."

"Now, Blanche," he remonstrated, "I really haven't said that our differences are of little consequence."

"Same thing," she snapped. "You said you didn't actually want a postmortem for Frank Favorite. All you wanted to accomplish was the creation of uncertainty and confusion. I take that to mean you have no real desire to learn the truth; your sole purpose has been to obfuscate the truth."

Bill Haines sniffed peevishly. "Well, of course, that's part of it. But I have to do what I can to cast doubt over the prosecution's version of the cause of death, the hard facts of the case."

She capitulated. "I understand it, dear. It's what you do. After all these years, I understand. But so far as Wilbur Thompson is concerned, I still don't like it much." She smiled at him. "Especially right now. I think I'm very close."

They chatted awhile about her confinement, their prospects for an uneventful delivery, potential names for the new baby, and all the other hopes and fears of expectant parents. Then, inexorably, their conversation directed itself back to the trial.

"You know," he remarked, "I could almost feel sorry for Slicker Knoop. This thing's been an ordeal for him too. He's the one whose life and freedom are at stake. If the jury convicts, he's the one who goes to the chair—or, if he's lucky, to jail for the rest of his life. I'll simply go back to the office and look into another file. I really have considerably less at stake here than he does. Truly, there's no comparison at all.

"The last few days he's been looking pretty discouraged—kind of dejected, almost forlorn. At the start of the trial his mother sat beside him every day. And one or the other of his uncles too. They'd be her brothers, the Knoop boys."

"They're not there now?" she asked.

"No. I had to identify them as prospective witnesses and the judge put them under the rule, segregated them. Now he's all by himself. Except for the lawyers."

"And they'd be poor company," she appended.

"True enough, love," he admitted. "He needs us, but we're probably not much moral support."

"Well then," she queried, "do you feel no compassion for the Favorite family? They've already lost their son. What do you feel for them?"

"They have all the sympathy in the world, Blanche. All that I can muster. The Favorites and the Rudys, too, are the only truly innocent parties to this whole farrago. Dan Favorite has long since collapsed from grief and poor Mary has spent almost every waking hour in the courtroom listening to the witnesses condemning her son as the town drunk. Both sides. And I acknowledge that's not the case. From all I can learn, he was a pretty nice guy, well-liked by about everybody. Sometimes he drank too much, but still a fairly decent person.

"Of course, Mary Favorite has now been identified as a prospective witness too, so she's been excluded also. That's probably just as well. For her sake, that is. This has had to be hard for her."

On Sunday afternoon, Bill Haines visited his client at the county jail. He arranged himself in the juvenile detention room while Sheriff Joe Barnett collected his prisoner and escorted him into the room. The detention room had not been designed for the purpose, but experience had shown it to be the most comfortable facility for attorney-client conferences. The necessary greetings were exchanged and the sheriff excused himself.

"All right, Slicker," began Bill Haines, "It's decision time. We've talked about it before, and you've had time to think about it. Now we need to decide which way we're going to jump."

Slicker Knoop drew himself up from his customary slouch. "There's no question about it, Mr. Haines. I intend to take the stand and testify. I'm innocent and the jurors want me to tell them so. I can see it in their faces."

"You're sure?" asked Haines.

"I'm sure," answered Knoop. "How would it look if I didn't get up there and tell my side of things. They'd think I had something to hide. Something bad I didn't want to tell about."

"They're not supposed to draw any inferences from your refusal to testify. The judge shall so instruct," Haines advised.

"Yeah, so I've heard," Knoop remarked sardonically. "And I don't believe for one minute they'll listen to that instruction. Besides, I want to look at them and tell them direct that I'm innocent."

"All right then, that's settled," said Haines. "You'll testify. But I want you to be careful. Don't get cocky. Don't try to outwit the prosecutors. You're clever, but you're not that clever. They'll probably put Campbell on you. He's their best man. He's never lost a case as a prosecutor, and there's a good reason for that. So you need to play it straight. Answer his questions as best you can—and don't get caught. All right?"

"All right."

Haines scrutinized his client thoughtfully, then pushed his chair back and climbed to his feet. He smiled ruefully. He was glad of his client's decision, thought it to be correct, but he still had apprehensions. He didn't want any clinkers at this stage of the game. He placed his hand on Knoop's shoulder. "Try to get a good night's sleep. It's going to be a grueling week."

THE WEEKEND WOULD NOT HAVE BEEN COMPLETE if there had not been a bit of excitement within the Haines household.

Late in the afternoon, Blanche called to her husband and asked him to summon Dr. Thompson. "You'll want to be quick about it," she said. "It's nearly time. And try to be nice to him."

Chapter Twenty-four

The penultimate day of January, the 30th, had provided a much needed respite for the participants in the Slicker Knoop murder trial. The grueling, tumultuous, and frequently tiresome activities of the previous week had taken its toll on the combatants. The litigants, the witnesses, the lawyers, and even Judge Jones himself, had all become both jaded with the trial and sorely enervated by their own efforts. The fortuitous intervention of that single day-long interlude had served as a welcome balm to their separate fatigues.

Monday morning, the last day of the month, found all of them refreshed and regenerated, ready to continue in earnest. Even Judge Jones seemed to be entirely refreshed by the weekend holiday. As he opened court for the morning session, he greeted the jurors cordially and expressed his fervent hopes that they had not been too greatly discommoded by their enforced segregation from their families.

Then, having accepted the mumbled assurances of the individual jurors, he nodded in their direction and turned his attention to the counsel tables. "And good morning to you, gentlemen, I trust that you also had an enjoyable Sunday with your families." He fixed his glance on Bill Haines at the defense table. "I apprehend, Mr. Haines, that congratulations to you are in order on the birth of a new child. Do I have that right?"

Bill Haines rose and replied respectfully. "You have it correctly, Your Honor. At precisely eight o'clock last evening, Mrs. Haines was delivered of a healthy, seven-pound baby boy whom we have named William Alverno Haines. The doctor had promised a son and that's what we got. I could not be happier."

Judge Jones rejoined, "The prophecy fulfilled, eh? That's as it should be. I'm glad for you. Is Mrs. Haines doing well?"

"Very well, thank you," replied Bill Haines.

"Might I ask who was the attending?" inquired Judge Jones.

"Of course you may. Dr. Wilbur Thompson attended to my wife and child. And, as might have been expected, he performed yeoman service."

Upon that pronouncement, Judge Jones nodded his agreement that Haines' expectation was fully justified, noted a subtle irony in the circumstance and reflected on the good doctor's total professionalism.

"If you're ready, counselor, you may call your first witness." The amenities had concluded. Trial would resume.

Bill Haines began the morning's proceedings with the testimony of the defendant's mother. Mrs. Burton told the jury that she had heard her son enter their home some time between twelve-thirty and one o'clock that Monday morning. Then, she said, between four-thirty and five o'clock that same morning, the police arrived and arrested him. Officer Harris told her only that Forrest had struck a man out by the fairgrounds. As soon as they left, she dressed and went to her brother's home. After conferring with her brother, L. P. Knoop, she returned to her home to await word. It was late afternoon when Officer Harris appeared and searched Forrest's room, including the dresser and washstand. When Harris had demanded Forrest's clothing of the previous evening, she told him that her son was wearing them.

There was no cross-examination of Mrs. Burton and she was excused

and thereafter was permitted to sit with the defendant at the counsel table.

Another ten witnesses were next paraded to the stand to recite their separate recollections concerning the activities of Frank Favorite on the Saturday before he was killed. The purpose of their appearance was to reinforce the defense contentions that the decedent was essentially drunk all day and that he had very little money on his person the entire weekend.

Then, after the mid-morning recess, Slicker Knoop was called to the stand to present his own version of the events of Sunday, June 27, 1915. He responded to Bill Haines' questions fully and appeared to be both candid and confident. He was an exceptionally handsome man, impeccably groomed, and he had an amiable charm that projected itself to the jurors and to the spectators alike.

At Bill Haines' gentle prompting, the witness identified himself as Forrest Knoop, known to most people as "Slicker." Until his incarceration last fall he had been employed as deputy county engineer. On the Sunday in question he and his friend Clyde Starry, who had slept over the preceding night, had gone first to the Harmon and Edwards Restaurant for breakfast, then they went to the Horace Smith poolroom, bought four decks of playing cards, and waited for the early car to the clubhouse. There was no one there when they arrived, other than Pony Favorite and his little boy. That would have been Russell, he said. He'd have been about eleven years old. There was a short, desultory conversation which ended when Pony sent the boy to town to buy some eggs and Slicker took a nap on Pony's mattress in the middle room of the clubhouse. A goodly number of men arrived while he slept and by the time he was awakened at about one-thirty in the afternoon they appeared to have consumed a considerable quantity of beer and whiskey. They had waked him, he said, to have a drink with them and to start a card game. From that time forward, until the game broke up just before eleven o'clock, he was never out of his chair or away from the table.

Knoop said that he had run the game for Pony Favorite and when it had ended he and Pony retired to the front room to settle the take-off; this consisted of five cents dragged off from each pot and it was to be divided equally between himself, Clyde Starry and Pony. After the split had been accomplished there was a crap game, lasting no more than five minutes, and Knoop had won three dollars and a half. Frank Favorite had been in that game and had lost all the money he'd had with him. Then, Knoop said, because he'd had a good day, he set up the drinks for the men still at the clubhouse. That would have been both Favorites, Starry, Ellicker and Heitman. A few minutes later they began to leave, first Starry and Ellicker, then Frank Favorite and Heitman. He had chatted awhile with Pony, perhaps five minutes or so, then left the clubhouse. He crossed over the canal on the log bridge, made his way to the cement highway and walked along the road towards town. When he reached the Lytle Road car stop he heard voices ahead of him and concluded that the other men had missed the last car and intended to walk back to town. He hurried along and soon overtook Starry and Heitman who had stopped at the north end of the fairgrounds. He spoke with them, then went along and caught Ellicker and Favorite at the end of the fence between the traction line and the road.

Surprisingly, he said, he had noted that Favorite was more than just mildly drunk; he had also seemed, inexplicably, quite hostile. He told Favorite, "You'd best be careful, you're pretty drunk, you could hurt yourself." And Frank had taunted him with, "I've got your girlfriend, Slicker. She's mine now."

Then, when Slicker had said he didn't have a girl friend, Frank had hooted at him, told him he'd spent Saturday with Peerless Mame and she'd told him she'd been Slicker's girlfriend, but now liked him, Frank, a lot better. That he'd rung her bell like Slicker never had.

"What happened next?" prodded Bill Haines.

"He called me a liar. Said I wasn't man enough to fight him for her. Then I said she wasn't worth fighting for; she was nothing more than a Saturday night plaything. A trollop. That seemed to make Frank really hot. He wanted to fight me right then and there."

"And?"

"And I told him he was too drunk to fight anybody. Then Bob Ellicker got between us to push Frank back a little. I thought it was over and there wouldn't be a fight, but Frank edged himself around Ellicker and came at me again. He called me a son-of-a-bitch, said if I wouldn't fight for her, by God, he would. Then he drew back his fist, like this," Knoop rose from the witness chair and demonstrated, "and I just up and hit him. Like this," and, still standing, he struck Bill Haines a hard blow to the chest. Haines, who had positioned himself directly in front of his client in anticipation of the demonstration, reeled from the force of the impact and only saved himself from falling by grasping the corner of the prosecutors' counsel table. "And Frank went over backwards. He must have hit his head on the cement highway."

"Then Charlie Heitman ran up and grabbed my arm. He cursed at me and asked why I'd done that. I got mad and told him to stay out of it—or something like that, I'm not sure what—I couldn't imagine what he was so hot about. He must not have heard the quarrel. Next thing was that the three of them, Heitman, Ellicker and Starry, tried to get Frank up off the ground. They couldn't get that done and I figured it was because he was too drunk. Then Charlie started ragging on me again and I thought he wanted to fight me too. Starry and Ellicker broke that up and Heitman said he'd see me later—after I was sober.

"Anyway, we got through all that and finally decided that Heitman would stay with Frank and the rest of us would go on into town and send a taxi back to pick up Frank. The three of us walked on to Harmon and Edmunds restaurant, called for a cab, had a bowl of soup together, and I went home to bed. I think Starry and Ellicker did too.

"Next thing I knew, my mother woke me up and told me Officer Harris wanted me to come downstairs right away. I put on my trousers and shoes and hurried down. Harris told me to go back up and dress because I was under arrest for assault. When we got to the sidewalk I saw officers Sharits and Landrey. Harris told me I'd hit Frank Favorite a hell of a blow with a stone. I asked him who'd said it was with a stone and he said it was Ellicker and Starry. Then as we passed the hospital on the way downtown, Harris chewed on me some more; he said, 'There lays the man whose head you crushed like an eggshell.' Then they put me in jail."

Now Bill Haines took control. "Tell the jury whether you had a blackjack that night."

"Never in my life did I have a blackjack."

"Tell the jury whether you struck Frank Favorite with any blunt instrument?"

"No sir. I didn't have a blunt instrument."

"Did you strike him with an instrument of any kind?"

"No sir. I just pushed him," and Knoop gestured with a forward motion of his hand and arm.

DURING THE NOON RECESS, Bill Haines made an occasion to stop by the jailhouse to tell his client that he thought his direct testimony had gone well. He nonetheless repeated his earlier caution to beware of Alvah Campbell's cross-examination. He hadn't meant to unsettle Knoop on that score, but he did feel it necessary to warn him. He considered Campbell to be a tough and incisive examiner.

Bill Haines'certainty that the cross-examination of the defendant would fall to Campbell was fully justified. The former prosecutor lost no time in getting to the issues.

"Slicker, did you have a gun with you that night?"

"No. I did not."

"Then what did you mean when you told Charlie Heitman you'd 'fill him full of lead'?"

"I said that—or something like that—because I was drunk. I'm not real sure what I said to him, but whatever it was, it was because I was drunk."

"You're a professional gambler, are you not?"

"At the time of my arrest I was deputy county surveyor."

"Oh, yes, I'm aware that you spent time in the surveyor's office, but you do know all about poker, don't you?"

"No sir. I don't know all about poker—or anything else, for that matter. I do know a good deal about it."

And then Campbell engaged the witness in a protracted and essentially meaningless dialogue about the card game, the stakes, the players, and who had won and who had lost. Knoop answered all the questions with ease and apparent candor. The examination seemed to lose direction and resolved itself into a series of random thrusts and ineffective parries.

"Frank Favorite was pretty drunk that night, wasn't he?"

"Yes sir."

"Yet you felt no compunction about getting him to shoot craps?"

"Well, I was pretty drunk, too."

"Were you drunk when you were playing poker?"

"I wasn't too drunk to run the game."

This last response engendered some restrained chortles from the spectators' gallery; several of the jurors seemed amused. A stern look from Judge Jones was sufficient to restore order. Now Alvah Campbell shifted direction.

"Why did you stop shooting craps after only a few minutes?"

"I wanted to shoot for a dollar or a dollar and a half, but Favorite wanted to shoot for a quarter. He said he didn't have much money."

Campbell next devoted an inordinate amount of time and attention to the crap game, demanding to know who was present, who participated and how much each of the players had won or lost. The purpose of his dwelling upon such matters was a mystery that defied Bill Haines' best efforts to see where, if anywhere, it was leading.

As the afternoon wore on, the prosecutor became yet more confrontational. "Didn't Bob Ellicker say he wanted to get Frank into the poker game because he was carrying a big roll of money?"

"No sir, I didn't hear anyone say that."

"Did you hear Pony Favorite testify that you and Ellicker were sitting together in a room by yourselves, conferring together?"

"I heard him say it. It wasn't true."

"Did you also hear him testify that you looked at your watch during the poker game?"

"Yes sir, but that wasn't true either. I wasn't carrying a watch that day."

"Do you mean to tell this jury you played poker all day without a watch?"

"Why, yes. You don't need a watch to play poker."

This time the laughter was unrestrained. Both spectators and jurors broke up. Judge Jones repressed a smile, then gaveled for order. In an effort to retrieve the situation, Campbell shot back, "There is no need of a blackjack to play poker either, is there?"

And Knoop responded quickly, "No sir, there is not."

Then Gilmer Thomas, whose participation in the trial had been minimal, supplemented the answer, "That's why he didn't have one, Alvah."

Judge Jones rapped sharply. "That remark will be stricken. Counselor, you know better than that."

Alvah Campbell, the astute prosecutor who had never lost a case, became flustered and his questions became more random. At one point he asked, "When you were on the road, could you see a man in front of you as far as your eye could reach?"

And Slicker Knoop quickly replied, "Why yes. If not, I couldn't have seen him, could I?" Which produced such an outbreak of laughter that Judge Jones found it necessary to declare a recess.

Alvah Campbell's cross-examination was resumed after the recess and droned on for another hour, during which time Knoop was merely required to rehearse, and to thereby fortify, the testimony which he had given on direct. Finally, mercifully, the dialogue between defendant and prosecutor ground to a halt. If anyone could be said to have won the encounter, it was not the prosecutor.

Bill Haines ended the day's evidence with Clyde Starry. His testimony was entirely consistent with that of the defendant. He had not seen any blows struck and he had tried to restrain both Knoop and Heitman after Frank Favorite had fallen. Alvah Campbell's cross-examination failed to make a dent in Starry's testimony.

Chapter Twenty-five

As though he had studied on the matter overnight, Alvah Campbell began Tuesday morning's session with the announcement that he had "just a few" more questions of Clyde Starry. He then proceeded to subject that witness to another two-hour grilling in a desperate effort to shake him from the story he had told the previous afternoon. He failed utterly to make any serious inroads on Starry's direct testimony and finally let him go.

Another handful of witnesses was called to the stand to fill out the time before the mid-morning recess. Their testimony was, singly and collectively, inconsequential and essentially insignificant to the real issues for trial. It consisted of a series of isolated statements concerning Frank Favorite's activities over the two-day weekend of his death, how much or how little money he had, how much he'd had to drink, who had been at the clubhouse on Sunday, when they had arrived, how long they had stayed and whatever else the witnesses had seen and heard. Very little controversy occurred and the taking of evidence in this regard became increasingly tedious for the spectators and, more importantly, for the jurors.

That tedium, however, quickly resolved when court was reconvened after the mid-morning recess. It had been known and widely circulated by the courthouse observers that Bob Ellicker would be called that day, which produced the largest crowd, seated, standing and waiting outside, in decades. It was generally appreciated that Bob Ellicker had been the one person who, by all accounts, had been in the immediate proximity of the defendant and the decedent when whatever it was the prosecution claimed had actually happened.

Ellicker presented a striking contrast to all of the witnesses who had preceded him onto the stand. He was by far the youngest member of the clubhouse group; he would not be twenty-one until February 9th, next week. He was handsome, clean cut, and formally dressed in a blue serge suit with a neat black bow tie; some of the spectators remarked that he lacked the hardened, man-about-town look that had characterized the other principals involved in the case.

He was seen to blush unashamedly as he glanced about the courtroom and was obviously abashed when he noticed that he was the center of attention of all the many onlookers, the jurors, the lawyers and the court personnel. He became more comfortable and progressively better at ease as he told first of his own activities on the Saturday evening and Sunday morning of June 26th and 27th, 1915. He seemed to gain confidence as he was called upon to relate matters which were neither in controversy nor of especial relevance. He said that he had spent some time Saturday night with his friend Frank Favorite. Then, on Sunday morning, he and his brother had ridden about the countryside on his motorcycle. He did not go to the clubhouse until after dinner, stayed there about an hour or so talking with other friends, and went to a baseball game with Squint Miller. He'd gone home after the game, had supper, and went to the corner of Main and Elm at about 6:30. He had encountered Frank Favorite and George McKenzie there and the three of them walked uptown together. Shortly afterwards, he said, they took a taxi to the clubhouse. Frank had paid for the ride and later gave him two dollars, one at a time, by way of staking him to the poker game. Frank declined an invitation to play himself, saying he didn't understand the game. He did, however, engage for a short while in a crap game with Clyde Starry. Frank had spent most of the evening drinking and talking with friends.

Ellicker remembered that when it came time to leave, Clyde Starry had been the first to cross the footbridge and he, Ellicker, was right behind him. Then Favorite had called to them to wait for him, and the three of them proceeded towards town together. They were soon overtaken by Heitman and then by Knoop. He said that Knoop's first comment, upon joining the others, was that Favorite was pretty drunk. Favorite remarked that he'd been with Knoop's girlfriend and Knoop answered that he didn't have a girlfriend. The conversation deteriorated rapidly after that and Favorite called Knoop a son-of-a-bitch and tried to provoke a fight. Knoop refused the challenge, telling Favorite he was in no condition to fight. Ellicker said he'd managed to restrain Favorite twice, and the third time Favorite tore off his coat and handed it to Ellicker; this time, Ellicker said, he'd grasped Favorite's left arm, but Favorite raised his right and made to strike Knoop. The next thing he knew, Favorite fell backwards, and hit his head hard on the cement road. Ellicker assumed that Knoop had struck Favorite, but didn't see it happen. He had no sense that any weapon had been used.

Haines asked his witness, "Did you, any of you, attempt to take anything out of Favorite's clothing?"

"We did not."

"Did you, or any of you, hit Favorite after he was down?"

"No sir."

Ellicker was able to recite the specifics of the quarrel that ensued when Charlie Heitman grabbed Knoop by the arm and demanded to know why he'd done what he had to Favorite. He recalled that Knoop had grown hot and snarled at Heitman, called him a son-of-a-bitch, dared him to cross a line in the road, and threatened to "fill him full of lead."

Ellicker confirmed their arrangement for Heitman to remain with Favorite while the others went into town to summon a taxi. At the corner of Main and Elm Streets they encountered Tot Spain and George McKenzie, spoke with them briefly, and then McKenzie accompanied them to the restaurant. He said that he had gotten home to bed at about 1:30.

"One last time, Bob," asked Bill Haines before releasing the witness, "Was there any understanding or agreement among the four of you that you were to meet at the fairgrounds, or anywhere else, and rob Frank Favorite?"

"No sir."

"Had you discussed the subject of robbing him, any of you—by twos, by threes, or by fours? Did you concert together at all?"

"No sir."

Bill Haines closed his file with a flourish, measured the jury for only a moment, and announced to the prosecutors, in a manner that bordered on the arrogant, "Your witness."

Bob Ellicker's testimony on direct had been concluded. Judge Jones adjourned court for the noon recess.

AFTER LUNCH THAT AFTERNOON Alvah Campbell began his cross-examination of Bob Ellicker by inquiring whether Ellicker had discussed his testimony with Bill Haines.

"Yes sir," replied the witness. "There've been several times when I've spoken with Mr. Haines over at the jailhouse. My lawyer, Mr. Thomas, and Slicker Knoop and Clyde Starry were there too."

"And on any of those occasions, did Mr. Haines ever tell you what he wanted you to say?"

"Yes sir."

"Mr. Haines is not your lawyer, is he?"

"No sir."

"All right then, if Mr. Haines is not your lawyer, your conversation with him cannot be privileged. So please tell the jury what it was that Mr. Haines told you to say on the witness stand."

"He told me to tell the truth, sir. They both did," came the swift response. "Mr. Thomas told me the same thing."

Visibly distressed by Ellicker's answer, Campbell changed the course of his examination. He next required the witness to rehash his testimony on direct, beginning with the events of that fateful Saturday afternoon and evening and progressing laboriously through Sunday morning, afternoon and evening. He accomplished little more than to buttress Ellicker's earlier account.

After he had pressed the witness to recount the details of the fracas between Slicker Knoop and Frank Favorite for the second time, Campbell became overtly confrontational:

"Do you want this jury to understand that you stood within two feet of these men, and did not see the lick struck?" he thundered.

"That's exactly what I want the jury to understand."

"Didn't you tell Clay Geisinger that same night that you'd seen Slicker Knoop blackjack Frank Favorite?"

"I did not."

Alvah Campbell gave up. He announced to the court, in exasperated tones, that he had no more questions.

But Bill Haines did. On re-direct, he asked Ellicker if he hadn't given the same account to Mr. Campbell on other occasions—months before the trial.

"Yes sir. That was last summer. Mr. Shipman was there too. And Mr. Bumbli."

"And what did Mr. Campbell tell you?"

"Mr. Campbell told me I shouldn't tell such a story to a jury; he said they'd never believe me."

"Did you discuss the matter with Officer Sharits?"

"Yes sir. John's my brother-in-law. He told me to tell the truth. And that's what I've done."

Bill Haines excused the witness; he'd been on the stand for more than five hours. And Judge Jones declared a mid-afternoon recess.

Twenty minutes later, when court had re-convened, Bill Haines rose to his feet and solemnly announced that the defense rested its case.

Then, in response to Judge Jones' inquiry as to whether the prosecution intended to produce any rebuttal evidence, Alvah Campbell produced B. C. Hardy, Clarence Duvall and Fred Smith, all of whom testified that despite Knoop's insistence that he had never owned a blackjack, they had seen him with just such an instrument on numerous occasions.

And Police Officer John Sharits testified that his brother-in-law, Bob Ellicker, had told him that "Knoop struck over his (Ellicker's) shoulder and hit Favorite; it sounded like a pistol shot, and Favorite fell like a ton of bricks."

Former Troy Mayor M.T. Dilts testified that Ellicker had told him that "Knoop had struck Favorite on the head with something."

The last rebuttal witness was perhaps the most damaging to the defense. William Rensch, a local farmer, told of a conversation he had had with Clyde Starry a few days after Favorite's death. "Don't worry," Starry had said. "We boys have a story all fixed up, and there'll never be anything come of it."

And try as he might, Bill Haines was unable to shake the witness. He was adamant about what Starry had said to him.

On that high note, the prosecution rested its case on rebuttal. There would be no sur-rebuttal. The evidence was all in.

Chapter Twenty-six

Bill Haines sat down to a solitary dinner that evening. Blanche was exhausted by her frequent ministrations to their two-day old son. Now the girls were spending the night with friends, the baby was asleep and Blanche had seized the opportunity to catch a small measure of sorely-needed rest. She had retired shortly before her husband had come home from his wars. Her sister-in-law, Bertha Bausman, had been helping with the new baby and with the household chores, but this evening Bill Haines had insisted she return to her husband and sons, and leave him to his own devices. He would manage, he assured her. Apart from his concerns about his wife and child, he was quite content to make his own dinner and to consume it in solitude. He had permitted himself a single pre-dinner cocktail.

He had not minded re-heating yesterday's left-overs and laying out the table service for himself. Those small exercises had afforded him both the time and the opportunity to organize his thoughts. He and the other defense lawyers had agreed to meet in his offices at eight o'clock that evening to prepare their requests for special charges to the jury. The rules of trial practice provided each side with the option of requesting that the court instruct the jury, prior to final argument, as to certain specific points of the law, and if the requests for such instructions were relevant to the issues, legally correct and otherwise appropriate to the case, the court was duty-bound to read them to the jury. These special charges, given before argument, were in addition to the general charge which the court was required to give after the arguments of counsel and before submission of the case to the jury for deliberation.

Seated at his customary place at the kitchen table, a newly-sharpened pencil and a fresh pad of foolscap at hand, Bill Haines wrote, struck-over, erased and otherwise formulated and revised his own first draft of the requests for special charges, all the while gnawing gamely at the rehabilitated and re-warmed slab of brisket he'd found in the icebox. A bowl of cold porridge and a glass of milk completed his meal; a moment later he completed his scribbles, surveyed his notes and tossed the pad onto the table by the door. An hour later, fully refreshed after a short nap on the davenport, he donned coat and hat and set off for the office. It was likely to be another in a series of late nights.

THE FOLLOWING MORNING found the entire courthouse teeming with people from all over the near part of the state. From within and without the county, there were spectators, those who would be spectators, new reporters, visiting lawyers and judges, students on leave, souvenir hunters and others who had followed the proceedings in the newspapers or by word of mouth. Many had arrived well before daylight and had camped, in the early February cold, on the courthouse lawn in hopes of finding a seat within the courtroom to watch the day's proceedings. Those who could not gain access to the inner sanctum would gather to wait patiently and hopefully in the huge third-floor atrium, beyond the big double doors that led into the courtroom, against the possibility of ultimate success. Collectively they comprised the largest such assemblage in the history of the county.

The attraction for this day's burgeoning crowd had nothing to do with the proceedings concerning the defendant's request for special charges. That which had attracted so large a crowd was the certain knowledge, gleaned either from word of mouth or from the rampant newspaper reportage, that the evidence had concluded and that the next and most exciting order of business would be the perorations of counsel, final arguments.

Few, if any, of the would-be onlookers had any conception as to what was happening when Judge Jones opened court before the jury was seated in its box. He would consider, he said, requests of counsel for special instructions to be given to the jury before oral argument. Those issues, strictly legal in their nature, would be treated by court and counsel outside the presence of the jury.

Predictably, the prosecutors had no such requests for instruction. Bill Haines' defense team had twenty, each of which was supported by legal citation, precedent and the arguments of counsel. After an hour and a half of wrangling and posturing on the part of the lawyers, and judicious consideration by the court, Judge Jones announced that he would give the jury fourteen of the requested instructions; the remaining six failed to state the law as he found it to be. Bill Haines entered his objections to the ruling, but was secretly well-satisfied. Fourteen out of twenty was a better percentage than he'd hoped for.

The jury was escorted into the courtroom by the bailiff and the judge advised them of the parties' right to special instructions before arguments. He swivelled his chair to address them directly, slid his wire-frames down his nose and began to read the charges. Utilizing the precise language written by the defense team and approved by the court, he advised the panel that:

"The allegations of the indictment charging the defendant with murder in an attempt to rob becomes a substitute for the premeditation normally required to ground a conviction of murder in the first degree, and if you find the assault was not made in an attempt to rob, the defendant must be acquitted of murder in the first degree.

"If you find by a fair preponderance of the evidence that Favorite assaulted the defendant, then the defendant was justified in defending himself, and if such defense could not reasonably be anticipated to cause death, your verdict must be 'not guilty.'

"The mere fact that Knoop purposely struck Favorite a blow that caused his death does not give rise to a conclusive presumption that the defendant intended to kill Favorite.

"If there is any reasonable probability of the innocence of the defendant, then a reasonable doubt of his guilt also exists, and the jury must render a verdict of 'not guilty.'"

Judge Jones' reading of the fourteen special instructions droned on for the better part of half an hour. As he paused between each of the fourteen charges he peered keenly in their direction as if to inquire whether they had understood. When no questions came, he assumed that they had. By the time he had finished, it was after ten o'clock and he declared the mid-morning recess. Final arguments would begin as soon as they reconvened.

AND ARGUE THEY DID. For the better part of two days the lawyers perorated. Alvah Campbell led off for the prosecution immediately after court reconvened. He reviewed the evidence, the testimony of each of the principal witnesses, and drew the attention of the jurors to the uniform consistency on the part of the state's witnesses and the irreconcilable inconsistencies in the several stories told by the defense witnesses. He reminded the panel that all of the key witnesses for the defendant, Heitman, Starry and Ellicker, had been indicted for the same offense and were slated to stand trial themselves in the months to come. Slicker Knoop was being tried first because it was he who had actually struck the fatal blow. These others were just as guilty as Knoop; they were themselves, in every sense of the word, accomplices to the robbery and murder of Frank Favorite. That they had all lied on the witness stand was precisely that which might have been expected. Their own guilt, as well as that of Knoop, was at issue in this case. It was obvious that the three of them had got their heads together in order to choreograph their evidence. Remember, Campbell told the jurors, that the state had shown that the stories they told on the witness stand had differed significantly from that which they told on prior occasions.

Consider also, he adjured, the fact that Favorite had been carrying a large sum of money the two days before his death, and that after his murder, he'd had no more than a nickel on his person. The defendant, together with his cronies, had conspired to hound him down the traction line and to strike him dead for his money. Campbell pointed an accusatory finger at Slicker Knoop and excoriated him in withering, thunderous tones, "You are a low-down dog. You have broken the commandment and taken a valuable human life. And you lied when you told this jury that you hadn't hit Frank Favorite, your friend, a savage blow, and then compounded your crime by taking money off his dying person."

Campbell's argument lasted more than two hours. He was as thorough as he was savage. And Slicker Knoop had paled visibly each time Campbell pointed at him and addressed him directly. Mrs. Burton cried softly the entire time and Knoop had no power to comfort her or to shield her from the force of the prosecutor's fury.

Gilmer Thomas took up the cudgel for the defendant immediately after the lunch break. He argued for two and a half hours, also reviewing the testimony, witness by witness, and frequently quoting verbatim from the record. Then, after yet another recess, Bill Haines began his own summation for the defendant. He was still on his feet when court adjourned for the day, and he held forth through most of the Thursday morning session. In total, he argued for an astonishing five and a half hours.

Bill Haines was thorough to a fault. He reviewed each witness's testimony on direct and on cross. Ask yourselves, he implored the jurors, was the witness credible? Was his testimony believable, was it reasonable? Was it consistent with common experience?

He was especially harsh with the doctors. They were all honorable men, he acknowledged. They were fine, capable, well-respected physicians. But they had failed on this one occasion. They had failed to accurately record their findings, failed to arrive at a consensus concerning the precise cause of death, and ultimately failed to insist on a proper postmortem examination. They had all agreed, right there on the witness stand, that an autopsy would have been helpful. With all due respect to their collective expertise, Bill Haines insisted, a proper post mortem would have been not simply helpful, but actually crucial to the expert opinions they were called upon to render. The plaster cast which the doctors produced was, in and of itself, ludicrous. Fabricated from recollection, did someone say? Or was it fabricated with the express purpose of demonstrating that the contours, sculpted from memory, precisely accommodated the blackjack? Which came first? The chicken or the egg? The plaster cast or the blackjack?

Remember the blackjack? There was no suggestion that Slicker Knoop had ever so much as laid eyes on the blackjack. That was produced here, in this courtroom, by the prosecutors. It didn't belong to the defendant. It actually *belonged* to the prosecutors. If it had been the *murder* weapon, did that point the finger at its owners? The prosecutors?

"And speaking of weapons," he continued. "Did any one of you, gentlemen of the jury, hear any testimony about a weapon? Oh, yes, I know that we've heard a great deal of speculation about a blunt object, a hard object, maybe a stone, maybe a blackjack similar to the one the prosecutors turned up; but did anyone actually testify that Slicker Knoop—or any of these other fellows—had such an object, a weapon, on or about them that sorry Sunday night last June?

"I can assure you, gentlemen, that if the state had any slightest evidence about a weapon, we'd have all heard about that from the day this trial began. The reason we've not heard about a weapon is because there is not, and never was, a weapon of any kind. The only hard, blunt object in the vicinity that night was the cement highway where Frank Favorite fell.

"He was drunk, gentlemen. And he should have been. He'd consumed an enormous amount of liquor those two days and he was falling-down drunk. Then when Slicker Knoop shoved him away to avoid a fight, he simply fell over backwards—like this." And with that, Bill Haines threw back his shoulders and fell to the courtroom floor, all the while taking great pains to avoid striking his head.

Then, while lying on the floor, he demonstrated, in slow motion, the mechanics by which Frank Favorite had hit the back of his head on the road surface. He lay there for an extra moment, for effect, then bounced back to his feet to continue the argument.

"Dr. Trowbridge is an eminent physician. He has maintained a successful practice right here in the county for many years. He was not involved in this case in any way, shape or form; he has no axe to grind with anyone here. He is completely independent, and the opinions he expressed in this courtroom are completely objective. He came here last Saturday and told us that it was very probable that an injury such as that sustained by Frank Favorite was produced by a backward fall to the pavement. And Dr. Ryan and Coroner McKenzie entirely agreed with him. These are people from Dayton and Montgomery County. They've both had a vast experience in these matters. All of these medical experts have agreed on one other point, and that is that it is most unlikely that such a wound as described could have been produced by an overhand blow to the top of the head as the prosecutors would have you believe."

As Wednesday afternoon bled over into Thursday morning, Bill Haines seemed to gather steam. Fortified by a fitful, anxious sleep, and a fresh rush of adrenalin, he argued with renewed intensity. He permitted no assertion or scrap of evidence produced by the prosecution to go unchallenged. If he seemed to be nitpicking, he apologized. He revisited the medical testimony and ridiculed the state's refusal to cause a proper autopsy; he jeered at the plaster cast and the prosecutors' prototypical blackjack. He characterized that portion of the state's case as "a sinister charade, a blatant attempt to manufacture evidence where none actually existed."

Most of all, he hammered repeatedly about the absence of the "slightest scintilla" of evidence concerning a weapon of any kind. It was dishonorable, he said, on the part of the prosecutors, to contend the existence of such a weapon against the harsh reality that there was no proof—of any kind—to support their contention. "Smoke and mirrors," he snorted.

Then, just before the morning recess, he finished. He thanked the jurors for their time and their attention. "It's been a long and difficult trial," he said. "And I know you've all had serious business of your own to tend to. I've watched you closely as the evidence has unfolded and I've found you to be interested and attentive. All of us, the prosecutors, defense counsel and the court, very much appreciate your help in resolving this case. I know that you will heed well the admonitions and instructions of the court, especially as to the concept of reasonable doubt, when you begin your deliberations. I know also that you will find the defendant Slicker Knoop innocent of all charges and set him free."

Chapter Twenty-seven

Frank Goodrich spoke for no more than an hour, which was a mercifully short period of time in comparison to that previously consumed. His argument added little or nothing to harangues and diatribes which had preceded his own relatively bland summation. He touched all the bases, the key points upon which the prosecution had rested its case against Slicker Knoop. Then, in perfunctory fashion, he admonished the jury to "do your duty," thanked them for their attention, and sat down.

IMMEDIATELY AFTER A LATE LUNCH on Thursday, February 3rd, Judge Jones delivered to the jury his general charge. Reading from a prepared text, he instructed the jurors concerning their procedure in first electing a foreman, then discussing the evidence and deliberating the issues soberly and thoroughly, and finally, voting as often as was necessary to produce a verdict. A verdict of guilty must be unanimous, he explained. If they had any questions, or if they required anything, they should summon the bailiff, who would be just outside the jury room to insure their privacy and to tend to their needs.

Judge Jones carefully and painstakingly explained the provisions of the Ohio murder statute, the implications of the so-called felony rule, and the specific elements which they must find to support a conviction, motive, intent, opportunity and the like. He also spoke to them about potential affirmative defenses to the charge, such as self-defense, provocation, unavoidable accident, et cetera. Then, too, he advised there were different degrees of the crime charged, murder first, murder second, manslaughter, or even simple assault. They would be provided with alternative verdict forms for their use when they had reached a verdict.

A considerable portion of Judge Jones' general charge was devoted to other legal principles which must guide them in their deliberations. He explained, in great detail, the concepts of "the presumption of innocence with which every defendant is clothed," "burden of proof," "direct evidence," "circumstantial evidence," "legally permissible inferences," "a preponderance of all the evidence," and he provided to them a detailed explication of that "reasonable doubt" beyond which they must be convinced of the defendant's guilt before returning a verdict of "guilty" as to any of the charges included within the indictment. The general charge to the jury had taken something more than an hour's time. As soon as it had been completed, Judge Jones added his own thanks for their service to that which had been expressed by counsel, and promptly consigned them to the custody of the bailiff. It was nearly two o'clock.

Except for the verdict, it was over.

TRIAL LAWYERS AND JUDGES have frequently remarked that the time which intervenes between the submission of a case to a jury and the actual announcement of the verdict is in the nature of an *entr'acte*, a surcharged intermezzo in a very real and usually an intensely human drama. In the case of *The State of Ohio vs. Forrest Knoop*, the lines had been clearly drawn and the stakes were abundantly high.

From time to time, the lawyers would venture out of the courthouse to visit their offices, take some refreshment, or invent some small task to pass the time, but they were soon drawn, irresistibly, back to the arena— the courtroom—which was for each of them at that moment the center of the universe. It is axiomatic with lawyers that time spent in waiting for a verdict is time spent in limbo. The moments themselves, and all the players, are as though frozen in both time and space. It was time taken out of time. The sensory impression was that all the players were locked into a state of artificially suspended animation, a condition which was itself preternaturally fraught with high-voltage tension and inordinate anxiety. And while that tension and anxiety may be self-induced and therefore artificial as well, no trial lawyer will ever admit it to be so.

Most of the spectators chose to remain in their seats behind the rail or in the aisles and window-wells. Some few elected to visit restrooms, sneak out for snacks or for exercise, but even these were unwilling to relinquish their seats for extensive periods.

The lawyers gathered in Judge Jones' chambers across the atrium from the courtroom. There, they milled about, offered remarks, both conciliatory and congratulatory, about one another's performance over the two weeks of trial, and whiled away the time. No one expected the jury to return within a short period. Experience had taught them that they were in store for a long wait. It had been a long, hotly contested trial; there was a great deal of evidence for the jury to weigh and evaluate, and it was of the utmost importance that they get it right. The first time. There would be no second chance. Forrest Knoop's life and liberty were clearly at risk, and it seemed that the verdict might go either way. There was little doubt that the jury would be out for a long time.

Shortly after ten o'clock, the bailiff brought word that the jury had sought—and gained—the court's permission to retire for the night. They were nowhere near a verdict and did not expect that to change for hours. They were tired.

On Judge Jones' orders the courtroom was cleared and the spectators and news reporters sent home. Slicker Knoop was taken back to his jail cell, the judge and the trial participants left the courthouse. Bill Haines returned to his office. He'd sleep there tonight. He hadn't the energy to go home to a warm bed and a fresh change of clothing. And, most of all, he knew he was too overwrought to sleep properly.

AT TWENTY-THREE MINUTES PAST ONE O'CLOCK Friday afternoon the buzzer sounded outside the jury room. After more than thirteen hours they had a verdict.

As if it were possible, the huge crowd of onlookers and reporters of the day before seemed to have grown by geometric progression. People, young and old, male and female, were crammed into places and spaces that couldn't have existed the day before. The lawyers and court personnel had taken their respective stations inside the bar, and Judge Jones was at the bench. At his discreet nod, the bailiff escorted the twelve obviously exhausted jurors into the courtroom and seated them in their box.

John Buchanan had been elected foreman of the jury. He rose in response to Judge Jones' inquiry, and announced that the jury had, indeed, reached a verdict. At a signal from the court he handed a folded paper to Clerk of Courts Brooks Johnson who read in loud clear tones, "We, the members of the jury, do find the defendant Forrest Knoop to be not guilty of the charge contained in the indictment." Nor, it appeared, of any lesser, included charge.

In a trice, Judge Jones thanked the jurors one more time, then turned to the defendant and released him, "Young man," he said easily, "you are free to go."

Slicker Knoop wrapped Bill Haines in an exuberant bear hug, shook hands with the other lawyers who had comprised his defense team and embraced his mother tenderly. After a moment, he released himself and approached the individual jurors, took each by the hand and thanked them warmly, one by one, for their verdict.

A half dozen conversations seemed to be taking place at once as the lawyers congratulated one another yet again on their eloquence, their grasp of the evidence and their professionalism. The disappointment of the prosecutors was greatly outweighed by the euphoria of the defenders. And Slicker Knoop, of course, was ecstatic.

By twos and threes, the players left the arena. Bill Haines conferred briefly with his client, who agreed to come around to Haines' office in the morning. This time, it was truly over.

Chapter Twenty-eight

Although it was scarcely two o'clock in the afternoon, Bill Haines had neither the energy nor the desire to return to his office. After two weeks of trial, he was bone-tired. He was also too preoccupied with the activities of those same two weeks, he told himself, to concentrate on any of the correspondence and other items, unrelated to the trial, which lay on his desk awaiting his attention. Monday would be soon enough.

He walked the few blocks to his residence, noted that Blanche was napping with the baby, the girls were still in school and Bertha had gone home. Greatly relieved to find the opportunity, he stretched out on the living room couch and fell into a deep sleep. Trial work is challenging and exhilarating, especially when the stakes are high—but it is also exhausting.

He awoke in time to begin preparations for dinner while Blanche nursed the baby. Then, over cocktails, he told her of the verdict. It was too soon to tell, he said, how the verdict would be received by the public. The defendant, his family and friends would certainly be elated, and the Favorites, their families and friends, would be disappointed. But no one knew what the general reaction was likely to be. Evenly divided, he guessed.

Their discussion continued into the dinner hour until it simply ran out of steam, faltered and died. Bill Haines finished his meal in silence. When he decided against both dessert and coffee, Blanche eyed him warily.

"Are you feeling poorly?" she asked. "Not catching anything, I hope."

"No love," he assured. "I'm just tired, I guess. I don't seem to have napped long enough."

"I'm sure you're worn out," she answered. "It's been a long, hard ordeal, and I know how hard you've worked."

Then, as he rose to gather the dishes, she looked at him obliquely and remarked, as much to herself as to her husband, "But you don't seem as excited about your verdict as I would have expected. It was, after all, what you wanted, wasn't it?"

"Oh yes," he answered quickly. "It was precisely what I wanted. It was the verdict I toiled and sweated to achieve."

"Then...what...?"

Bill Haines smiled at her wryly. "Do you know the expression 'The game is not always worth the candle.'?"

"I've heard you use it often, and I have a general idea what it means, but I don't understand what you're telling me now."

"Of course you don't," he said wistfully. "I'm not really trying to tell you anything. I only meant to reflect that there are times when the victory comes at too great a price."

"I don't understand," she said. "Do you mean to say that winning the Knoop case wasn't worth the time and effort you expended?"

"Something like that," he mused. "But not quite."

"I don't understand."

"Neither do I, love. Neither do I." He rose from his chair, kissed her cheek, and mounted the stairs toward the bedroom. The conversation was over.

His energies seemingly restored by his afternoon nap and a good night's sleep, Bill Haines was in his office early the next morning. By eleven o'clock he had made a respectable dent in the mound of papers that covered his desk. Then, true to his promise, Slicker Knoop appeared, sought permission to enter, and greeted his lawyer effusively.

"Mr. Haines...Good morning," he began in a boisterous tone. "I can't tell you how much I appreciate everything you did for me. I'm quite certain I'd have been convicted without your help. My mother, too. She says she knew I was innocent, of course, but she said they'd have gotten a verdict if it hadn't been for your efforts and abilities."

Then, without missing a beat, he extracted an envelope from his inner coat pocket, extended it to the lawyer, and continued, "Mother insisted that you be paid your entire fee at once. That is, we all agreed on that. So mother borrowed the money from her brother, my uncle, and we got a cashier's cheque for you as soon as the bank opened this morning. The whole family believes the amount of your fee to be quite reasonable. You most certainly earned it."

Bill Haines took the envelope and opened it sufficiently to examine the cheque, ascertain that it was in the correct amount, and placed it in his top desk drawer. His manner was less than cordial, almost aloof.

"Thank you," he said coldly. "The amount is correct. I think that we achieved the result that you wanted."

Slicker Knoop was more than a little perplexed at his lawyer's stiff formality. He had believed, during the entire course of the trial, that they had a congenial rapport and that Haines had harbored a genuine affection for him. Now, it seemed, all that had changed and Haines' treatment of him was strictly professional, but decidedly cool.

"Absolutely, sir," he blustered. "It was most certainly the desired result."

And when his broad, self-conscious grin was not returned, he assayed another tack. "I'm sorry, sir. Did I say something wrong? I sure didn't mean to give offense. I only meant to express my gratitude for all you did for me."

"As well you might," said Haines severely. "I did more for you than I should have, and I can't say that I'm especially proud of it." Haines sat back in his swivel chair, folded his arms across his chest and stared coldly at Knoop.

"I don't understand. What are you saying to me?" asked a very stunned Slicker Knoop.

Bill Haines directed a stony look at his client. "I guess you haven't noticed my newest artifact," he drawled, while pointing to the fireplace mantel behind his desk. "Have you?"

Slicker Knoop had been standing since the interview began. He had not been invited to sit. Now he surveyed the mantel behind Haines, hoping to find and identify whatever it was Haines referred to. There were framed photographs, a model automobile, a bicycling trophy and an assemblage of other meaningless bric-a-brac, none of which he could recognize. Finally, when Bill Haines pointed it out to him, he reacted.

"What's that?" he inquired.

"You don't recognize it?" demanded Haines.

"Uh...no...I don't. What is it?"

"What's it look like?" Bill Haines' voice was as harsh as his manner.

"I guess it looks like a bottle."

"Not *a* bottle, you murdering son-of-a-bitch. It's *the* bottle. It's the beer bottle that you used to beat poor Frank Favorite's brains out."

Slicker Knoop literally staggered at Haines' disclosure. "What...?" and couldn't finish.

Now Bill Haines' contempt for his client was obvious. "Right after your mother called me that morning—it was well before daylight, probably before Frank Favorite died—I rode my bike out to the ticket house. I had a light with me. It didn't take long to find the exact spot. There was broken glass everywhere. I picked it all up, every grain, every bit and shard of it. Put it all in my pocket. Then when I was sure I had it all, I came back here and pieced it back together. That's the only way I could be sure I had every last piece of the damned thing. I needed to be real sure before I dared challenge Frank Goodrich to try to find evidence of a murder weapon. So I glued the whole bottle back together. I'd got it all. It's all there now."

Slicker Knoop stared dumbly at the bottle. No words formed themselves.

Now Haines was on his feet. "Go ahead," he taunted. "Look at it. It probably still has your finger prints on it."

The two men glared at one another for a long moment. Then Bill Haines broke the connection, settled back into his chair and sighed audibly. "Probably has my prints on it too," he conceded morosely, "...now."

Slicker Knoop sank into the wooden arm chair in front of his lawyer's desk. For a moment he tried to look Haines in the eye. He couldn't. He could only stare at the floor. Minutes passed in silence. Finally, in a voice that was barely audible, he said, "I never meant to kill him."

"I'm sure you didn't," said Haines.

"I guess I hit him too hard."

"You said that to the police," reminded Haines. "What you didn't tell them is that you hit him a truly *savage* blow—with a hard, solid weapon. Like that bottle. You didn't tell them that, did you?"

"No," came the guilty response. "I didn't."

Bill Haines leaned forward in his chair, placed his elbows on the desk and fixed his client with a hard stare. "I paid a high price for your acquittal. Much too high. I shouldn't have done so, and I won't do it again. So if you should ever find yourself in a predicament again, don't come back to me. I won't help you. Is that understood?"

"Yes sir, but...."

Bill Haines didn't let him finish. "Goodbye, Slicker. Close the door on your way out.

Epilogue

Immediately after the entry of the verdict in Slicker Knoop's separate trial, the prosecutors dismissed the parallel murder charges against Charlie Heitcamp, Bob Ellicker and Clyde Starry. A few days later, the perjury charge against Pony Favorite was also dismissed.

The verdict itself was not received well by the Favorite family, the press, the local citizenry or the local clergy. The Very Reverend T. G. Eiswald of the First Baptist Church summed up public sentiment the following Sunday when he advised his congregation that the real blame for Frank Favorite's death fell to the people of Troy. In allowing such dens of iniquity (the river clubs) to exist within their community, he charged, the people had sowed the tares which were certain to mature and, finally, to be reaped in the form of lawlessness. And for so long a time as the demon rum should run rampant in their midst, it was the people themselves who must stand at the bar of justice.

Slicker Knoop never went afoul of the law again. In what seemed a dramatic metamorphosis, he became a sober, moderated, uncharacteristically diffident person, no longer the confident, swaggering, young man-about-town he had been before. After the trial he returned to the county surveyor's office for a brief period until he was called into the army for a fourteen-month stint during World War I. Mustered out of service less than 30 days after Armistice Day, he found a job in the bookkeeping department of a local industry, married an ordinary girl, dwelt in an ordinary house, and lived an ordinary, unexciting life. He died May 14, 1965, and is buried next to his wife, Gladys Howell Knoop, in the Casstown cemetery. Shortly before his death he arranged to have his mother's remains moved from Troy's Riverside Cemetery and re-interred next to his own waiting grave.

Merle Miller, a long-time acquaintance of the reconstituted Forrest Knoop tells of his own experiences, years after the trial, when he and his wife would socialize with the Knoops in their home. It sometimes happened that a cavalcade of automobiles would drive past the house, with lights flashing and horns blowing; on such occasions Forrest and Gladys would douse the lights, pull the shades and all four of them would sit, fearfully, on the floor until the procession had cleared. No explanation for these sometime phenomena was ever offered.

Author's Note

Times change. And so do perceptions. Bill Haines' unabashed spoliation of evidence, the harvesting of the shards of the beer bottle with which Slicker Knoop crushed the skull of Frank Favorite, was for many years considered to be a clever, possibly even admirable, stratagem in the jurisprudential game played by lawyers, with their clients' lives in the balance. Initially, that which he had done was a well-kept secret, one which he himself was not particularly anxious to see revealed. He had, after all, tampered with the evidence in a capital case, a felony in and of itself. His conduct, even by the somewhat looser standards of 1915, could have subjected him to very harsh criminal sanctions; it could also have resulted in his disbarment from the practice of law. Add to all that the fact that he was not entirely without scruple. I have no doubt that he was greatly troubled, from a purely ethical standpoint, by the enormity of his duplicity.

Nonetheless, his secret would eventually out, and by the time it did, he made no apologies. The potential for sanction having waned, and his own conscience having been salved by the passage of time, he freely, though privately, acknowledged what he had done. He kept the reconstructed bottle on the mantel behind his desk for all to see and, if pressed, would recount its history.

I have previously referred to Bill Haines as one of the truly pre-eminent criminal trial lawyers of his day. That judgment stands. He was, indeed, a veritable master of his trade. However, one of the characteristics that made him so formidable an advocate was his intense, compelling desire to win—at all costs. Sadly, there were occasions when he crossed the lines of propriety, legal ethics and sound judgment. The Slicker Knoop case was such an occasion.

LOADED HIS SHOTGUN WITH TWO SHELLS...

July 7th
1938

FOR AS LONG AS HE COULD REMEMBER Lonnie Hight had been a devoted Laurel & Hardy fan, and he seldom missed a chance to catch one of their films. The town boasted two movie-houses; the seedy, bare-bones Jewel theater (admission ten cents) and the tonier, more modern Mayflower (twenty-five cents). Whenever either of them offered a Laurel and Hardy feature Lonnie found the chance to go. There were times he had traveled all the way to Dayton or Springfield just to catch one of their "shorts." Featured films or short presentations, whatever was offered, Lonnie wanted to be there. He had already seen most of their productions three or four times and it seemed unlikely he would ever tire of them.

His wife Elizabeth was nearly as much a fan as he was and the two of them usually attended the shows together. This week, however, was different. She'd told him she had other things to do all week and now, on a Thursday evening, time was running out. Because both of the local theaters routinely changed their featured presentations on Fridays, tonight's showing at the Mayflower would have been their last opportunity to see it together. That was an especial shame because this week's film was a brand new, just-released Hal Roach production called *Swiss Miss,* and Lonnie had been anxiously awaiting the chance to see it.

And Elizabeth couldn't find the time to go. She'd catch it the next time around, she said. "It'll be back," she assured him.

So Lonnie Hight went to the picture show alone and tried to follow mousetrap salesmen Stan and Ollie to Switzerland where they believed the abundance of cheese produced in that country would attract a corresponding number of mice for their traps. As it happened, however, Lonnie fared no better in his efforts to follow the Messrs. Laurel & Hardy than did the two comedians as the purveyors of mousetraps. Although he would have been unwilling to admit to any feelings of resentment, he soon realized that he was more than a little disaffected by his wife's stubborn refusal to accompany him. And the longer he thought about it, the more disaffected he became, to the point that his appetite for the feature soured and his interest in the slapstick antics of the popular comedy team flagged. Twenty minutes into the film he was wholly preoccupied with the cause of his discontent and was not enjoying the movie at all.

The owners kept it dark in the rear part of the theater where the colored people were required to sit and Lonnie hadn't seen her at first, but there, across the aisle and two rows behind him, sat Elizabeth. He had no idea how she'd got there or whether she had arrived before or after him. She was just there when he'd happened to look in that direction. And it didn't seem like she was alone either. He could just barely make out a dark silhouette on either side of her, and it looked like her head was pretty close to the one on the right. Too close together, he thought. And as he watched the two silhouettes he became aware that there was a whole lot of lip-sucking, and maybe even a little poorly concealed groping activity, going on between them.

Whatever little interest in the movie Lonnie still had very quickly dried up and he lost all focus on his surroundings save only the activities of his wife and that other person seated beside her. He wasn't real sure of it, but he thought he knew who that person was, too. Howie Quisenberry had been sniffing around his place, and his wife, for a couple of weeks now and Lonnie had warned him off. Several times. He was just another randy young buck from the neighborhood, maybe had a thing for Elizabeth, and Lonnie thought it had passed. Apparently he was wrong. And from the looks of things Howie was receiving more than a little encouragement from his wife.

At nineteen, Howie was a full eight years younger than Elizabeth, and Lonnie hadn't believed she would have been interested. Perhaps, he reflected, he needed to think that one over. That difference of eight years paled in significance when compared with the disparity in age between himself and his wife. His fifty-five years were more than twice her twenty-seven. Funny, he hadn't thought much about it until Howie started hanging around. Even then he'd convinced himself that Elizabeth considered the kid as nothing more than a damn nuisance. If that had ever been true, it was obvious that she had reconsidered the matter. The thing that bothered him most was their shamelessness; that the two of them, his wife in particular, would grope and fondle one another, without embarrassment, right under his nose, was more than he could stomach. He'd seen no sign that she was aware he was watching their dalliance, but she had known very well he'd intended to come to the Mayflower to the movie this evening. One way or the other, it was clear enough that she didn't give a good goddamn whether he knew what she was doing or with whom she was doing it. And that hurt.

Predictably, and within a very short interval, the hurt evolved into anger.

Rigidly, and without wanting to make eye contact with anyone, Lonnie rose from his seat and strode up the carpeted aisle and out of the theater.

Chapter Two

Nearly four hours later, just before midnight, Elizabeth and Howie could be heard before they could be seen. The two of them, along with Elizabeth's teenage niece, were making their way raucously down West Market Street towards Vornholt Avenue. All three seemed to be in high spirits and their progress was intermittent, frolicsome and marked by considerable hilarity. Three steps forward, one backwards, a pregnant pause, a round of laughter and then reluctantly homeward again. It was slow going, but seemingly harmless.

Vornholt Avenue was probably the shortest street in town. Underdeveloped and poorly maintained, more like a broad alley than a municipal thoroughfare, it stretched a single block from West Market Street to Peters Avenue. Elizabeth's sister, Gertrude Williams resided at number 440, the last house on the west side, just around the corner from 509 Peters where Lonnie and Elizabeth lived with their three kids, his two and her little boy. Actually, because they were just around the corner from one another, the backyards of the two houses enjoyed a common boundary.

Gertrude's house was dark, everyone in bed, when the merry-makers reached her front gate. The third member of the party, Elizabeth's niece Annie, took her leave and headed off in the direction of her own home. Left to themselves again, Elizabeth and Howie collapsed playfully into the lawn swing in the side yard and renewed their amatory attentions to one another. It had not occurred to either of them that their activities were being observed.

But of course they were. Lonnie Hight had been quietly seated in the back porch swing of his own house for more than three hours. Across his lap he cradled an old, weather-beaten, side-by-side shotgun. He had already loaded it with two 12 gauge shells, number six shot pellets, which he had borrowed that same evening from one of his neighbors. During the entire time he had waited, Lonnie had nursed and nurtured his pique. He had been embarrassed and humiliated by the scene so brazenly played out in front of him at the theater. He was certain that there had been snickers and laughter at his expense and his shame had soon begun to feed on itself. Inevitably the pique, his humiliation and shame, gave way to a cold rage.

He watched the smoochers for as long as he could stand it, then quietly rose to his feet and lumbered menacingly across his yard towards Gertrude's lawn swing. He was directly in front of the two love birds when Elizabeth came up for air and caught sight of him.

"Lonnie?" she gasped. "Is that you? What do you want?"

"You'll see in just a minute," Lonnie replied, then completed his answer by blowing away half her mid-section. She took the full charge at close range, collapsed immediately and fell backward into the swing. The momentum of her fall knocked the swing over and spilled Howie out onto the lawn. He then rolled to his feet and took off running. He almost made good his escape. Even though Lonnie's second shot shattered his forearm, Howie managed a couple of hundred yards before he too collapsed.

MOMENTS LATER LONNIE HIGHT KNOCKED on the front door of Ellen Abshire, one of his neighbors. He asked her to dial the police department for him, and when she had done so, he took the phone from her, reported what he had done and asked that they send a car for him. He also requested an ambulance for Elizabeth.

TROY POLICE OFFICER Bert Arthur had the dispatch desk that evening. He had already received a report concerning a severely injured man lying on the pavement in front of the Sunshade Company and had sent Patrolman John Buckles, the only other officer on duty, to investigate. Then when Lonnie's call came in, Arthur had no alternative other than to telephone the Chief, alert him to the situation, and then to respond to the call himself.

As Arthur approached 509 Peters Road, the address provided, he found Lonnie Hight standing in the center of the street, holding his unloaded shotgun over his head with both hands and awaiting the officer's arrival. The old double-barrel had done its damage and was now broken open at the breach, and Lonnie promptly handed it over as commanded. At the officer's request he repeated his account of what had occurred, this time in greater detail, then docilely climbed into the rear seat of the patrol car for the trip to the station house.

Within moments of Arthur's arrival a small crowd had gathered.

Initially awakened by the twin shotgun blasts, then emboldened by the flashing lights of the police cruiser, the neighborhood denizens had cautiously emerged from their houses to see what was happening. Gertrude Williams quickly discovered her sister's inert form on the grass, directly behind the overturned lawn swing, and held her close as they waited for the ambulance.

Officer Buckles had already located Howie Quisenberry and had taken him to the nearby Stouder Memorial Hospital. Elizabeth arrived there a few moments afterward and both received prompt medical attention. Howie was given a tetanus shot and the expectation was that he would probably survive, but might well lose his arm. There appeared to be little that could be done for Elizabeth and she was expected to die within hours.

POLICE CHIEF RED SMICK, rudely aroused from a sound sleep by Bert Arthur's call, was already at the station, working on his second cup of wake-up coffee, when the officer brought in his prisoner and placed him in the small, seldom-used cell at the rear of the city building. Smick conferred briefly with Arthur, instructed him to write out his report, and went back to talk with Lonnie Hight. When it became apparent that Lonnie freely acknowledged all that had transpired and announced that his only regret was that he hadn't had another shot with which to make Howie run faster, Smick sent for City Solicitor Robert S. Miller and Police Officer John Hennessey. Then, in the presence of those several worthies, a full written confession was prepared, read aloud to the prisoner, approved and signed.

Lonnie Hight was booked on an open charge of shooting with intent to kill. As soon as Elizabeth died, the charge would be amended to murder in the first degree.

Chapter Three

Over the course of the next several days, the police officers, the county prosecutor and the local newspapers waited for Elizabeth

Enraged Negro Shoots Wife, Young Companion

Mrs. Lonnie Hight Near Death In Troy Hospital and Husband Jailed In Open Charge—Arm of Howard Quisenberry Shattered By Jealous Gun User

Lonnie Hight, 54, colored, residing at 509 Peters avenue, is being held in the county jail by city police on an open charge as the result of his having shot with a shotgun about 10:30 p. m. Thursday his wife, Mrs. Elizabeth Hight, 27, and Howard Quisenberry, 19, 502 Lincoln avenue, as they were sitting in a lawn swing at the home of Gertrude Williams, 440 Vornholt avenue, a sister of Mrs. Hight.

Mrs. Hight is in a critical condition at the Stouder Memorial hospital with a gaping wound in her right side where the entire charge of the shotgun entered her body. Little hope is held for her recovery.

Youth's Arm Shattered

Quisenberry is suffering from a shattered left arm. The charge from the gun, fired at close range, hit his arm below the elbow shattering the bones. It is possible that the arm will have to be amputated at the elbow.

After shooting the pair Hight returned to his home and called the police. He told them what he had done and asked them to come and get him. When Patrolman Bert Arthur arrived he calmly handed the officer the empty gun and surrendered himself.

Hight told Police Chief E. J. Smick that "Quisenberry had been too friendly with Mrs. Hight and a week ago had warned him to stay away. Last evening Hight said his wife refused to accompany him to the picture show and that he went alone. In a short time Hight told the chief he saw his wife enter the show in company with Quisenberry and Annie Mitchell, 19, niece of Mrs. Hight.

Waits On Pair With Gun

He was so angered, Hight stated, that he immediately went home, loaded his shot gun with two shells and awaited the return of his wife and Quisenberry. When the party returned home they stopped at the Williams home which adjoins the rear of the Hight property. Miss Mitchell left, while Mrs. Hight and Quisenberry sat in the swing.

Hight, according to his story, approached the couple and as his wife asked what he wanted, opened fire at close range. The first shot penetrated the side of Mrs. Hight. She screamed, ran a few steps and fell in a faint. Quisenberry started to run but Hight fired again at close range, the charge striking the youth in the left arm. Quisenberry continued to run but finally fell exhausted near the plant of the KitchenAid Manufacturing Co. several blocks from the Williams home where he was later found by the police.

Police are holding Hight on an

JAPANESE PROTEST EJECTIONS FROM U. S. DEFENSE DISTRICTS

Attempt To Search Chinese Suspects Brings Action By Marines

to die. There was no hope for her recovery and they needed to get on with the prosecution. Lonnie Hight had been transferred to the Miami County jail and had spent the weekend calmly and submissively in his new quarters. He knew he'd be there for an indefinite period of time and he was fully resigned to his circumstance. He understood the nature and the potential consequences of his acts and had declared himself prepared to accept whatever punishment was meted out to him. He appeared to have no remorse for what he had wrought and he seemed to be essentially unperturbed over the prospect of his wife's imminent demise.

The only thing that seemed to concern him was the welfare of his children, Lonnie Jr. and Julia, and also that of Elizabeth's little boy by her former marriage. With Elizabeth in the hospital and himself in jail, there was no one in the home to care for the kids. He did seem to be placated when sheriff's deputy Ralph Hawn assured him that the matter had been attended to; his sister-in-law, Mrs. Williams, had taken all the children into her home and had assumed full responsibility.

Apart from his frequent inquiries about the kids, Lonnie spent his time with reflections about his own personal history and that of his marriage. Born in Chattanooga way back in '83, he had first come to Cincinnati at age eleven. He'd entered the work force shortly thereafter and had held a variety of jobs both before and after migrating to Troy. For the last ten or eleven years he had been employed as a maintenance man for the Hobart Manufacturing Company. The pay was good for depression times and he enjoyed the work.

Lonnie's first wife, Lois, had borne him his son and daughter, but had died just three years after their marriage. Then, seven years ago, in 1931, he had married Elizabeth. She was just twenty years old and had a baby boy by her own previous marriage; Lonnie was forty-eight, widowed with two children, aged seven and three.

For the most part it had been a good marriage. They had loved each other and had been fairly compatible despite the considerable age difference. Elizabeth was a good housekeeper and a good mother to all the children, his as well as hers. There were, of course some rough spots; especially over the last year or so when he thought she might have encouraged the attentions of some of the young hot-bloods around the town. God knows, they didn't really need much encouragement. Elizabeth was an attractive item, straight black hair, good cheekbones and a stunning figure. Lonnie could understand her allure to the young wolves by whom they were surrounded. That didn't mean that he liked it, but he could certainly understand it. He had almost deluded himself into believing that the subtle encouragements she'd offered were unintentional on her part. She was, after all, a friendly, outgoing person and something of a natural coquette; that was part of her charm. It had been one of the things that had attracted Lonnie to her in the first place. And because he had considered it to be a part of her nature, Lonnie had almost convinced himself that her suggestive remarks and her small flirtations were all perfectly innocent.

All that had been true, of course, until recently. Over the last two or three weeks, she'd begun to tease him about his age, hint to him that maybe he didn't have it anymore. There were a couple of times she'd let him know she was attracted to one or another of the younger men around the neighborhood. When she'd told him right out, a week or so ago, that she wanted to go out on dates, Lonnie knew he had a problem. He'd told her no, in unequivocal terms, and he'd thought that was the end of it. More accurately, he'd hoped that was the end of it.

And that hope had proved to be false this last Thursday night.

MIRACULOUSLY, ELIZABETH WAS STILL ALIVE on Monday. Over the weekend she had regained her senses long enough to make a statement for the police investigators. Then she had relapsed again and passed in and out of consciousness sporadically. Awake or otherwise, she was surrounded by her sisters, nieces and friends, all of whom combined to maintain an intensely vigilant death watch.

Late Monday morning, during a lucid interval, Elizabeth asked that her husband be brought to her bedside. In her own words she made it clear that she bore him no ill will, had already forgiven him, and wanted to grant him absolution before she died. Her request was quickly relayed to Chief Smick and he arranged for Deputy Ralph Hawn to escort the prisoner to his wife's bedside. No one could have been more surprised than Lonnie Hight when he learned that he was to have a deathbed audience with his wife. All the same, he welcomed the opportunity to see her one last time. In spite of everything, he still cared for her and he realized, perhaps for the first time since the shooting, that he didn't really want her to die—most of all, he didn't want her to die without benefit of a final, mutual absolution.

THE DEATHBED SCENE AT STOUDER HOSPITAL played out much as might have been anticipated. Lonnie and Elizabeth came together guardedly. In halting terms they separately expressed contrition for what they had done. She told him that she didn't want him to blame himself for what had happened. It was all her fault, she said. She had goaded and provoked him to do murder. And she was profoundly sorry for everything. Lonnie, who was as much overcome by emotion as his wife, blamed himself and his own uncontrollable temper. He insisted that he should have been man enough to overlook her conduct. Given the chance, they agreed, they could have worked it out.

Ultimately, they held one another, kissed and cried together. And said goodbye.

LATE IN THE AFTERNOON of the same day, Lonnie Hight was formally arraigned on a charge of shooting with intent to kill Howard Quisenberry. He entered a plea of not guilty and was remanded to the custody of the sheriff. Bail was set at $10,000 and the matter was continued for preliminary hearing. No formal charges were filed with reference to the shooting of Elizabeth. The authorities intended to wait until she died.

Chapter Ten

Contrary to the studied medical predictions of her attending physicians, and against all odds, Elizabeth Hight refused to die. Her refusal to accommodate in that regard was so pronounced that the doctors were initially forced to upgrade her condition from critical to stable and a few days later, to fair, and finally, within two weeks of the shooting, she was determined to be out of danger and on the road to recovery.

Lonnie Hight had been kept closely apprised of his wife's medical condition and was much gratified to learn that she was now expected to survive. Quite apart from the fact that they had made their peace with one another, and expressed their abiding love for each other, the potential for a first degree murder trial diminished with each day's improvement in Elizabeth's condition. As Elizabeth continued to thrive, Lonnie's prospects brightened. He was certain that she would not accede to his being charged with any offense against her, and that meant that he had only to contend with the pending charge of shooting with the intent to kill Quisenberry. Given the circumstances, he was sure he would receive a light sentence, if not an outright acquittal, on that charge. So great was his confidence on that score that he had not even seen fit to engage a lawyer.

On balance, life had become very good for Lonnie Hight. Even the closeness of his jail cell in the July heat was powerless to daunt his new-found euphoria. The children, all three of them, visited with him as often as Sheriff Miller would allow, and his friends and neighbors came to see him also. And though he could neither read nor write, and was thereby denied those occupations, he could play cards with one or two of the other inmates and, on rare occasion, with chief deputy Ralph Hawn. He had known worse summers.

AND THEN THE MUSIC STOPPED. On July 22nd, Sheriff Kenneth Miller brought him the unwelcome news that Howard Quisenberry had died that afternoon. No one could offer any explanation. Howie's life had never been thought to be in danger. His arm, maybe, but not his life. In fact, the doctors had already said his arm could be saved and he'd been released from the hospital. And now they said he was dead. But how? What had he died of? And ultimately, did Lonnie really care?

Surprised, perhaps not unpleasantly, by the Sheriff's report, Lonnie did not immediately grasp the significance of this new information. "Good," he remarked flippantly. "I wanted him dead in the first place. He'd been messin' around with my wife. Now that's over."

"No, Lonnie" remarked the Sheriff, "that's not so good. You shot him and now he's dead. That makes it murder."

"Yeah, I shot him all right," acknowledged Lonnie. "But I didn't kill him. I didn't aim good enough."

"Mhmm," was the sheriff's response. "We'll see what the prosecutor says. But don't get your hopes up."

ELLIS W. KERR WAS THE MIAMI COUNTY PROSECUTOR. Tall, handsome and athletically constructed, he came from one of the oldest and most prominent families in the county, not a few of whom were lawyers. At thirty-one years of age, he carried about him an aura of congenial confidence. He was a dedicated and intensely capable prosecutor.

Kerr had spent the weekend mulling over the circumstances surrounding the death of Howard Quisenberry. What he had learned, primarily from the hospital staff, was that Quisenberry had received a routine shot of tetanus antitoxin on July 7th, directly after he'd been shot. His recovery had been essentially uneventful until last Thursday when he began to

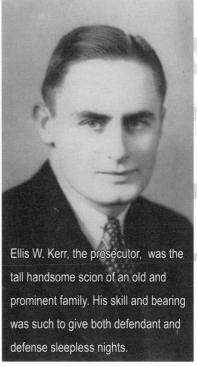

Ellis W. Kerr, the prosecutor, was the tall handsome scion of an old and prominent family. His skill and bearing was such to give both defendant and defense sleepless nights.

exhibit the symptoms of developing lockjaw. On Friday his attending physicians, Drs. Norton Lindenberger and Joe Hance, responded to his worsening condition by administering a second tetanus shot. Within minutes thereafter their patient died from an adverse reaction to the serum.

Kerr's legal research told him—quite correctly—that because the injury inflicted by Lonnie Hight had set in motion the chain of events that ultimately resulted in Quisenberry's death, and because that progression of events was reasonably foreseeable, Lonnie was both morally and legally responsible for the consequences of his actions. It was a clear case of first degree murder.

An affidavit charging that capital offense was prepared and filed by Kerr the first thing Monday morning and Lonnie Hight was arraigned forthwith. A plea of not guilty was entered on his behalf and when he waived preliminary hearing, he was bound over to the grand jury and once again remanded to the custody of the sheriff.

All of a sudden, Lonnie Hight's perspectives had changed dramatically. His earlier sense of well-being suddenly transformed itself into a new and unwelcome recognition that he just might be in more trouble then he had realized. As the deputy sheriff escorted him across the street, back to the jail-block that had been his home these past weeks, he became aware of a rapidly growing sensation of peril that had begun to overcome his earlier confidence. And for the first time since the shooting it dawned on him that he did, indeed, need a lawyer. He needed one bad.

Chapter Five

Harley D. Enyeart had been hopelessly and irretrievably crippled virtually all his life. He had contracted infantile paralysis, the dreaded poliomyelitis, as a very young child—at age two, actually—and the ravages of that disease had permanently destroyed the function and the usefulness of both his legs. As he neared maturity he came more and more to resent his enforced dependence on the wheelchair in which he'd spent most of his childhood, and he ultimately disdained its use altogether. He vowed to himself that he would never again be victim to that horrid contraption. As a result, then, of his obstinance, he'd had to learn to drag himself about awkwardly, in exquisite agony, with his entire weight supported by steel leg braces and a pair of wooden crutches. Each step involved the swinging of his contorted frame from one side to the other and then catching himself with the off crutch a carefully calculated moment before disaster.

His progress was slow and torturous, and when he fell, a not infrequent occurrence, he was rendered entirely helpless and could not get up again without assistance. And if this obvious disability were not a sufficient curse, it was compounded by the constant back pain with which he was doomed to live out his lifetime.

Harley Enyeart's response to the afflictions visited on him by a cruel and impersonal destiny was to crawl and scratch his way through high school, college and finally law school, and then to set up a solo practice with offices as near the county courthouse as could be found. By the summer of 1938, he was just months shy of his fortieth birthday and he had already earned a reputation as one of the more redoubtable criminal lawyers in the county. His physical infirmities and the tribulations that constantly plagued him had taken their toll on his persona and his mannerisms. Caustic and acerbic in his approach to hostile witnesses and to jurors alike, he was surprisingly effective in the courtrooms. Thickset, with coal black hair parted in the middle in the style of his time, he glared outward from under heavy, beetled brows, and commanded the full attention of his listeners, friend and foe alike.

Precisely because of who and what he was, it came as no surprise to him when his secretary relayed to him the sheriff's message that one of his current prisoners, a colored fellow named Lonnie Hight, wanted to see him. Harley Enyeart had read the newspapers and was well aware of the charges filed against the sheriff's prisoner. He had anticipated the call.

"Tell them I'll be over after lunch," he fairly growled. "Be damned if I'll talk with him on an empty stomach."

SHERIFF KENNETH MILLER generally made a point of being on hand when Harley Enyeart came to visit one of his inmates. Because of the attorney's obvious infirmities, Miller made an especial effort to accommodate him in the small ways available to him. He knew from prior experience that when Enyeart had said he'd be there after lunch, he could be expected at one-thirty P.M. He also knew that the meal in question would have consisted of a sandwich, a banana and a cookie packed in a paper sack by his wife and eaten at his desk. And finally, he

The defense attorney, Harley D. Enyeart, was a man who had suffered greatly from polio. His formidable courtroom skills, however, more than made up for his physical disadvantages.

knew that it would have taken the better part of a quarter hour for Enyeart to crab his way along some fifty feet of South Plum Street and diagonally across the intersection to the county jailhouse. Ironically, the intersection at Plum and Main Streets was known, colloquially and insensitively, as Cripples' Corner, for the very cogent reason that there were no fewer than three crippled attorneys, Enyeart included, and one crippled justice of the peace, who maintained their offices within a fifty yard radius of the intersection.

Harley Enyeart would have been accompanied by his secretary, Zelma Motter, who carried his briefcase and helped him cope with doors, steps and other potential impediments to his forward progress. Then, upon his arrival at the entrance to the jail, Sheriff Miller would customarily take over, shepherd him into the ground-floor juvenile detention room and help him arrange himself into a chair behind a weathered oaken desk, ready to meet with his prospective client without having to apologize for his obvious physical inadequacies. Neither man acknowledged the rationale for the special consideration.

"I know what you're up to, Kenny," Enyeart growled at his host. "You're not willing to let me out of your sight because you're scared to death I'm gonna steal something of value from right under your nose."

"Something like that," chuckled the sheriff. "Can't trust any of you damned lawyers."

"Well, let me tell you something, Mr. Sheriff," countered Enyeart. "There's nothing in this dilapidated old building worth stealing. And, in the second place, I'm not just another one of your ordinary, run-of-the-mill lawyers."

"Yeah, I know," answered Miller. "You're an honest to God, good old American Injun. That makes you a lot better risk than if you were just a regular attorney."

Because of Enyeart's dark, blunt facial features and his thick mane of black hair, it had been frequently suggested that one or more of his ancestors might have been of Indian extraction. Enyeart went along with the canard.

"That's right, Kenny. I'm a certified member of the *Sue* tribe. Have been ever since I got my law degree."

"I'm pretty sure you're certifiable, all right," conceded the sheriff as he made ready to leave the room. "I'll go get your miscreant for you. If you're ready?"

"I'm ready, Kenny. Thanks."

Half a dozen minutes later, Sheriff Miller and Deputy Hawn escorted

Lonnie Hight into the detention room. Miller performed the perfunctory introductions and both of the officers withdrew. "I'll be right outside," he announced as he closed the door. "Just holler when you're done. Or if you need anything."

Harley Enyeart spent a long moment sizing up his prospective client. Approaching six feet in height, the man's lean muscular physique made him appear twenty years younger than his actual age. Dark skinned and clean-shaven, he possessed good facial bones and a strong, firm jaw-line. He seemed genuinely concerned, but not the least abashed, by his present predicament. Most importantly, he appeared quite willing to place his trust—and his life—in this severely handicapped lawyer whom he had known, heretofore, only by reputation.

Enyeart waved a hand towards the single chair on the opposite side of the table, "Have a seat, Mr. Hight," he said, "And tell me what happened. All of it. I can't help you if I don't know everything there is to know."

Three hours later Harley Enyeart concluded the interview and summoned the sheriff. He didn't yet know everything about Lonnie Hight, his history, his marriage or about the shooting itself, but he was satisfied that Hight had been forthcoming and candid with him. He would be back, he said, and there would be other interviews, but for the moment, he felt he had learned enough to undertake the defense. They agreed on a retainer of two hundred fifty dollars. It wasn't enough for a murder defense, but it was the best that Hight could manage.

As Sheriff Miller and Deputy Hawn led their prisoner back to the jail-block, Harley Enyeart issued one final admonition to his client, "In the meanwhile," he commanded, "I don't want you to say a word to anyone about anything unless I'm present. And that includes the weather. Is that understood?"

Lonnie Hight nodded his acquiescence, "Yes sir. I understand."

Chapter Six

From Lonnie Hight's perspective there wasn't much happening from the last week of July through the middle of November. Time passed very slowly within the overheated, over-populated confines of the Miami County jail. Apart from the occasional visits from Mr. Enyeart and the weekly appearances of friends and family members, there was very little to relieve the stifling monotony of confinement. In view of his circumstance and the fact that he had already been charged, he could scarcely console himself with the old saw that "no news is good news." He could only await developments in the inexorable process that would ultimately lead to a trial on the murder charge. And that waiting time weighed heavily on him and constituted, in and of itself, a punishment of some order.

Then, on October 8th, the October grand jury returned and filed the indictment upon which he would be tried. The indictment charged, in language both plain and (relatively) simple, that:

...Lonnie Hight, on the 7th day of July, in the year of our Lord one thousand nine hundred and thirty-eight at the County of Miami, aforesaid, unlawfully, purposely and of deliberate and premeditated malice, killed Howard Quisenberry, by shooting said Howard Quisenberry with a shotgun on the date aforesaid, and the said Howard Quisenberry died on July 22nd, 1938, as a result of the unlawful, purposeful and deliberate and premeditated shooting by the said Lonnie Hight....

By virtue of the inclusions of the several terms of art, "purposeful," "deliberate," and "premeditated malice," the charge was that of first degree murder. Omission of any one or more of those terms would have resulted in a lesser charge such as second degree murder or even manslaughter.

Harley Enyeart had hoped that the grand jury, because of the circumstances, might actually return an indictment on one of those lesser included charges and that his own job, that of defending his client, might thereby become somewhat less challenging. As it happened, however, the fact that the charge was that of murder one created a serious problem for him. He had agreed to represent Hight for the sum of $250—which was all the money his client could raise—but Enyeart could not realistically undertake the full responsibility for a first degree murder defense for that amount of money. The time and effort, not to mention actual expenses, required for such a defense would prove to be too great a burden. But Enyeart had a contingency plan—one which he had already discussed with Hight against the possibility that the charge would be murder in the first degree.

Directly after the filing of the indictment, Lonnie Hight was arraigned in open court and Harley Enyeart entered a not guilty plea on his behalf. Judge Paul T. Klapp assigned the case for trial to a jury beginning Monday, November 14th, and directed the clerk to require the Miami County Jury Commissioners to assemble on the 18th of October, in company of the clerk, the sheriff and the Judge of the Common Pleas Court, for the purpose of drawing a special venire of 75 jurors for the trial.

That directive was observed to the letter and a special panel was indeed drawn on the 18th. Two days later, on the 20th, Harley Enyeart implemented

his contingency plan with the filing of an application for the appointment of additional counsel:

This applicant states that as attorney for Lonnie Hight he has received the sum of $250, which is insufficient to defend this action since he has already expended a considerable portion thereof for necessary expenses. Said Lonnie Hight is unable to pay or secure additional funds for his defense. This applicant, because of the seriousness of the charge, and because of the lack of funds of said defendant, Lonnie Hight, solicits the appointment of additional counsel, the same to be paid by the State of Ohio, in order that justice may be served and said defendant adequately protected, and further because of the expense necessary for proper defense, which will involve a great amount of research and legal effort and preparation, which a case with one's life at stake demands.

Judge Klapp promptly granted the application and appointed local attorney Baird Broomhall as additional counsel for the defendant, at state expense, and Mr. Broomhall endorsed his acceptance of the assignment on the order filed with the clerk.

Chapter Seven

Baird Broomhall was a real sweetheart. Literally. The scion of an exceptionally cultivated and locally prominent family, he was himself well-educated, properly-spoken, congenial and convivial to a fault. His father, Addison Broomhall, was a lawyer of considerable talent and a richly deserved reputation for probity. The father had taken extraordinary pains to insure that the son would receive the finest preparation available to the end that he might ultimately prove to be a worthy associate in the law practice that would become known as Broomhall & Broomhall. And although the son, Baird, would later protest that his real calling should have been to the Shakespearean stage, he'd shown no reluctance whatever in following the course his father had so carefully charted for him.

He had, in fact, taken an under-graduate degree from Yale College in 1908 and a law degree from the University of Michigan in 1910. He passed the Ohio State Bar examination that same year with the highest score of any of his fellow candidates and was immediately admitted to practice. Then, after two years as a fledgling lawyer in partnership with his father, and because he truly did have an abiding interest in the arts, he returned to Yale to earn his Master of Arts degree in English Literature in 1913. One of his four classmates there was a tall skinny young man with a full head of red hair named Sinclair Lewis and on one occasion their instructor, after grading their separate efforts at short story writing, passed judgment. "Mr. Jones, Mr. Bascom and Mr. Seymour, you may in time become writers, but for you, Mr. Lewis and Mr. Broomhall, there is no hope."

And while Mr. Lewis refused to accept his instructor's verdict in the matter, Mr. Broomhall did. He contented himself with the satisfaction of having achieved the masters degree and returned home to rejoin his father in the practice of law.

More than a quarter century later, in the fall of 1938, Baird Broomhall was not only one of the more distinguished attorneys in the county, he was clearly the best regarded and the most popular of them all. Amiable and gregarious by nature, his manner and his appearance were of a Dickensian cast. In rare fashion, he combined the courtly demeanor of a medieval player with a native sense of humor in a way that was at once disarming and irresistible. Tall and thickly constructed, he had a wide, plain face set off by the bulbous nose of a circus clown and the shiny tonsure of a Franciscan friar. Most of all he possessed a persistent twinkle in his eye that suggested both an intelligent mischievousness and a kindly, caring understanding of humankind.

Finally, of course, his legal training combined with his love of the arts and his flair for the dramatic to produce the consummate trial advocate. Throughout his long career at the bar Baird Broomhall was consistent in that he craved nothing better than the opportunity to harangue and cajole a jury, to tell a story, or to argue, sometimes with tongue in cheek, a fine point of the law.

It was no accident then that it was Baird Broomhall who was appointed by the court to assist Harley Enyeart in the defense of Lonnie Hight. Enyeart had specifically requested the appointment and Judge Klapp had accommodated. Broomhall, of course, accepted the assignment with alacrity. He had worked with Enyeart before and welcomed the opportunity to do so again. The two of them, on rare occasion, had also been known to get drunk together.

Baird Broomhall lost no time in bringing himself up to speed concerning the posture of the state's case against Lonnie Hight. In company with Harley Enyeart, he paid a visit to their client at the Miami County jailhouse. The interview lasted several hours, during which time both men explored their client's background, his history, his likes, dislikes and preferences; they reviewed with him all the significant events leading up to and including the events of July 7th , and discussed with him the potential for pleading out to some lesser included offense. They ended that interview with a consensus that their best option was to stand trial.

Baird Broomhall also interviewed the local police officers, friends and family members of the defendant—as well as those of the decedent, Howie Quisenberry—and he reviewed the court records with reference to the proceedings to date.

Because both defense lawyers were aware that Lonnie Hight had made a full statement to the police officers on the night of his arrest, they promptly served a formal written demand on Prosecutor Ellis W. Kerr for "the privilege of inspecting and copying the purported signed statement, or statements, confession or confessions, if any, made by the defendant, Lonnie Hight, on the 7th day of July, 1938, or upon any subsequent date." Included within the same pleading was an additional demand for a written "Bill of Particulars" setting out in detail a complete and chronological specification as to the evidence which the prosecutor intended to offer at trial. Then, when Kerr refused to comply, the two attorneys filed a formal motion with the court to require him to do so. And Judge Klapp, relying on the authority of the 1925 decision of the Ohio Supreme Court in *State vs. Yeoman*, 112 O.S. 214, denied the motion.

Undaunted by Judge Klapp's refusal, the two attorneys immediately filed their motion for reconsideration, pointing out to court and counsel the fact that both the Ohio General Assembly and the Supreme Court had

changed the rule laid down in the *Yeoman* case. Section 1344-1 of the Ohio General Code had been enacted in July of 1929 and the Supreme Court had just decided the matter of *State vs. Fox* in January of 1938. By virtue of those changes in both the statutory and the case law of Ohio it was clear, they argued, that defense counsel in a criminal prosecution were now entitled to inspect and copy any and all statements made by the defendant.

Their arguments on the point were sufficiently compelling to convince Judge Klapp of his error, and he modified his earlier ruling so as to order the prosecutor to produce the requested statements; he did not, however, require the production of a

Baird Broomhall was the additional counsel, a well-bred man with a literature degree from Yale.

Bill of Particulars. Enyeart and Broomhall were satisfied; they had gotten what they really wanted.

LATE IN THE AFTERNOON ON MONDAY of the following week, Harley Enyeart was at his desk, busily engaged in the review of the court files of yet another criminal matter. This one involved only a theft, as opposed to an assault or a murder, a crime against the person. He was excited about his client's prospects in this latest case because he had found a procedural technicality which he believed would lead to a dismissal of all charges.

Because he had no client with him and because there was no one in his reception room other than his secretary, he had allowed the doorway connecting the two rooms to remain open. That way, if he needed his secretary, he had only to call out to attract her attention. It was a primitive, but effective interoffice communications system.

His own attention, however, was suddenly diverted by a mild commotion in the outer office. He heard the front door slam and a boisterous, flamboyant address to his secretary. "Good afternoon, Mrs. Motter. How, indeed, are you this fine autumnal afternoon? It has been far too long a time since these weary eyes have had the pleasure of feasting upon your lovely countenance, and I take full responsibility for the omission. I really should have come to visit with you long ere now, but the opportunity to do so has been denied me. Please assure me that you have missed me also."

Harley Enyeart readily identified, and quickly interrupted, his colleague's facetious and wholly meaningless blather. In his own strident, slightly nasal, tone, he commanded his secretary, "Zelma, don't get caught up in any of that drivel; send that big, over-inflated windbag in here and shut the door behind him."

Then, when that had been accomplished, he waved his visitor into one of the three armchairs opposite his desk. "Well, Baird," he greeted amiably. "Aside from that load of crap you just laid on Zelma, what brings you over here today? Something to do with our local Othello?"

"Would-be Othello, more like," Baird Broomhall corrected. "I acknowledge that our guy is the right color and that his motivations were essentially the same, but you'll remember that the real Othello managed to kill his wife, but spared her suspected lover. Lonnie Hight failed in his attempt on his wife, but killed her paramour."

"By accident," appended Enyeart. "I don't think he intended to kill the Quisenberry boy."

"You're quite right," said Broomhall. He only meant to sting him with a few pellets, 'to make him run faster'." Baird Broomhall stroked his shiny, bald pate, then added. "Besides, I don't think Lonnie Hight really killed Quisenberry. He only wounded him. We're talking about a few shotgun pellets in his arm, not nearly so serious an injury as was first reported. Quisenberry died of other causes."

"Come on, Baird," came the rejoinder from the more cynical Harley Enyeart. "You know the law better than that. No matter how slight the initial wound, if the victim dies of it, it's still murder."

"Ah yes, so I remember from law school," said Baird Broomhall. "But I also seem to recall that one of the three principal elements of first degree murder is that of intent, and if Lonnie Hight didn't actually intend to kill Quisenberry, it's second degree."

Harley Enyeart snorted. "He meant to kill somebody, and if he missed Desdemona and hit Cassio, its still murder one. And you know it as well as I do. Nice try, but it'll never get past Kerr—or Klapp either, for that matter."

Baird Broomhall nearly pouted. "It just doesn't ring true for me. Howard Quisenberry didn't die of the few pellet wounds to his arm; he died of *complications*."

"Forget all that stuff. It doesn't go anywhere," demanded Enyeart. "We're gonna have to come up with some realistic theory of defense. And we'd better be quick about it. Trial date's approaching."

"Actually," mused Broomhall, "that's what I came over to talk with you about. I spent the whole weekend going over Lonnie Hight's statement. I even went over to see him at the jailhouse to review it with him."

"And?" queried Enyeart. "Did you find any daylight?"

"None whatsoever. Hight says they got it right. It happened just like he says in the statement. In fact, he says, he's told the same story to anybody and everybody who's asked."

"Maybe he can't read or write?"

An informal portrait of three of the court's major characters: City Solicitor Robert Miller, Harley Enyeart for the defense, and Judge Klapp for the people.

"Actually he says he can read and write very well. But he also said he couldn't read the statement that night because he didn't have his glasses. But that doesn't help us either. He made the statement freely; the officers took it down just as he told it, and then they read it to him. He says they've got it right. He's not going to repudiate it."

Both men were silent while they contemplated their options. Then Harley Enyeart articulated their predicament, "Kinda looks like we're gonna have to live with it."

Chapter Eight

Trial of the matter of *The State of Ohio vs. Lonnie Hight* began on Monday, November 14th.

Elizabeth Hight, who appeared to be fully recovered from her injuries, arrived at the courtroom well before the time court was due to convene. She, and their three children, his and hers, greeted the defendant affectionately. Husband and wife locked one another in a protracted, fond embrace and the little ones took turns sitting in their father's lap.

Then, precisely at nine o'clock, Bailiff Louis Paul proclaimed court to be in session, and the honorable Paul T. Klapp, Judge of the Common Pleas Court of Miami County, swept through the tall, walnut-paneled, swinging door from the clerk's office, mounted the dais and arranged his robes about himself as he assumed his place at the bench. Although Judge Klapp was still in his mid-thirties and was just completing the second year of his judgeship, he was nonetheless very much in control of the courtroom. He was of prepossessing appearance with a leonine head of full, prematurely silver hair and the presence of a veteran, distinguished jurist.

Once he had ensconced himself in his high-backed leather chair behind the bench and the courtroom had settled down, Judge Klapp called the case and addressed himself to the panel of prospective jurors. He explained that the court was fully cognizant of the inconvenience that their summons to jury duty had occasioned and that for this he was truly sorry, but that it was necessary to the American system of jurisprudence for its citizens to perform this service when required. He proceeded from that short and oft-repeated introduction to a brief description of the circumstances which had required their presence, the fact that this would be a first degree murder trial, what it was that was expected of them if selected as jurors, and the manner in which the trial would be conducted. Then, with no further ado, he required that the entire panel be sworn, introduced the participants, and turned the proceedings to the lawyers for *voir dire* examination, the close questioning of each of the prospective jurors by counsel to determine their individual qualifications to weigh the evidence impartially and to render a judgment in accordance with the law.

That process moved along quickly and a jury consisting of nine men and three women was selected and sworn just before 3:00 in the afternoon. Out of a total panel of seventy-five veniremen summoned to appear, only thirty-five had been examined for cause, rejected or seated. Judge Klapp instructed the empaneled jurors as to their duties and the constraints which the law imposed upon them. Immediately thereafter they were taken by Sheriff Miller and Bailiff Louis Paul to view the scene of the shooting, in order that they might better understand the evidence, and were then excused until Tuesday morning.

THE SPECTATORS' GALLERY had been no more than half filled for Monday's preliminary proceedings. In contrast, the courtroom was teeming when the Tuesday session began at 9:00 o'clock the following morning. It appeared almost as though Lonnie Hight's mood swings were a function of the size of the crowd which observed them. While he had seemed to be in high spirits throughout all of Monday's activities, and smiled constantly at friends and acquaintances as though he were enjoying the experience, his attitude and demeanor took on a more serious aspect Tuesday and he was thereafter seen to pay especial attention to all that was said and done during the rest of the trial.

Opening statements for both sides were short and perfunctory. Prosecuting Attorney Ellis Kerr recited briefly the events of the night of July 7th which had led to the death of Howard Quisenberry, fifteen days later on July 22nd. He promised that the evidence would show, unequivocally, all three of the principal elements of first degree murder: actual malice, an intention to kill and premeditation on the part of the defendant. Harley Enyeart opened for the defense. He did no more than reaffirm the defendant's original plea of not guilty.

In only his second year at the bench, Judge Paul Klapp was assured and self-possessed. It was clearly understood that it was *his* bench.

"Pay close attention to the evidence," he admonished.

Prosecutor Kerr began the presentation of the state's evidence with the testimony of Troy Police Chief Red Smick, Officers Bert Arthur, Ralph Buckles and John Hennessey. All four had been present when Lonnie Hight made his confession; all four agreed that the defendant had said he could read and write, but was unable to do so because he didn't have his glasses; and all four agreed that he freely signed the confession after it had been read to him by City Solicitor Robert Miller. Officer Bert Arthur told of Hight's having telephoned him at the police department the night of the shooting, his peaceful surrender, and the story he heard from Hight at the scene. Officers Buckles and Hennessey testified to their having found Howard Quisenberry near the KitchenAid plant, badly injured, and having taken him to Stouder Memorial Hospital. As a part of the testimony from the several police officers, the defendant's written confession was read to the jury and offered as an exhibit.

Harley Enyeart undertook a desultory and wholly pointless cross-examination of each of the police officers. His attempts to undermine their testimony were more a feckless adherence to custom than a serious attempt to challenge their stories. It didn't really matter anyway because he knew that Lonnie Hight was fully prepared to confirm all his prior admissions.

City Solicitor Miller also identified the confession, which he had reduced to writing and read to the defendant. On motion of Prosecutor Kerr, and over the objections of defense counsel, the confession was admitted into evidence. It would go to the jury when they began their deliberations.

In its essence the confession contained Lonnie Hight's statement that he had been having trouble with his wife for some time and that he had warned Quisenberry to stay away from their home. On the night in question he had asked his wife to accompany him to the picture show; that she had refused; that he was deeply humiliated when he later saw her there with Quisenberry; that he went home, got his shotgun, and borrowed two shells from a neighbor; that he waited for the couple to return from the show, and when they came to the home of her sister he shot her; and finally, when Quisenberry started to run, he shot him too.

PROSECUTOR KERR NEXT CALLED to the witness stand Dr. Norton Lindenberger and Dr. Joe Hance, the two physicians who had participated in the treatment of Howard Quisenberry after he had been taken to the hospital. Both testified that the immediate cause of Quisenberry's death was shock from the injection of an anti-toxin administered by Dr. Lindenberger on the morning of July 22nd, some two weeks after the shooting. It developed that Dr. Lindenberger

had given Quisenberry a similar shot at the hospital on the night of July 7th and that such treatment was standard procedure for the prevention of tetanus, or lockjaw, in cases involving gunshot wounds. Then, on the 22nd, when Quisenberry began to exhibit symptoms of developing lockjaw, Dr. Lindenberger gave him another massive dose of the same serum. Their patient's reaction to this second, and much larger dosage, was virtually instantaneous and the young man died within twenty minutes of receiving it.

Both doctors were adamant in their insistence that if the anti-toxin had not been given—on either occasion—Quisenberry would have died of lockjaw. Dr. Hance, who testified right after Tuesday's lunch break, emphasized that lockjaw, in the absence of treatment, is invariably fatal, and that the administration of the anti-toxin serum, after tetanus has actually developed, is the only known treatment that is capable of curing the disease. He also expressed his opinion that Quisenberry would have developed lockjaw if Dr. Lindenberger had not administered the initial injection on the night of the shooting. The serum is a preventative, he said, but despite its usage the patient nonetheless contracted the disease; therefore, he concluded, if the shot had not been given, the patient would have contracted the disease and died.

"You mean to say," asked Harley Enyeart with asperity, "that with or without the tetanus shot, he would have died anyway?"

"I do," answered the witness.

"From a few shotgun pellets in his arm?"

Dr. Hance bridled at the question. "No. He would have contracted tetanus and died of lockjaw."

"Doctor," pressed Enyeart, "How many shotgun pellets would it take to cause death under the circumstances you've described? One? Two? Would it take more than two? Tell the jury, if you can, precisely how many of these tiny lead pellets are required?"

Chapter Nine

Ellis Kerr rested the state's case against Lonnie Hight at 2:45 Tuesday afternoon. It had taken less than six hours to present the totality of his evidence in support of the indictment for first degree murder. And it took less than six seconds for Judge Klapp to rule on Harley Enyeart's written motion to dismiss the charges.

"Overruled," he intoned harshly. "There is more than enough evidence to sustain the indictment. Court's in recess 'til 3:00 o'clock. The defense should be prepared to call its first witness."

OVER THE COURSE OF THE PAST THREE WEEKS, as the trial approached, Harley Enyeart and Baird Broomhall had been engaged in a running debate about whether or not they should allow their client to take the witness stand in his own defense. Predictably, Enyeart was adamantly opposed to the tactic. Most of the people he defended were guilty as charged and for that reason, if for none other, they usually got caught out on their own testimony. Now they had reached the crossroads. They, and their client, needed to make their decision and run with it.

"Goddammit, Baird," Enyeart railed at his co-counsel. "It's the state's job to prove him guilty. Why the Hell should we let our client do it for them?"

To which Baird Broomhall replied, "Harley, the state has already carried their burden. They've already proved their case. And," he mused, "everything Lonnie Hight has said or done thus far has helped them convict him."

"Absolutely," agreed Enyeart heartily. "So why put him on the stand and let him finish the job? He can't help himself. He's already admitted everything they need to prove. Besides, we both know he won't repudiate his confession. He'll simply confirm what he's already told the police. So, one more time, why put him up there as a ripe target for self-destruction?"

Baird Broomhall, his elbows resting on their conference room table, thumped his smooth dome with a stubby middle finger as though he were trying to stimulate some newly awakened cerebral activity. "Two reasons, my friend," he began. "And very compelling ones at that. First and foremost," he stopped his head-thumping long enough to raise an index finger, "our client has insisted on his right to testify in his defense. And he does have that right. We cannot, in good conscience, prevent him from doing so."

Enyeart snorted derisively. "And the second reason?"

"That one's easy," Broomhall answered wistfully. "He's already given his case away; he can't really do himself any more damage than he already has."

"You question him then," said Enyeart with obvious resignation. "I can't make myself lead him to the slaughter."

"Huh-uh," demurred Broomhall. "You're lead counsel. You're gonna

have to do it. Otherwise the jury will conclude we've abandoned our client in his hour of need."

LONNIE HIGHT SURPRISED THEM BOTH. From the moment he took the stand he appeared to be the most composed man in the courtroom. With only minimal guidance from Harley Enyeart, he first detailed his history and his circumstances up until the night of the shooting. He had been born in Tennessee, he said, and as an orphan at age eleven, he came to Cincinnati with friends. He had worked at odd jobs there until he was twenty-seven when he found his way to Troy and eventually went to work as a janitor for the Hobart Manufacturing Co. He was married for the first time in 1928 and had two children, a boy, Alonzo and a girl, Julia. Tragically, his wife had died just three years into the marriage. Then, just a few months later he married his present wife, Elizabeth; she had had one child, a boy, by her first marriage. The five of them had lived together happily at his residence at 509 Peters Road until Howie Quisenberry turned up last spring.

Calmly, and seemingly without emotion, Lonnie Hight told the jury that he had warned Quisenberry repeatedly to stay away from his wife, but the boy refused to take him seriously. On one occasion, he said Quisenberry forced his way into the house and would have attacked him but for the intervention of his neighbors.

In response to Enyeart's surprisingly gentle questioning, he told the jury how his wife had refused to go to the theater with him on the night of the shooting, but later appeared there with Quisenberry. He spoke of his shame, his total humiliation, and all that he had done thereafter. The story he told on direct examination elaborated upon, and confirmed in every way, the matters testified to by the police officers and contained in his "confession." He did tell the jury that he could sign his name, but that, despite conflicting testimony to the contrary, he could not otherwise read or write.

"Don't really matter none," he said. "It happened just like they said it did. I already told 'em that."

He did claim, however, that he had not meant to kill either his wife or young Quisenberry. He had meant to hurt his wife, he admitted, but had only fired at Quisenberry to "sprinkle him a bit" as a warning to stay away from Elizabeth. He expressed no remorse over his death, but remarked only that it was not what he had intended.

Lonnie Hight's direct testimony lasted nearly a full day. He had been called to the stand as the first witness for the defense—late Tuesday afternoon—and lasted until early Wednesday afternoon when Enyeart announced that his direct examination of the defendant was concluded and invited Ellis Kerr to cross-examine.

On cross, the prosecutor made Hight re-confirm his confession in all its particulars and then attempted to induce him to admit that he really had no serious objections to his wife's keeping company with younger men, that it was a pattern of conduct in which he had long since acquiesced. Lonnie Hight bridled at the suggestion and objected strenuously. He loved his wife, he declared, and was unwilling to share her with any man, young or old.

AFTER ELLIS KERR HAD CONCLUDED his cross-examination, Baird Broomhall finished out the day by calling five witnesses to the stand to testify concerning the defendant's character and his reputation as a hard-working, respectable and peaceable man. These were all men of substance and standing in the community, and included Charles Trostle, John Calloway, R. N. Burnwell, John M. Spencer and Johnson West. Spencer was the president and chief executive officer of the Hobart Manufacturing Company, and West was the corporation's house counsel. It was, indeed, a distinguished array of character witnesses.

ELIZABETH HIGHT WAS THE FIRST WITNESS CALLED at Thursday morning's session and the last called by the defense to testify in the trial. She acknowledged the truth of her husband's account of the events of the evening of July 7th and his assertions about her dalliances. He had indeed remonstrated with her about her going out with younger men, mentioning Quisenberry in particular, but said that she had paid no attention to him. She declared that she had had numerous dates with Quisenberry without her husband's knowledge, and she admitted that she had refused to accompany the defendant to the picture show that evening because she already had an engagement to go with Quisenberry. Her testimony was an obvious attempt to assume the blame for the shootings and to thereby exonerate her husband.

"It wasn't Lonnie's fault," she declared. "None of it. I got hurt too, you know, but it was all my fault. It was my own wickedness that made him do what he did. I taunted him too much. There's only so much a man can take."

When pressed, on cross-examination, she assured the prosecutor that her husband hadn't really intended to hurt anybody.

"He shot both of you at close range with a twelve gauge shotgun and

you don't believe he intended to hurt anybody?" Kerr persisted.

"No sir, I don't," came the response. "He didn't have no way of knowin' how much damage a shotgun can do. I got hurt pretty bad myself, but he didn't mean for that to happen either. It was like an accident, a freak accident, and I forgive him."

Then when Kerr confronted her with a host of conflicting statements which she had made to the police officers while in the hospital, she seemed to have developed memory problems.

"I don't remember saying anything like that," she said. And demurrers such as "I don't remember it that way," "Don't think I'd have said that," or "If I ever said that, I sure don't recall it. I was in pretty bad shape there for awhile, you know," quickly became her principal currency. And after more than a dozen similar responses, the prosecutor let her go.

And the defense rested its case.

Chapter Ten

Final arguments to the jury began right after the lunch break and, for the most part, ran pretty much to form. At least they started out that way. Everything that Prosecutor Kerr had to say, and all that Harley Enyeart pitched to the jury, were fully predictable. It was almost as though their remarks had been scripted in accordance with the established, if not hackneyed, traditions of courtroom procedure.

Ellis Kerr simply rehearsed the state's evidence against the defendant. He reminded the jury of the testimony of the police officers, the damning admissions contained in Lonnie Hight's confession, and the findings of Drs. Lindenberger and Hance. The defendant, he said, had convicted himself out of his own mouth and had never once repudiated his confession or denied any of the facts.

"Simply put," he charged, "Lonnie Hight armed himself with a 12 gauge shotgun, purposefully loaded it with two borrowed shells, and waited patiently for the errant couple to walk into his trap; then, at point blank range, he shot first one, and then the other, of his two victims, seriously wounding both; and, finally," Kerr's eyes bore into the jury as he completed the syllogism, "the small wounds which he had deliberately inflicted on Howard Quisenberry ultimately proved to be fatal and resulted in his death fifteen days later."

The state had carried its burden, he argued, of proving each of the principal elements of the indictment for murder in the first degree, i.e. malice, premeditation and intent. "Your duty is clear," he admonished.

"The mores of a civilized society and the laws of the State of Ohio demand that you perform that duty by returning a verdict of guilty of the offense charged in the indictment."

Harley Enyeart led off for the defense. His arguments were no less predictable than had been those presented by Kerr. He began by alluding, subtly and by intimation, to the so-called "'unwritten law'" which is so frequently invoked to insulate a wronged husband from the consequences of criminal acts committed in the sudden torment of anguish. "Every man among us," he proclaimed, "has the God-given right to protect the sanctity of his home and family."

And, from that point of departure, he embarked glibly on a series of attacks on the prosecutor's assertions. There was no evidence on the issue of malice, he pronounced. It would be wrong for the jury to leap to the unsupported conclusion that Lonnie Hight had acted out of any motive other than to protect his hearth and home from the depredations of an intruder. And, glibly ignoring the evidence, he insisted with equal vehemence that there was no evidence to support a finding of either premeditation or an intent to kill. The defendant's response to the suddenly discovered perfidy of his wife and her paramour was instantaneous and unplanned, an autonomic, knee-jerk reaction. "What Lonnie Hight did, in the heat of the moment," Enyeart postulated, "was wholly understandable and, just perhaps, fully justifiable. We don't ask that you pin a medal on him; we simply ask that you send him home to his family."

Baird Broomhall, batting second for the defense, seemed to have abandoned the script. Prancing about the courtroom like a player in an off-Broadway production, he invited the jury to look into the minds and motives of all the participants, the provocative wife, the interloper—and the tormented, cuckolded husband. "Who among us," he demanded reasonably, "would have been able to resist the compelling urge to inflict some small injury on the offenders? An urge," he insisted, "not to kill, but rather to remonstrate against their flagrant, hurtful conduct against him. To inflict some slight punishment to them both in a token retaliation for the pain which he himself had felt so acutely."

Now Broomhall brought himself to a standstill directly in front of the jury box. Lowering his voice and leaning towards the box, he spoke in a conversational tone, "And that's exactly what he intended to do. He intended to injure them, an eye for an eye, an injury for an injury. That, in fact, ladies and gentlemen, is precisely what he did. He worked a very serious, nearly fatal injury on his wife. She nearly died of her injury, but of course she didn't. And she has forgiven him. She has come into this courtroom on her husband's behalf and acknowledged her own fault in the matter. Lonnie Hight is not on trial for the injuries he wrought upon his wife. No such charge exists on that account.

"But this case is about Howard Quisenberry, and all the same considerations apply. Lonnie Hight intended to injure him as well—here again, an eye for an eye, an injury for an injury. And here again, that's precisely what he did. Lonnie Hight fired at Howard Quisenberry, hit him in the arm with no more than a handful of pellets, and caused an injury. Not nearly as serious an injury as that inflicted upon Elizabeth Hight, but nonetheless an injury."

Then, without missing a beat, came the admonition: "Bear in mind, ladies and gentlemen of the jury, that the defendant in this case, Lonnie Hight, didn't *kill* anybody. While it's most certainly true that he injured him, Lonnie Hight did not *kill* Howard Quisenberry..." Baird Broomhall looked away from the jurors, surveyed the courtroom, then turned back to the jury, drew himself up to his full height, shot both hands upwards toward the high-domed ceiling and pronounced, in stentorian tones, "DOCTOR LINDENBERGER DID IT!"

Pandemonium broke out in the courtroom as Harley Enyeart, from a seated position in his counsel chair, swung one of his crutches like a ball bat and soundly thwacked his co-counsel in the knee. Broomhall howled in pain as Judge Klapp pounded his gavel for order. "This court is in recess until further notice," he roared. "Bailiff, escort the jury to their quarters and clear the courtroom. I'll see counsel in chambers immediately."

IT TOOK LESS THAN TEN MINUTES for Bailiff Louis Paul to carry out his instructions and for counsel to appear in Judge Klapp's inner sanctum. Harley Enyeart, because of his disability, and Baird Broomhall, limping with an intensely sore knee, were the last to arrive. It was obvious that the judge was in high dudgeon. "For Christ's sakes, Baird," he thundered. "Have you lost your mind? Do you realize what you just did?"

And when Broomhall stammered uncertainly, Judge Klapp answered his own question. "You—just this moment—accused this town's most respected physician of homicide," he roared. "In front of all the news reporters and more than two hundred spectators, most of whom are Dr. Lindenberger's patients. That's what you just did."

"But, I didn't mean..." Baird Broomhall protested.

"Baird, I don't give a damn what you meant. An entire courtroom full of people heard what you just said."

For one of the few times in his life, Baird Broomhall was genuinely abashed. He hadn't considered his remarks to have been quite so egregious as all that, but there was no mistaking the fact that everyone else in the courtroom apparently did. "What should I..." he began when Klapp interrupted a second time.

"I strongly suggest," he commanded, because it was indeed a command, "that you haul your ass into the law library, call Norton Lindenberger on the phone and tell him what you just said to the jury—before he hears it on the street. And I'd advise that you make it sound like an abject apology."

Then as Broomhall skittered towards the doorway that led to the county law library, Judge Klapp added, "While you're doing that, I'll talk to the reporters. Let's see if we can't keep the lid on this thing as best we can."

DR. NORTON LINDENBERGER was more than a little annoyed at having been called from his busy practice to answer the telephone. He listened stoically to Broomhall's report concerning the charge he had just made to the jury, but interrupted the intended apology with a tolerant snort. "Jesus Christ, Baird, I don't give a good goddam what you or any other damn lawyer told the jury. Nobody believes anything you bastards say anyway. Now, if that's understood, I've got a patient here with a real problem. Good luck with your case and goodbye."

Chapter Eleven

The jury returned a verdict of manslaughter after no more than two hours of actual deliberation. They had gotten the case just after 4:00 P.M., enjoyed dinner at county expense at 5:30, and reached their unanimous verdict at 7:20 that same evening.

Lonnie Hight paid close attention, but showed no emotion whatever as Deputy Clerk Ethel Christie read the verdict. He had, he acknowledged later, expected to be acquitted entirely, but had nonetheless been prepared to accept whatever the jury decreed.

The first ballot showed the jurors at eight for acquittal and four for manslaughter. It was ten to two before they were taken to dinner and they reached full accord less than fifteen minutes after they returned. They never considered first or second degree murder.

Immediately after receiving the verdict, Judge Klapp imposed the sentence prescribed by law, that the defendant serve from one to twenty years in the Ohio penitentiary.

ALL OF THE PARTICIPANTS WERE INTERVIEWED Friday morning. Prosecuting

Attorney Ellis Kerr professed himself to be well-satisfied with the jury verdict. He reminded the news reporters that he had never asked for the death penalty.

Defense counsel Harley Enyeart and Baird Broomhall simply announced that they would be filing the customary, but usually feckless motion for a new trial. It was nonetheless obvious that they, too, were pleased with the outcome.

Lonnie Hight was in good spirits and specifically asked that the reporters convey to the jurors an expression of his appreciation for their consideration and for their deliberations. He said that it was a great relief to have the trial over and the issue resolved. He assured everyone, the reporters, his jailers, lawyers and family members, that he intended to be a model prisoner so that he might be paroled at the earliest possible time.

Epilogue

Lonnie Hight was conveyed to the Ohio State Penitentiary by Deputy Sheriff Ralph Hawn on November 25th, 1938; Warden J.C. Woodward issued a formal receipt, that same day, to evidence the delivery of the prisoner into his custody. He was assigned Inmate Number R74787 and became, indeed, a model prisoner.

Three years, four months and nineteen days later, on April 14th, 1942, Lonnie Hight was released and returned to Troy. Elizabeth Hight had left their marital home at 509 Peters Road two weeks before his release. She had moved to Dayton and adamantly refused to live with him ever again. They were divorced on his petition six months later.

Lonnie Hight went back to work at his old job as a maintenance man for Hobart Manufacturing Company, raised his son and daughter alone, and died of natural causes in November of 1954. He was never in trouble with the law again.

Author's Note

I have been intrigued by the story of Lonnie Hight's murder trial from the time I first heard it from Baird Broomhall himself. Some fifty-plus years ago, when I first entered into the practice of law, I was befriended by that very distinguished, congenial and much-admired gentleman. Although still practicing the profession he loved so well, he was already on the dark side of seventy and had relaxed the tempo of his activities to a level that he found both comfortable and rewarding. And because he had the time, and the natural inclination to do so, he soon became something of a mentor to me and I, in turn, became a sort of protegé to him.

In addition to his many other attributes, Baird was the consummate teller of stories, most especially, those stories that involved the practice of law and its many twists, quirks and vagaries.

It is probable that I was the more intrigued by Baird's version of the tale of Lonnie Hight's travails because he had embellished the same, either intentionally or by reason of a faulty memory, in the telling of it. In any event, the way I heard it from Baird was that Lonnie had come home from work one afternoon to find his wife and Howie Quisenberry together in the swing on the back porch of their home; that Lonnie had picked up his shotgun as he made his way through the house and Howie made for the back fence; then, just as Howie dove over the top of the fence, Lonnie touched off a load of sixes and struck the boy in the leg with a single pellet; and finally that Dr. Lindenberger administered a tetanus shot from which Howie died, and Lonnie was put on trial for murder.

I recognize, now, that that's not quite the story I've just related. It is, however, the story that I've repeated over these many years.

In my endeavors to research the facts and to set the story down correctly, I have become aware of the several discrepancies between Baird's version and that which is historically verifiable. As stories go, I really prefer Baird's, with all its separate and seemingly incredible ironies. Be that as it may, I've tried to tell it as it happened. Life has enough irony to go around.

BANDAGED AND HANDCUFFED, CHARLES KENNEDY, JR.

February 9
1964

As is the case with any trial lawyer, the lot of a criminal defense attorney is not an easy one. But then it's not supposed to be easy. It can be, and usually is, arduous, onerous, demanding, time-consuming and intensely challenging.

In addition to the requirement that he possess a knowledge and understanding of the criminal code, with all its myriad complexities and nuances, as well as a thorough conversancy with courtroom procedure, the criminal defense lawyer must also be prepared to stir his stumps in order to seek out and learn all that can be known about the peculiar facts of the case at hand. That reality has spawned, among the brethren at the bar, the somewhat trite, but nonetheless accurate, aphorism to the effect that the "the law is easy; the facts are hard."

The task of learning all the pertinent facts necessary to the defense of a major criminal case, arduous at best, is rendered the more difficult with the passage of time, so that the longer it takes to involve defense counsel in a case, the tougher is his job in acquiring, marshaling and processing all the data pertaining to the specific events of the crime and, often of equal importance, the history leading up to those events.

I had, of course, read the newspaper reports of the murder of thirteen year old Danny Bolden at his home in nearby Piqua, Ohio and the concomitant abduction of an elderly neighbor as a hostage on Saturday, February 1st, 1964. It would have been difficult to avoid the blatantly prominent and shockingly lurid press coverage. Complete with photographs of the sordid scene where the boy's body had been discovered and the devastated interior rooms of the residence where the actual killing was purported to have occurred, the newspaper accounts contained graphic descriptions of the boy's savaged and bloody corpse and all the gruesome details that could be gleaned from the havoc which had been wreaked within the home.

So, at the time, I was at least aware of the events as reported by

173

the local newspapers. And then, in the days immediately following this first account, I read of the apprehension and arrest of a young black man named Charles C. Kennedy, Jr. who was reputed to have been the deceased boy's step-father. He had apparently made a full statement to the authorities and admitted to having stabbed the boy to death with a ten-inch hunting knife.

And that's essentially all I knew about the matter at the time. What's more, I had paid no more than scant attention to the published reports and soon dismissed them entirely from my mind. I had other things on my plate.

IN ALL FAIRNESS, it was scarcely more than two weeks after the killing when the call came from Judge Porter and that would, under ordinary circumstances, have been soon enough. This time, however, because of the unique circumstances which developed, the 16 day hiatus between February 1st and the 17th became quite crucial.

David S. Porter had been appointed Judge of the Miami County Common Pleas Court in 1948 to fill the vacancy created by the premature death of Paul T. Klapp. He had thereafter been elected and re-elected to a series of four-year terms. In February of 1964, then, he was in his 17th year on the bench. A physically fit, wiry man in his mid-fifties, and totally bald for as long as I had known him, he was congenial, readily approachable and jurisprudential to the core; a judge's judge, if there ever was one.

"How busy are you?" he asked as soon as my secretary had put him through.

"Never too busy, Judge. You know that," I replied. "What did you have in mind?"

"Well," he temporized, "I'm sure you saw that Bassett Avenue homicide in the papers?"

I experienced a moment's sudden exhilaration as I guessed where this was leading. "Yes, sir, I did. It would have been hard to miss. Sounds like it was a hell of a mess," I answered.

"It sure does, John," he said. "But I expect you'll be able to sort it out soon enough. The sole suspect, a fellow named Charles Kennedy, has apparently admitted the crime and he's already been indicted by the grand jury. Jim DeWeese filed it with the clerk about an hour ago."

"That happened pretty quick," I mused aloud. A lot of procedural matters would have had to occur in order for the case to have reached that point so soon. Someone in authority would have had to file a charge, or charges, with a court of original jurisdiction in criminal matters (in this case, since the situs of the homicide was Piqua, the appropriate court would have been the Piqua Municipal Court), the defendant would have had to have been arraigned in that court, a preliminary hearing would have been held, or waived, and the accused would have been bound over to the grand jury; that body, if not then in session, would have had to have been convened to hear the evidence and make a determination whether or not to return an indictment. In the ordinary course of events, that process might take anywhere from a few weeks to several months.

"It does seem that way," Judge Porter agreed. "As you know, the defendant was arrested the same day and made a full statement. The prosecutor's office filed the charges within hours that same afternoon, two weeks ago Saturday. The timing worked out just right and here we are. I've scheduled the defendant to be arraigned on the indictment charging him with first degree murder on the 17th, that's this Thursday.

"As you may have guessed by now, this young man—he's only twenty-three years old—is both indigent and unemployed. He simply cannot afford to retain a lawyer. As you know, that means I've got to appoint counsel to represent him at county expense. And that, of course, is the reason for this call. If you're willing, I'd like to appoint you as his counsel. Is that okay with you?"

"That's fine with me," I answered quickly. "Sounds like a challenge."

"Maybe, maybe not," came the reply. "Remember, he's already made a full statement. Do you think you can be ready for the arraignment by Thursday?"

"I would think so," I guessed.

"If you need more time we can re-schedule. There's no rush."

"Thank you, Your Honor," I replied. "I'll holler if I develop a problem."

"Oh, one more thing," he caught himself. "You'll want co-counsel. It's been my practice to appoint a second chair. Who would you like?"

"Judge, I'll take all the help I can get. Who would you suggest?"

Judge Porter knew what my reaction would be before he asked the question. "How 'bout Mike Norris?"

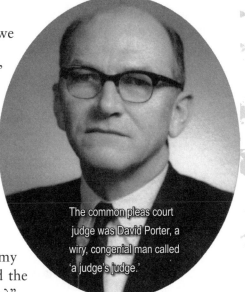

The common pleas court judge was David Porter, a wiry, congenial man called 'a judge's judge.'

"Super!" I responded with enthusiasm. "There isn't anyone I'd rather work with." Mike Norris was one of my favorite colleagues. He was also the *de facto* dean of Miami County's trial bar. Despite the thirty year age difference between us, we were good friends and had tried a number of cases together.

"If he'll take it," cautioned the judge. Mike was past age 65 and though he had no intention of ever retiring, he had begun to ease back on his practice because of its demands upon his time and energy. Had it been otherwise, Judge Porter would surely have asked him to serve as lead chair in the first place.

"He'll take it," I replied with total assurance. "Want me to call him?"

"That'd be good," Judge Porter chuckled. "If I don't hear from you by Thursday, I'll put the order on."

Chapter Two

"One condition," Mike Norris admonished when I put the question to him. "I'll expect you to do all the heavy lifting."

I had called Mike within minutes of my conversation with Judge Porter. I told him only that I was to be appointed to defend Charles Kennedy for first degree murder and that His Honor had offered to appoint co-counsel of my choice. I didn't mention the first chair/ second chair alignment and, as it happened, I didn't need to.

By the time I had sketched for him the little bit I remembered about the case from the newspaper accounts together with what Judge Porter had told me I had Mike's full attention. Old warhorse that he was, he could not have failed to be intrigued by the prospect of becoming involved, at some level, in the defense of what might well prove to be a nearly hopeless situation.

"John, I think you know as well as anybody that I'm trying to lighten up my practice a bit," he remarked. "In fact, you've handled a number of cases I've turned down lately."

"I know all that, Mike," I interjected. "But I expect this is one you'll want to take a look at."

"It does sound like a challenge," he temporized. "I just might sit in as second chair, but I'd want you to do most of the hard stuff. I'm not as young as I was yesterday—or even the day before that. Truth of the matter is I've grown too old and too lazy to want to take the lead anymore. The ravages of time, scars from bygone battles, all that rigamarole.

"And Judge Porter knows that. I'd guess he intended that you take primary responsibility for handling the defense of this young fellow with whatever small assistance you might be able to wring out of this old gray head of mine. If that's an understanding you can live with," he continued, "you can count me in."

"You're on," I accepted without further ado. "Arraignment's set for Thursday."

"Thursday? Jesus Christ! That doesn't give us too much time, does it?"

"Judge said he'd move it if we asked him to," I mollified. "Want me to request a continuance?"

"Let's play that one by ear. We might have time enough," he said. "I suppose we ought to try to interview our client as soon as possible. When can we do that?"

"I can do it anytime. How about you?"

We agreed to meet with our new client at the Miami County jail at 4:00 o'clock, twenty minutes later. We didn't need to consult with our client concerning the time for the interview; he wasn't going anywhere soon.

The jailhouse, located at the corner of Main and Plum Streets, was almost exactly equidistant from Mike's office on Cherry Street and my own quarters on Plum Street, about fifty yards in both cases.

"I'll meet you there at four," I assured him, intending to end the conversation.

"Well, John," he drawled before I could break the connection, "I'll do like the beleaguered Confederate general said to his troops when they found themselves surrounded by half the Union army. He told them their situation was hopeless and they'd have to retreat, honorably, of course, and in orderly fashion. 'As for me,' he said, 'I'm a bit lame; I'll start now.'"

"If I do that," he added, "I ought to be able to make it by four."

MIKE WAS AS GOOD AS HIS WORD, and when I got to the sheriff's residence, office and jail complex, I found him in the kitchen seated at the plain metal table that served as a gathering place for the kitchen staff and the off-duty deputies. He had his hands cupped around the half-finished cup of coffee he had cadged from the kitchen staff and was fully engaged in the business of swapping stories with Sheriff Chet Paulus and Chief Deputy Moose McMaken. The latter's given name was James, but I can't say that I ever heard anyone call him anything other than "Moose." Neither, for that matter, did I ever learn how he came by that moniker; he wasn't an especially large man, as the name would seem to imply. An inch or two south of six feet in height, he was strongly-built, stocky in fact, and the name did seem to fit.

I helped myself to a cup and settled in long enough for Mike to finish the story he was weaving. Then, when the opportunity presented itself, I broached the subject of Mr. Kennedy. The sheriff and his deputy expressed mock condolences when I mentioned that we'd been appointed to represent him.

"You guys are gonna have your hands full with that one," McMaken offered ominously.

"Oh," I reacted. "Is he giving you trouble?"

"No, no, nothing like that," Moose answered quickly. "He's been a model prisoner—very tractable. You might even call him polite. And a good thing, too, 'cause he could be a lot of trouble. He'll weigh about 235 pounds and he looks to be strong as a damn bull. But no, there's been no problem there.

"What I meant was it ain't gonna be easy for you fellas to help him out much. He's already admitted the whole thing; made a full statement. What's more, you wouldn't believe the way he carved that boy up. Worst thing I ever saw. Must have been thirty stab wounds in him; looks like he'd be stabbing him yet if the last thrust hadn't driven him out the window. That's where we found him, you know. Lying on the ground—in a pile of busted glass—just outside the shattered window. There was blood all over hell. It was on the kid's clothes, his body, and inside the house, all over the floors, the walls, the furniture—absolutely everywhere. You get a chance one day, I'll take you up there and show you; it'll make you sick to your stomach.

"Point is, it was a horrendous killing of a pretty decent young kid and your guy's already admitted to it. And, as if that wasn't enough, there'll probably be a kidnapping charge on top of it. That old man got clobbered with a tire iron and shanghaied off to Springfield. Prosecutor's gonna file on that one too. Strikes me there ain't much you two can do for your newest client except tell him to kiss his ass goodbye."

"You make it sound pretty bleak, Moose," I told him. "But we'll need to find out more about this thing before we can address it properly. We haven't seen the files yet and we've not had a chance to talk with our client."

"You want to do that about now, I suppose?"

"Now's a good time," said Mike genially. "I've had about all this stale coffee I can stand. Why don't you trot him out for us?"

MIKE AND I HAD NO SOONER SETTLED ourselves in the sparsely furnished conference room located on the second floor of the jailhouse complex when Moose and another deputy escorted Charles Kennedy, Jr. into our presence, introduced him to us and beat a hasty retreat. He was a big man, perhaps five nine or ten, two thirty-five or forty, and even the loose-fitting prison garb could not disguise his powerful arms and shoulders. Because his blunt, black, facial features were difficult to read in the dim light emitted by the single low-wattage ceiling fixture, Mike and I were glad to note that he was both shackled at the ankles and manacled at the wrists. He did look dangerous and we had already been apprised as to his capabilities.

At the same time there was nothing particularly menacing about his demeanor. He stood before us as though riveted to the floor, his eyes downcast and his expression unreadable. I asked him to sit down in the only unoccupied chair in the room, just opposite the tired, battle-scarred oaken table from where Mike and I had taken up station. Shackled as he was, that exercise was not readily accomplished. When he had finally achieved a sitting position, feet flat on the floor, thick forearms on the table and cuffed hands folded together in front of him, I waited for him to raise his eyes to meet my own. I needed his full attention.

"My name is John Fulker, and this gentleman is Mike Norris. We're lawyers. Okay?"

"Yes sir."

"And because you seem in be in some trouble, and because you apparently cannot afford to retain a lawyer, the judge has asked us to represent you, to act as your counsel. Our job is to help you through this thing as best we can. Is that all right with you?"

"Yes sir. Seems like I could use some help." To my considerable surprise, his manner was open and almost docile. I had expected hostility, sullenness and resentment. I saw none of it.

"You understand, don't you, that you've been indicted for first degree murder?"

He nodded. "That's what they say."

"And, if convicted, you could be put to death?"

"Yes sir. They told me that, too."

"All right. Now, before we go any further with this," I said, "I need for you to understand the precise nature of our relationship. That is, your relationship with Mr. Norris and with me, and our relationship with you."

Then, with Mike's assistance, I explained the various ramifications and nuances implicit in the attorney-client relationship, specifically including matters pertaining to confidentiality, our duties to him and all that we expected of him. "Any questions on that score?" I asked.

"No sir," he answered deferentially. "I understand."

"That's good," I pronounced. "Now, you need to understand also that if we are to be able to help you, we'll need to know everything that happened that day—February 1st, two weeks ago last Saturday—and why it came down the way it did. Okay?"

"Yes sir."

"By the way, do people call you Charles,—or Charlie—or Chuck? Which do you prefer?"

"It's just Charles. Nobody ever called me anything else."

"All right then, Charles it is. Now tell us what happened. We'll probably interrupt with questions as we go along, but tell it as best you can."

As though about to begin a long narrative, Charles Kennedy removed his arms from the table, folded them across his chest and sat up straight in his chair. "Well sir," he began, "They say I killed that boy with a knife..."

Mike couldn't stand it. "Wait a minute, son," he remonstrated. "We don't want to hear what 'they say.' We need to hear, from you, what happened. Okay?"

"Yes sir."

"All right," Mike told him. "Let's try it again."

Thus instructed, Kennedy rolled his eyes toward the ceiling as if the truth were written in the cracked and peeling plaster. Then, with seemingly great effort, he took another run at it. "Well sir. I guess I stabbed him, maybe twenty times, with a knife..."

"What do you mean 'you guess'? Did you or did you not stab him?" demanded Mike tartly.

And though it shouldn't have, the answer truly stunned us both. "I don't remember."

Now Mike fairly bristled with incredulity. "You don't what?"

"I don't remember, sir. But everybody says I did it, so I guess I must have. I just don't remember nothin' about it."

With more than a little effort Mike composed himself, let out a long sigh and had at our client again. "Look son, you've already made a statement to the officers. You've told them what happened. Now you need to tell us too. We've already told you we can't help you if you don't level with us. Understand?"

Charles Kennedy looked as though he'd been slapped. "Yes sir," he said. "I understand."

Mike was not in the least mollified. "All right then," he barked. "Let's try it one more time. And keep in mind that 'I don't remember' doesn't get it."

I may have imagined it, but I thought I saw a tear begin to form in Charles Kennedy's left eye as he strained to comply with Mike's stern directive. "I'm awful sorry, Mister, but I just can't remember anything about it. I'd tell you if I could, really I would, but I just can't."

That was enough for Mike. "This interview is over," he snapped. "I didn't walk over here to spend the afternoon playing games. You're scheduled for arraignment on Thursday. One of us will be back to see you before that and I strongly suggest to you that your memory needs to improve a whole bunch before that time." He stomped towards the locked door of the conference room and called for a deputy to let us out.

My own response was similar to Mike's if only a bit more temperate. Before I joined Mike at the doorway I put a hand on our client's shoulder and said to him, "You'd be wise to think real hard about what Mr Norris just told you. You also need to try real hard to remember everything that happened that day so that we can help you. I'll bet if you really put your mind to it these next couple of days it'll all come back to you. We'll see you in a few days."

"Do you believe him?" Mike asked as we conferred briefly on the sidewalk outside the jail-house.

"Not for a minute," I said. "He just doesn't trust us yet. Let's let him think about it awhile. Meanwhile, let me check out the court file, get a copy of the indictment and a transcript of the preliminary hearing, and see what other information I can develop. Then we can come see him again and see if he's ready to talk with us."

"You do that," Mike responded dourly. "And while you're gathering information, I'll check around with some of my farmer friends and see who's raising strawberries this season."

"Strawberries?" I queried, wondering if I'd heard him right.

"Yeah, strawberries," he answered. "Isn't that what you do with horseshit? Put it on strawberries? With a load like we just got from our client, we oughta be able to bring in a hell of a crop.

Chapter Three

By way of establishing a beginning point in my research concerning our client's several transgressions, I first revisited the contemporary newspaper accounts which I knew to have appeared in the *Troy Daily News* and in *The Piqua Daily Call*. From these, I learned that on Saturday morning, February 1st, at approximately 10:00 a.m. the body of 13-year old Danny Lee Bolden had been found lying on the ground between his home at 220 Bassett Avenue in Piqua and that of the house next door to the north. The boy was reported to have been an eighth grade student at Bennett Junior High School and the son of Mrs. Joan Kennedy who lived at the Bassett Avenue address. Death was attributed by Coroner William N. Adkins to multiple stab wounds in the back. Early reports indicated that an unidentified man was seen to have run from the house and to have seized an elderly hostage, a neighbor named David Love, and fled the scene in Love's automobile. As of press time that afternoon an all-out search of the southwest Ohio area for a suspect "whose name was being withheld" was in progress.

The reports for the following day, the 2nd, indicated that 23-year-old Charles C. Kennedy, Jr., had been apprehended by police officers in nearby Springfield, Ohio, at a house where his father roomed. Kennedy was identified as the step-father of the deceased boy by virtue of his marriage to his mother, Joan Kennedy. The *Springfield News-Sun* ran a front-page photo of the "suspect" as he was escorted from the house by four police officers. The arrest itself was described as a "quiet surrender" and the photo revealed that Kennedy's right wrist was bandaged "from a fresh cut, believed to have been self-inflicted."

As a result of its own investigations, the *News-Sun* was able to report that "Piqua authorities theorized" that the boy had been killed as the culmination of a struggle which occurred when he had come by the Bassett Avenue house to pick up his newspaper route bag. None of the family members had actually been in residence there at the time; Joan had been estranged from her husband for the last few weeks, and she and Danny had been living with neighbors for fear that her husband might do them harm. Charles had been living with his father in Springfield because he'd been under a restraining order requiring him to leave his wife alone.

The *News-Sun* went on with its report to the effect that after having killed Danny, Kennedy went to the nearby home of David Love and attempted to escape in Love's 1956 Oldsmobile. Love attempted to prevent the theft of his automobile and Kennedy struck him forcibly on the head with some sort of weapon, threw him in the rear seat, and drove to Springfield. He abandoned both Love and the automobile in a Holiday Inn parking lot and proceeded on foot to the Mary Dean residence where his father had a room.

Springfield police detective Joseph Barcelona learned that Kennedy's father resided at the Dean residence and, acting on a hunch, actually arrived there before Kennedy did. Mrs. Dean told him she hadn't seen the younger Kennedy in several days and that his father had gone to the store for groceries. They weren't home. Barcelona was skeptical and returned to his squad car to radio for assistance and while thus occupied he actually saw the culprit approach the house and sneak in through a side door. Moments later, and backed by four armed, uniformed police officers, Barcelona summoned Mrs. Dean to the door and asked whether Kennedy was in the house. Although she answered, as loudly as she could, that she had not seen him, she nodded her head vigorously and pointed towards the upper part of her house. Guns drawn, the officers entered the house, charged up the stairs and kicked in the door to the second-floor bathroom. They found Charles Kennedy lying face down on the floor, his arms wrapped around a small gas heater. The gas had been turned on, but the device had not been lit. A blood-soaked cloth had been wrapped around his right wrist as what appeared to be a makeshift bandage.

The police officers rolled him over onto his back, but noted that his eyes were squeezed shut. He seemed to be straining to keep them closed until Lieutenant Billie Schlagle nudged him and commanded, "Get up, Charlie. There's nothing wrong with you."

Kennedy opened his eyes, got to his feet and meekly allowed the officers to lead him to their cruiser. He had a dazed look about him and kept his head down, not daring to glance at the small crowd that had gathered to watch the arrest. Because he was bleeding from the deep cut to his wrist he was taken to Springfield's Mercy Hospital where he was treated and admitted with a 24-hour guard.

Coincidentally, the injured hostage, David Love, had been found by other officers at about the same time as the arrest had taken place, and he too was taken to Mercy Hospital. He was admitted for treatment of the deep gash in his head; later that evening his condition was listed as "satisfactory."

That same issue of the *News-Sun* carried separate interviews with Charles Kennedy, Sr. and Mary

Charles Kennedy goes quietly with the authorities, his arm bandaged from a cut thought to be self-inflicted.

Dean. The elder Kennedy had been grocery shopping for Mrs. Dean and had not returned home until the excitement was over. He shook his head sadly when told about the slaying. "You just never can tell, can you?" he asked Lieutenant Schlagle. "He and that woman been havin' trouble; she was 33 and he was only 23. I tried to talk to him, but he just wouldn't listen."

Mrs. Dean had echoed her tenant's sentiments. "That boy's daddy is a good, hard-working man. He'd never do no wrong. But that boy of his, he just wouldn't listen to nobody."

THE NEXT STEP IN MY QUEST to learn about Charles Kennedy's current predicament involved an examination of the court documents on file in the office of the Miami County Clerk of Courts. The official who held that title, Earl Mishler, was a solid, stone-bald and thoroughly intimidating-looking man in his mid-fifties. Despite his forbidding appearance, he was not only knowledgeable and efficient as the keeper of the court records, but he was also the most amiable person in the courthouse.

"I expect I know what you're looking for," he drawled in his easy way when I entered his office Tuesday afternoon and approached the counter that separated his own inner sanctum from the separate area reserved for the public. Even though Judge Porter had not filed the order appointing us as counsel for Charles Kennedy, Jr., Mish was well aware that Mike and I were on board. He also knew that we had tried a number of cases together in the past and that we enjoyed a pretty good rapport. "You suppose you and Mike'll be able to get along all right?" he asked with his customary good humor.

"Oh yeah," I assured him. "We won't have any problems. I'm a lot bigger than he is."

Mish had already pulled the official court file in Case No. 8614, entitled *State of Ohio vs. Charles C. Kennedy, Jr.* He handed it across the counter and offered, "If you like, you can use my desk to review it now and when you're finished I'll have one of the girls copy it for you."

It took no more than a few minutes for me to examine the three documents that comprised the thus-far skimpy file which nonetheless contained a record of everything that had been filed to date in the case against our client. The first item was a transcript, or summary, of the proceedings held in the Piqua Municipal Court in Case No. 16278 on the docket of that court. My review of the transcript revealed that the prosecution of Charles Kennedy, Jr. had been initiated on February 1st with the filing of the affidavit of James P. McMaken charging that young Kennedy had, that same day, "unlawfully... purposely and with deliberate and premeditated malice" killed Daniel Bolden, contrary to Section 2901.01 of the Revised Code of Ohio. Based upon that affidavit, and on the same day, a warrant was issued by the clerk commanding the bailiff to arrest the defendant and to produce him before the court forthwith. That task would be easily accomplished inasmuch as the defendant was scheduled for transfer from Mercy Hospital to the Miami County jail the following day.

The transcript also showed that Kennedy did, indeed, appear before Bernard S. Keyt, Judge of the Municipal Court, on Monday, the 3rd and that a plea of not guilty was entered on his behalf. Judge Keyt set the matter for preliminary hearing on Friday, the 7th, and the defendant was remanded to jail.

Finally, and to the surprise of no one, the transcript showed that a preliminary hearing was held on the 7th and that Judge Keyt entered a finding to the effect that it had appeared from the evidence that the offense charged had been committed and there was probable cause to believe that the accused was guilty as charged. Predicated on that finding, the judge ordered that he be bound over to the grand jury and that he once again be remanded.

The second item in the file was the original copy of an indictment returned by the grand jury and filed with the clerk on February 17th. The indictment was couched in the same language contained in Moose McMaken's affidavit and effectively charged the defendant with first degree murder. It was signed by John C. Grubb as foreman of the grand jury and by James H. DeWeese in his capacity as Miami County Prosecuting Attorney.

And the only remaining item in the file was an order directing Sheriff Paulus to serve a copy of the indictment on the defendant. On the reverse side of that document was the sheriff's return, dated on the 16th, showing that service had been made as ordered.

I returned the file to Mish, swapped fishing stories with him while we waited for copies, thanked him for the accommodation and returned to my office. There was much more to be learned.

I knew from my review of the transcript that there had actually been a preliminary hearing; it had not been waived as was so often the case. That meant that the prosecution had presented evidence, in the form of testimony, upon which Judge Keyt could base his order of probable cause. Rather obviously, I needed to review that testimony.

Helen Foley was the best and most popular court reporter in the county. In addition to being the official reporter for the common pleas court, she frequently served, on a case by case basis, as the stenographer for some of the other courts and for private depositions. Because it seemed likely that she had been asked to record the testimony taken at the preliminary hearing, I telephoned her that same evening to inquire. She had, she replied, and she had provided the original typed transcription to the prosecutor. She agreed to deliver a copy to my office the first thing in the morning.

Chapter Ten

As a general rule the only evidence to be considered by the court at a preliminary hearing is that presented by the state. Because the burden thrust upon the state to show that a crime has been committed and that there is probable cause to believe that the accused perpetrated the crime is a slight one, the hearing itself usually consists of the testimony of only one or two witnesses called by the prosecution. And while we do expect those witnesses to be cross-examined by counsel for the accused, it is virtually unheard of for the accused, himself, to either testify or to call any witnesses. If he does so, any testimony offered on his behalf may come back to haunt him at a later date. It can be used against him in any subsequent proceeding, specifically including an eventual trial on the merits.

For that reason, I was somewhat surprised to note that of the two witnesses called to testify at Charles Kennedy's preliminary hearing, one was called by each side. Piqua attorney J. Richard Gaier had been appointed by Judge Keyt to represent Kennedy at the preliminary hearing and he had done so *pro bono*, i.e. without any expectation of payment for his time and effort. I knew Dick Gaier well and had a great respect for his talents and his dedication to any cause in which he became involved. Short in stature and pudgy in girth, he possessed both the physiognomy and the tenacity of a bulldog. He neither asked nor gave quarter in any contest, and his courtroom manner was consistently and irritatingly confrontational, and frequently acrimonious to boot. And because I knew all that, I assumed that there had to have been a very good reason why he had seen fit to call a witness to testify on behalf of the accused.

At that early stage of the proceedings, the state was represented by the Piqua Municipal Solicitor, Richard K. Wilson, whom I also knew well. That probably need not have been articulated, because in a county the size of Miami, with perhaps no more than 60 lawyers, we all knew each other pretty well. In any event, Dick Wilson was tall, spare and blond, studious in his habits and pleasant by nature. He began his presentation by offering the official death certificate for Danny Bolden. It attributed the cause of death to "multiple stab wounds" and was admitted into evidence by stipulation.

As I worked my way through Helen Foley's transcript I was mildly surprised to note that the first—and only—witness called by the state was Robert J. Huffman, the chief assistant prosecuting attorney for the county and the person whom I had every reason to believe would be in charge of the prosecution of our client when the case ultimately reached the trial court. Here again, like poor Yorick, I knew him well. Huffman testified that he had been called to the crime scene directly after Danny Bolden's body had been discovered. He had seen the body, observed the multiple stab wounds and asked the usual questions of the police officers and sheriff's deputies. He next learned that Charles Kennedy had been apprehended and was under guard at Springfield Mercy Hospital and, upon receipt of that information, he accompanied sheriff's deputies James McMaken and William Kiser to the hospital to interview Kennedy.

In response to Dick Wilson's careful questioning, Huffman described the circumstance and the appearance of the defendant as he found him upon his arrival. He said that Kennedy was still in the emergency room when he and the deputies had arrived and that he had been thereafter transferred to a well-guarded hospital room designated as the "solarium" where he was placed on a bed, covered with a sheet and strapped, all four limbs, to the bed rails. He also said that Kennedy's right wrist was bandaged and that he was receiving oxygen by way of nasal tubes. Huffman said that he was told that the oxygen was being administered because Kennedy was believed to have inhaled a considerable amount of natural gas from Mrs. Deane's bathroom heater and the doctors were attempting to purge his system of carbon monoxide. Huffman had spoken to a nurse and with all three of his treating physicians in order to ascertain whether their patient had been given any medications which might have sedated him or affected either his memory or his cognitive abilities and was assured that no such medications had been given.

Huffman testified that his interview with Kennedy began at approximately 2 o'clock in the afternoon and continued for perhaps an hour and a half. He said he had been identified to the prisoner by Deputy McMaken as a lawyer who wished to speak with him. Huffman first asked whether his name was indeed Charles Kennedy and whether he knew that he was under arrest. Upon receiving affirmative responses to those questions, and having introduced himself by name, he then took pains to explain that he was not merely an attorney, but that he was the assistant prosecutor of Miami County, Ohio. He said that he expressly advised Kennedy that he was under arrest; that he did not have to make a statement; that any statement that he made could be used against him in court, and that he was entitled to an attorney. He also said that he asked whether there was an attorney or family member he wanted to contact or whether he wished to use a telephone. Kennedy replied that the only person he wanted to telephone was his father, but that he didn't know where he was or how to reach him. He freely consented to continue the interview.

Huffman's direct-examination testimony as to admissions made by Kennedy was succinct and to the point:

Q. Will you relate now to the Court just what Mr. Kennedy told you?

A. He told me that he had killed Danny that morning.

Q. State whether or not he made any statements to you with regard to taking another person to Springfield.

Q. Yes, he first related the events that took place in the Kennedy home there in Piqua and then he told me that after he killed the boy that he left the Kennedy home by the back door and went across the street and down two or three houses to the home of David Love; that he went into Mr. Love's home through the back door and that he had struck Mr. Love on the head. He told me that he didn't recall what he had hit Mr. Love with; that he had been there a brief time and that he then told Mr. Love to get out of bed and get his clothes on, that he was taking Mr. Love's car and that Mr. Love was going with him. He told me that he had forced Mr. Love into his car and had taken it from the rear of the Love home and driven to Springfield with Mr. Love in the car.

Taken as a whole, Bob Huffman's testimony on direct examination, together with the death certificate which had been admitted by stipulation, was sufficient to make the state's case for purposes of the preliminary hearing. Dick Gaier made a perfunctory and essentially fruitless attempt, on cross, to induce the witness to contradict himself with reference to the admonitions which he had given the defendant prior to receiving his confession. At one point in Gaier's cross-examination:

Q. Could Mr. Kennedy have looked upon you, Mr. Huffman, as his attorney?

A. I don't believe he could have, Mr. Gaier, because I told Mr. Kennedy that I was a prosecuting attorney and that I would probably be representing the State of Ohio in some capacity against him.

That which was of value—to me anyway—in Gaier's cross-examination of Bob Huffman was the additional information adduced concerning the murder of Danny Bolden and the circumstances which had preceded the event itself. From that exchange, I learned that Charles Kennedy's entire work experience had been as his father's helper in the masonry trades; that because of the seasonal nature of that occupation, he was currently unemployed and required to look to his father for subsistence. I also learned that because he had been jailed within the past few weeks, on his wife's complaint, for threats of violence and had been ordered to stay away from their marital home on Bassett Avenue, he was currently sharing his father's room at Mrs. Deane's home in Springfield. Apparently Joan Kennedy, despite the court order, had been still concerned for her own safety and that of her two children because she had arranged that they all take temporary refuge elsewhere, with the result that no one was actually in residence at the Bassett Avenue home at the time of the homicide.

Still on cross-examination, Bob Huffman testified that Kennedy had told him that on Friday evening, the last day of January, his father came home from work shortly after suppertime and took him, in company of a friend of his father—a man with some kind of funny name—to a bar in nearby Urbana and then to another bar located in Piqua, a place called Barneys, on Bassett Avenue. Kennedy said that he had not entered Barneys with his father and his companion, but only looked in through the window. He saw only one person he knew, 'Fats' somebody or other, whom he had no desire to see and he returned to the car for a nap. Then, later that night or maybe early Saturday morning, when the two men re-appeared and signaled their intention to return to Springfield, Charles asked them to drop him off at his Bassett Avenue home. All three of them had been drinking whiskey, both in the bars and in the car, and Charles was too drunk to make the trip back to his father's room. He said he'd spend the night at his own home and come back to Springfield the next day.

There was no one in the house when he arrived and he sat down in a chair in the living room—the one with the television in it—and promptly fell asleep. The next thing he remembered was that he was awakened the next morning when his stepson Danny came into the house to get his newspaper bag. He asked the boy where his mother was and the only answer he got was that she wasn't there. Then when Kennedy pulled himself out of the chair and

A heavily-manacled Kennedy is brought into court where he pleads not guilty by reason of insanity, then is transported to Lima State Hospital for 30 days.

said he was going to wash his hands and face, the boy told him he couldn't wash up there. He said he wasn't even supposed to be there and should just "get out." They argued and then Danny grabbed a heavy wooden figurine from off the television set and struck Kennedy in the head with it. A struggle ensued and the boy produced a knife; Kennedy said that he managed to wrestle the knife away from him and stabbed him with it.

At that point Huffman said that he had asked one of the attending physicians to examine Kennedy's head for signs of injury; none, he said, were found.

And finally, Huffman told Gaier that so far as he was aware the defendant had not given or signed a written statement of any kind, either at the time of his interview or afterwards.

DICK WILSON RESTED THE STATE'S CASE at the conclusion of Bob Huffman's case and Gaier called Deputy McMaken as a witness for the defense. It quickly became obvious that his purpose in doing so was to impeach Huffman's testimony to the effect that Kennedy had been fully informed that Huffman was an assistant prosecuting attorney and that Kennedy was not required to speak with him. The effort failed and McMaken fully corroborated everything that Huffman had said in that regard. He also said that there were other sheriff's deputies and Springfield police officers present during the interview.

McMaken said that he had also had a conversation with Kennedy after Huffman had finished. During that conversation, which had been taken down by Sgt. Kiser, Kennedy reiterated his earlier admissions. For some reason or other, however, Kennedy had not been asked to sign Sgt. Kiser's notes or any other statement of any kind.

Additional information obtained from Deputy McMaken concerned physical evidence delivered to him by the Springfield police, including a knife, Mr. Love's automobile and a series of photographs taken by the officers. He said the knife was of the standard hunting variety, 9- to 10-inch blade, brown handle with a carved head, and had belonged to one of the two Bolden brothers. It had been sent to the state crime lab, the BCI, for examination.

Dick Wilson had waived cross-examination of Deputy McMaken and, as soon as Gaier rested the defense case, he moved the court for an order binding the defendant to the grand jury on the charges of murder and kidnapping. The kidnapping charge was withdrawn and Judge Keyt ordered that Kennedy be held for further proceedings by the grand jury. Because the charge was a capital offense, there would be no bond.

Chapter Five

I telephoned Dick Gaier, told him that Mike and I would be representing Charles Kennedy in the trial court proceedings and asked him to share whatever relevant information he thought might be helpful.

"It's all in the transcript, John. Have you seen a copy?"

"I have one, Dick, I've just spent the morning going through it," I answered.

"Then you know as much as I do. I never really talked to the man. Judge Keyt asked me if I'd appear for him at the preliminary and I did. The only thing I could do was to try to protect his rights, make sure his confession was admissible, and see what we could learn about the state's case. From what I heard it looks like they've got him by the nuts."

"Kinda looks like it," I agreed. "But it's early days and we're still trying to get our arms around it. Our client hasn't been helpful. Says he doesn't remember a damn thing."

"That's stupid," he snorted. "He's already confessed in front of about forty witnesses. Told the whole story from start to finish."

"Yeah, I know," I admitted. "But he insists he can't remember."

"It may be early days for you, but it strikes me his amnesia developed a bit late in the game. I think he's just trying to be cute."

"I think you're right," I sighed.

"And you and I both know it ain't gonna work."

MY NEXT CALL WAS TO MIKE NORRIS. I briefed him, as best I could in a telephone conversation, as to what I had gleaned from my investigations thus far. That exercise was not swiftly accomplished because there was a lot to tell.

When I had finished my protracted oral report, he said, "Sounds like you've been busy. You didn't have to do it all; I could have helped, you know."

"I know, Mike. I wanted to do it myself," I assured him. "Besides, I agreed to do the heavy lifting."

"That's right," he confirmed. "You did."

"But it hasn't really spared you all that much. You're going to have to go over it all again anyway. I'm having copies made of everything and I'll have someone drop them off to you. Then, after you've had a chance to review them we can get together and talk about our next step. When's convenient?"

"Well," he answered in a manner that was almost casual, "it probably oughta be later this afternoon. I seem to remember we're scheduled for arraignment tomorrow and I expect we'll want to talk with our client again before that time. How 'bout 5 o'clock? Will that work?"

BY THE TIME MIKE AND I had compared notes, exchanged ideas concerning our Mr. Kennedy, and arrived at the county jail, the sheriff's kitchen staff had managed to feed the inmate populace their evening meal and was engaged in the process of cleaning up afterwards. Sheriff Chet Paulus himself, a small wiry man in his late thirties, brought our client to us while we waited in the same conference room we had used just two days earlier. We found him pretty much as we'd left him. Mild to the point of meekness, deferential in every way, and wholly unhelpful. Even after Mike had rehearsed for his benefit all that we had learned about his savage tussle with Danny Bolden, he continued to deny any recollection.

"Now look, son," Mike insisted, "it's pretty obvious that you remembered the whole thing that Saturday afternoon, right after it happened, and that you described it to more than a half dozen police officers. You can't have forgotten something that important, that traumatic, in a matter of a couple of weeks."

Kennedy looked at him without emotion. "I can't remember nothing, sir. I musta done what they say I done, killed that white boy and run off with that old man. But I just can't remember it."

Mike's Irish dander began to rise. "I don't believe you." he persisted. "I think you've managed to convince yourself that you can't be convicted of a crime if you 'can't remember' what you did. And," he continued, "you'd better get that idea out of your head right now."

Now Kennedy looked as though he'd been struck. The color rose into his cheeks, his lower lip trembled and his eyes glistened. "I'm tryin', sir, but I just can't. Maybe it'll come to me in a day or so."

And I tried also. "Charles," I addressed him with all the patience I could muster, "you need to understand that we're trying to help you. We really are. That's our job. You also need to understand that there is no advantage to you in not being able to remember. That doesn't help you; it doesn't help us. Understand?"

"Yes sir."

"But it will help—a whole lot—if you can remember what happened well enough to tell us about it so we can help you. Do you understand that?"

"Yes sir."

"All right. We're due in court tomorrow for arraignment. That means that the judge will ask you how you plead, guilty or not guilty. Mike and I will be there with you, both of us. We'll tell the judge that you're not guilty. You don't have to say a thing. Okay?"

"Yes sir," he answered softly.

"In the meantime I want you to think real hard about what we've been telling you. You need to trust us. We're on your side in this thing. And, most importantly, we need for you to try, as hard as you can, to remember everything that happened. Will you do that?"

"I'll try, sir. I really will," came the respectful response.

"DID YOU CATCH HIS REFERENCE to his having killed a 'white boy'?'" asked Mike after we'd stepped outside and engaged in a short sidewalk reprise of our latest session with our client.

"Yeah, I did," I answered, "but I'm not sure it means anything. Nobody's accused him of killing anyone other than his wife's son and he scarcely qualifies as a white boy. Maybe he said that on purpose to convince us that he really doesn't remember killing anybody."

"I'm sure you're right," Mike agreed. "I suspect our guy has gotten some very bad advice from some of the resident 'jailhouse lawyers.' They seem to think they're smart enough to beat the system."

"And they're sure as hell willing to offer free advice to anyone who'll listen to them," I added.

Mike grimaced ruefully and prepared to return to his office. "I think I'd better keep looking for my strawberry farmer. It doesn't seem like we've gotten through to this guy yet." There followed a rueful sigh. "In the meantime, I guess we'll have to play the hand we've been dealt."

THERE WAS NOT A GREAT DEAL of business to come before the court on Thursday morning. It was to be a "light calendar," a couple of arraignments, a probation violation and a misdemeanor sentencing. There were scarcely a dozen people arranged about Judge Porter's commodious, wood-paneled courtroom. The session began promptly at 9 a.m. and because of the seriousness of the charge, our case, that of the State vs. Charles C. Kennedy Jr. was called first. We noted that Miami County Prosecuting Attorney James H. DeWeese had appeared for the state.

As the first order of business in that matter, Judge Porter signed the order finding the defendant to be in "indigent circumstances and unable to employ counsel" and therefore appointing the two of us to represent him in the present proceedings. That order, of course, merely formalized that which had already occurred, but it was essential to keep the record straight.

Then, with the defendant standing at the defense counsel table, flanked by Mike and myself, Judge Porter read the full text of the indictment and inquired how the defendant pled to the charge.

"If it please the Court, the defendant says that he is not guilty," I responded, "and the defendant further says that he is not guilty by reason of insanity. We have prepared a written plea to this effect, properly executed by the defendant, for filing if approved by the Court." I had simply articulated that which Mike and I had agreed upon. We'd had no difficulty inducing Kennedy to sign his name to the plea. And that latter fact had encouraged us; perhaps he was beginning to trust us.

Just prior to the defendant's arraignment on the murder charge in Case No. 8614, the prosecutor had filed an "information" charging him with the additional offense of kidnapping Mr. Lowe. That charge had been separately docketed as Case No. 8616. By agreement of the parties, the same pleas were entered as in No. 8614. It was understood that the two cases would be consolidated for trial.

After the judge had accepted the pleas, we had an informal discussion between court and counsel concerning the several implications of the insanity plea. First and foremost was the statutory requirement that upon receipt of a "suggestion" that a criminal defendant might have been insane at the time of the offense or that he might be presently so mentally impaired as to be unable to assist in his own defense at trial, the court was required to refer him to Lima State Hospital for a period of 30 days for observation and evaluation. And although we did not disclose our client's questionable claims of amnesia, the insanity plea was sufficient to trigger the statute.

Pursuant to Judge porter's directive, I prepared a journal entry, approved by court and counsel and filed with the clerk. The entry provided that:

The defendant appeared in Court for arraignment this 20th day of February, 1964 with his attorneys, Michael E. Norris and John E. Fulker, and the indictment having been read to him, the defendant filed his written pleas of not guilty and not guilty by reason of insanity.

The defendant having filed his written plea of not guilty by reason of insanity, the Court orders that the defendant be committed to the Lima State Hospital where he shall remain under observation for a period not exceeding one (1) month, and Dr. T. J. Reshetylo is hereby appointed to investigate and examine into the mental condition of the defendant and to prepare a written statement, under oath, concerning the defendant's mental condition, which report shall be forwarded to this Court and filed herein.

It is further ordered that the sheriff of this county shall forthwith transport the defendant to the Lima State Hospital for such examination.

Chapter Six

Our client's conveyance, the following day, to Lima State Hospital had the corollary effect of denying us access to him for the next thirty days. There was certainly no harm in that because we weren't getting any help from him anyway. What it did accomplish, however, was to give us a little time within which to conduct our own investigations into the homicide itself and into the histories and backgrounds of the *dramatis personae* involved.

And, because we'd just been notified that the consolidated cases had been assigned for trial on the merits on April 26th, it looked as though we'd need all the time available.

To be perfectly candid about it, I had always intended to do the witness interviews and the document-digging myself, then share the results with Mike. Not just because I had promised to do all the heavy lifting, but because it works better for me. If I personally speak with all the persons of interest, one on one, and if I personally run down all the leads and examine all the available materials, I seem to be better able to assimilate the information gained and organize it into a single intelligible skein than if it were to come to me in bits and pieces, some direct and some indirect.

And so, for that reason, I was not in the least distressed when Mike disappeared, apparently from the face of the earth, shortly after the arraignment. Neither was I particularly surprised. Mike Norris was an alcoholic. These days he was a pretty well-controlled alcoholic, but he was nonetheless an alcoholic. On occasion, happily not too often, he would simply disappear for periods ranging from a few days to a couple of weeks. Then, of course, he'd resurface, seemingly none the worse for wear and he'd be fine for months or even years until the demon bit him again.

As might be expected, he'd paid a price for his affliction. His marriage was in shambles and his only daughter had all but repudiated him. He had literally no home life at all. Because he was a staunch Roman Catholic in the traditional sense, divorce was out of the question, so he simply persevered. He made his confessions, said his rosaries, counted his beads and got on with his life. There were a few times when he had done his drinking locally, been arrested and had to spend a day or two in the county jail for driving while intoxicated. On those occasions, he had unabashedly arranged for his office to send his clients to the jail house and he had conferred with them there in the same second floor conference room in which we had visited with Charles Kennedy. I should not have thought that a lawyer who worked out of the local jail would have inspired a great deal of confidence in his clients, but it seemed to work out all right.

It did not work, however, with everyone. Banking institutions, insurance companies, private corporations, professional people and the town's socially elite seldom consulted with him. Now and then, if in serious need of his trial advocate's skills, some of our more prominent locals would call upon him, but for the most part his practice was limited to the less desirable, and the less lucrative, sector of the local client pool.

Despite his addiction, however, and the personal and professional handicaps it inflicted on him, he was well-liked as a person and highly-respected for his professional abilities. A consummate story-teller with an elfin sense of humor and a ready grin, he had about him an engaging charisma that was virtually irresistible. As an attorney, he was a devout student of the law and a formidable adversary in the courtroom.

Once upon a time, much earlier in his career, Mike's very considerable personal charm had combined with his rough-hewn good looks to win the affections of a goodly number of the young women with whom he came into contact. Unhappily, and because he was an optimist of the first water, he often pushed his advantages too far. There was one occasion, at a time when his doomed marriage still had a chance, on which he became hotly involved with his secretary. The affair lasted for more than a year before his wife, Joanne, learned of the situation and took him to task about it. Completely undaunted, Mike somehow managed to convince himself that he could have his cake and eat it too. After all, each of the three players in the triangle were in love with him, so it seemed as though they should be able to subsist together harmoniously as a single happy menage. With that in mind, he took his wife and his secretary to dinner one evening and actually sold them the package. Ultimately, as a result of his blandishments, the two women reluctantly agreed to share his attentions, at home and at work, as a sort of divided harem. Predictably, their detente did not survive the evening. They left the restaurant in agreeable fettle, Mike at the wheel of his late-model automobile, his secretary in the middle and his wife in the passenger seat, arms locked about one another in a show of shared affection, but before they'd progressed a quarter mile, Mike, in a sudden moment of euphoria, squeezed his secretary and gave her a slurpy kiss. That seemed a bit much for Joanne and she had a sudden moment of her own. She reached across the secretary, yanked the steering wheel to the right and ran the car off the roadway and directly into a stout oak tree. Mike got the worst of it and carried a scar, which proceeded diagonally across his face, from hairline to jawline, for the rest of his life. Characteristically, he wore it without apology and, like an old dueling scar, it actually enhanced his masculine attractiveness.

That episode had happened long before I came to practice and virtually no one knew how it was he had earned the cicatrix that he wore, almost heroically, as a subtle badge of his masculinity. Apart from that history, I had never actually known Mike to have a secretary. What he did have was a very charming associate who sometimes served him in a secretarial capacity. Marie Schmuecker, a self-described "spinster lady," was only a few years younger than Mike and had been admitted to practice in Ohio long before Mike first met her. Although she had been born and raised in Minster, Ohio, a strong German Catholic community located some 35 miles north of Troy, she had never actually practiced law in Ohio. Mike had found her working in an insurance company office in Indianapolis. He made her acquaintance effortlessly, charmed her as only he could have done, and induced her to come to Troy and join him in his practice. Despite the fact that Marie was a confirmed teetotaler, the arrangement had worked very well. She established living quarters in the rear portion of Mike's office building on North Cherry Street and, inevitably, it happened that Mike soon came to share them with her.

It was Marie, then, who brought me the news of Mike's disappearance. She was very certain that he was on a protracted binge, she said, but she wasn't entirely sure where he was. She suspected that he was in a whorehouse "up north somewhere," but couldn't be more precise than that. Because of the intimate nature of her own relationship with Mike, it was obvious that she was more than a little perturbed at him. She nonetheless apologized for his absence and assured me he'd be back on the job in plenty of time. I told her I hadn't doubted it for a moment. I knew that despite his occasional lapses, he could always be depended upon to re-appear when we needed him.

"In the meantime," she said, "I'll help anyway I can. I guess I'm responsible for him."

"I appreciate the offer, Marie," I assured her, "and I may take you up on it. But I'd really rather work it out myself. I'll get a better handle on it that way. We'll be okay; don't worry about it."

DESPITE THE FACT that I had other fish to fry, cases to try and a fairly healthy civil practice to manage, I had no difficulty in finding the time to conduct my inquiries concerning the Kennedy matter. As a practical matter, it was easier and more time-efficient to work alone. I didn't need to concern myself with the logistical problems attendant to the task of scheduling interviews and document searches with an eye to two separate professional calendars, and, best of all, when I suddenly found myself with an unexpected opening in my schedule, I was free to seize the moment without the necessity of coordinating with my co-counsel.

Just such an opportunity presented itself early in the week following the arraignment. An evidentiary hearing on a motion in a domestic relations case, set for Tuesday morning, was scrubbed when the couple reconciled of their own accord, and I developed a half-day's opening in my calendar. Remembering that Moose McMaken had offered to show me the crime scene at convenience, I telephoned him at the jail. It was a good time, he said. He'd pick me up in 10 minutes.

Although I'd seen some pretty grizzly-looking newspaper photos of the interior of the Bassett Avenue home, I was still wholly unprepared for the horrid, gruesome scene with which I was confronted when Moose had unlocked the front door and escorted me into the single story, dilapidated house where Danny Bolden had died. It looked as though a malevolent giant had lifted the entire building off its rudimentary foundation, shaken it like a pair of dice in a backgammon cup and rudely slammed it back to the ground. As far as I could tell, no single item from any room in the house could possibly have been in its original condition or location. The bed had been destroyed, its mattress on the floor and the box-springs sprawled crazily across a splintered table with its legs broken and awry, a handful of wooden chairs had been reduced to kindling, cupboards and cabinets overturned, their contents strewn in angry fashion throughout the house. It was unlike anything I had ever seen or could have imagined. And the blood. There was blood virtually everywhere—it had dried now for nearly four weeks, but it was literally ubiquitous—on the carpet, the bedclothes, the furniture fabrics and on the floors. But it was the walls that marked the house as an abattoir. They looked like drab, unprepared screens upon which a giant had painted enormous, incarnadine Rorschach splotches with a huge straw broom.

There was a single broken window on the north side of the house, the trim also liberally spackled with paint from the giant's broom, and Moose showed me the place, just outside, where the boy's mutilated body had been found on the ground amid a riot of bloody shards and the brown remnants of last summer's uncropped weeds.

It was not a pretty scene. It depicted for me, with unsettling eloquence, the tableau of a struggle of such unimaginable savagery that I shuddered in contemplation.

THEIR CONTEST HAD NOT BEEN ENTIRELY UNEQUAL, Moose assured me as we traveled back to Troy in his cruiser. Although Danny Bolden was still shy of his 14th birthday, he was big for his age and pretty strong to boot. At 5 feet ten, 180 pounds, he had already distinguished himself as a gifted athlete. Charles Kennedy, though some fifty pounds heavier and ten years older, was nowhere near as fit or as agile as the boy was and would almost certainly have had his hands full in a man-to-man combat with him. "But I guess it's clear enough," he conceded, "who won and who lost."

Moose also reprised for me his recollection of the statements Kennedy had made to Bob Huffman and to the other law enforcement officers at Springfield Mercy Hospital directly after his apprehension. "He was meek as a lamb and fully cooperative," he said, "and he sure as hell didn't have any memory problems then. He knew exactly what he'd done. That's why he was trying to kill himself."

And, in response to my questions, he told me about the physical exhibits the department had collected as a part of their investigation. I already knew that the hunting knife had been sent to the Ohio BCI for study and that Mr. Lowe's automobile had been impounded. Moose also enumerated other items of evidence that had been sent to the BCI, such as bits and pieces of the boy's perforated clothing, Kennedy's blood-stained shirt, another two knives, a hatchet, a hammer, a club, two wooden figurines, blood samples, fingerprints, a slew of photographs and a raft of other items he couldn't remember offhand. I'd need to see Bob Huffman for the complete list, he said. "And," he added, "I know you're gonna want to look at the photographs. They're pretty graphic."

Then, just before we got back to Troy, we began to pick up radio transmissions from the sheriff's office in San Diego, California. They came in loud and clear, and they overrode the local chatter and static we'd been hearing all morning. "Happens every so often," he assured me. "Has something to do with the weather." He pulled the cruiser off the road and we wasted a little time listening to the staccato-like reports of troubles besetting another city some 2500 hundred miles removed. It was an interesting diversion and a comfort to be reminded that we were not unique in the trouble department.

Chapter Seven

.

I found time the following day to visit the photographers for the two local newspapers, the *Troy Daily News* and the *Piqua Daily Call*. Both papers had featured the homicide prominently and had included photos depicting the house and environs. I suspected they had a great many more which had not appeared in print. And, as it happened, they did. Between the two offices I reviewed nearly a hundred pictures of the Bassett Avenue home, interior and exterior, the location where the body had been found and its immediate surroundings, the body itself *in situ*, and random shots of just about everything else imaginable.

Having just visited the cold scene yesterday, it was helpful to see what it had looked like when the authorities, and the news people, had first arrived. I purchased copies of those prints which best represented the various aspects of the original scene and ignored the rest.

There would be other photographs. I knew that the sheriff's department had taken a set of their own and that those had already been delivered to the prosecutor's office. I'd review those when I talked with Bob Huffman. That interview would come later.

I ALSO ANTICIPATED THAT a far more gruesome set of photos would be in the possession of the Miami County coroner. And, of course, when I visited with Dr. William N. Adkins later in the week, my expectations were confirmed. Bill Adkins was only a few years older than I, but it seemed as though he'd been county coroner forever. He was an exceptionally fine physician and surgeon with a busy office schedule. He was also an ardent student and an able practitioner of the so-called photographic arts.

Although he was under strict instructions from the prosecutor that he not provide copies of either his photographs or his "preliminary" report, he had no reluctance whatever in sharing his findings and showing me his pictures.

"Now that I've read this thing, Bill," I said as I handed the impressive-looking, extremely esoteric sounding "preliminary" report back to him, "tell me what it says—in language I can understand."

"I can do that," he answered with a wry grin. "What would you like to know?"

"Can you tell me specifically what the cause of death was?"

"Sure. Which one do you want to hear first?" he answered.

"Meaning...?"

"John," he said, "I counted five separate stab wounds in that kid's body, almost any one of which could have caused his death. Your guy really did a number on him." He thumbed through the pages of his report and marked several phrases. "In the final analysis, and reduced to simplest terms, I found that the cause of death was—get your pencil out—here we go: 'internal hemorrhage due to lacerations of the aorta, the lower lobe of his right lung, and both lobes of his left lung, all of which appear to have been caused by multiple stab wounds.' How's that sound?"

"Well," I marveled, "I think I can understand it. But, wow! What a job!"

"Oh, yeah. It was a job all right. A hell of a messy job," he agreed heartily. "This kid bled out like Caesar at the forum. He'd have been dead before he hit the ground. Let me show you some pictures."

And he did. They were professional-grade, full-color 8 by 10 photos. They included the house and grounds, the blood-stained walls, the chaotic disarray within, the body, fully-clothed on the ground, and—more to the point of our discussion—the boy's naked body on the autopsy table. These latter pictures, showing a veritable plethora of cleansed, but nonetheless grisly, gaping wounds to the boy's well-developed torso, will remain with me for the rest of my life. Each separate puncture appeared as an obscene crater in an otherwise impressive physique, a horrid intrusion into the core of his existence.

I couldn't even begin to imagine how a jury might react to them.

OVER THE COURSE OF THE NEXT WEEK or so I kept pretty well occupied with my attempts to educate myself as to all that was relevant, and knowable, with reference to our client's case. We certainly weren't likely to learn much from him—not so long as he continued to insist that he couldn't remember.

One morning I drove to Springfield to talk with the police officers who had participated in Kennedy's apprehension and arrest. My interviews with detective Joe Barcelona, Lieutenant Billie Schlagle, and Officers Robert Kerr and Keith Gundolf yielded little more than that which I had already seen in the newspapers. Kerr and Gundolf did tell me that Kennedy had seemed "dazed and unaware" when they found him in Mrs. Deane's bathroom. So much so, they said, that he'd had to be helped to get up off the floor and down the steps. Neither of them was prepared to attribute his somnambulistic condition to the inhalation of fumes from the unlit bathroom heater. Although they said they had heard its hissing sound and could smell the gas, both were satisfied that the heater hadn't been on for very long.

The same two officers had delivered their prisoner to the hospital in their cruiser. They told me that they had not heard Kennedy utter a single word the entire day. They were present when he'd spoken to prosecutor Huffman, but they hadn't heard any part of the conversation.

I also stopped, that same day, to see Mrs. Dean at her residence at 116 Lohnes Street. She told me that she was 84 years old and essentially house-bound. She remembered that a police officer had come to her home that Saturday to inquire about the younger Kennedy and she had told him that Charles, Sr., had gone to the grocery for her and would probably be back in an hour or so; she hadn't yet seen the younger Kennedy. Then, within a very few minutes after the officer left, she said, Charles, Jr. slipped in through the side door, his wrist bleeding, and ran upstairs. He said he'd been in a fight with a white boy, and when she asked him about it, he said he'd come back down, but first he had to go to the bathroom.

Less than five minutes later, four or five officers came back to ask again if Kennedy, Jr. was there. This time, she said, she'd nodded affirmatively and pointed upstairs, all the while telling them in a loud voice that she hadn't seen him. She did say, quite gratuitously, that he "didn't look right" that day; that he "seemed kind of off" and had a "crazy look about him."

Mrs. Dean told me that Charles, Jr. was a sometime resident, and a frequent visitor, in her home; that he had always conducted himself "like a perfect gentleman; that he had, from time to time, brought his wife's two boys with him and that she thought they had a good relationship with one another.

MY NEXT EXERCISE INVOLVED A TRIP to the Piqua Municipal Court where I managed to catch Judge Keyt at a leisurely time. Because he would have no further role to play in the proceedings against Charles Kennedy, Jr. he was at perfect liberty to discuss the matter with me candidly. We examined the extant records concerning the Kennedys on file in his clerk's office and found the jacket for Municipal Court Case No. 16214. That case was initiated on January 17th, just fifteen days before the homicide, with the filing of an affidavit by Joan Kennedy alleging that Charles had "assaulted or threatened to assault her in a menacing manner." It also appeared that Charles had been arrested the next day and remanded to jail for want of $100 bond. A trial on the charges was held three days later, on the 21st, and the defendant was found guilty. He was sentenced to 5 days in jail and required to pay costs of the proceedings in the amount of $12.70; both the jail-time and the costs were suspended on condition that the defendant make no threats and commit no act of violence against his wife for a year. He was released the same day, a mere 11 days before he would kill Danny Bolden.

Judge Keyt said he remembered the case well. The testimony had been to the effect that Kennedy had threatened his wife frequently and had, most recently, menaced her with a knife. It had seemed that the principal source of contention between them had been Joan's drinking. The judge had a specific recollection that there was no testimony that Charles had ever actually struck her or harmed her in any way; neither, he said, was there any assertion that either of the two boys had ever been threatened or harmed. There seemed to have been no animus as between the defendant and the two step-sons.

Contrary to the current misconception on the part of the media, and perhaps even shared by the prosecution, Judge Keyt advised me that he had not issued any orders requiring Kennedy to vacate the marital home—or that he stay away from it or his wife. He did suggest that the parties might want to avoid one another until they, and their tempers, had cooled off a bit. His own apprehensions on that score were assuaged by Kennedy's willing assurances that he had absolutely no intention of returning to Bassett Avenue and that one or the other of them would be filing for a divorce.

"Maybe I should have seen it coming, John," he commiserated, "but I didn't."

I BUMPED INTO DICK WILSON as I was leaving the municipal building. Although he maintained private offices for the practice of law, his responsibilities as city law director brought him to the seat of government on a daily basis, and I had hoped to find him there.

Even though I had read the transcript of Kennedy's preliminary hearing, I wanted to hear Dick's candid opinion as to whether his confession had been sufficiently voluntary to pass constitutional muster.

"Oh yeah," he replied with a grin. "It was obvious, both from the testimony and from my private conversations with Huffman and McMaken, that they both took great pains to identify Bob as a prosecutor and to provide Mr. Kennedy with all the requisite admonitions.

"Actually," he added, "There was a reason for that. Huffman had just had a confession thrown out in another case because McMaken's warnings to the defendant were found to have been inadequate. I heard him ask Moose if he'd learned anything from that experience."

I had no reason to argue the point. "It sounded pretty solid on the record," I acknowledged. "If Gaier couldn't impeach it..."

Dick recognized that I didn't need to finish my pronouncement. "Actually," he said, I was impressed by Huffman's overall treatment of Kennedy. He can be very intimidating, you know, when he wants to be. But this time he was respectful and considerate, almost to a fault. And then, after Kennedy had freely confessed to a really brutal crime, Huffman asked whether he wanted or needed anything. Was he comfortable? Hungry? Thirsty? He even offered him a candy bar and offered to unwrap it for him."

Chapter Eight

I had no difficulty whatever in locating Charles Kennedy, Sr. He found me. "I understand, sir," he said as soon as my secretary had put his call through, "that you and some other lawyer are representing my son, Charles, Jr. It's a murder case. Do I have that right?"

"Yes sir," I answered. "The other lawyer is Michael Norris and he has offices in Troy also."

"I wonder if it'd be all right if I was to come and talk with you awhile. I don't know a whole lot about these things and I've got some questions maybe you could help me with. That be okay?"

"It'd be better than just okay, Mr. Kennedy. I'd like very much to talk with you as soon as we can get together. I've been meaning to make contact with you and just haven't gotten it done yet," I told him. "When can we do it?"

He agreed to come to my office the following afternoon. He'd be off work because of the weather. "One more thing," I interjected before we broke the connection, "do you know where I can find your friend, the man with the funny name?"

"You mean Snake-Eye Crow?" he asked. "Yeah, he's a good friend of mine. I can find him easy. Want me to bring him along?"

I PROBABLY GARNERED more meaningful information and gained a better understanding of our client from my session with his father—and Snake-Eye Crow—than from all the other sources I had tapped thus far. Charles, Sr., was small in stature, no more than 5 foot 5 in height, and he carried no excess weight. He was probably in his late fifties, clean-shaven and neatly dressed in a checkered shirt, freshly-pressed slacks and tweed jacket. His manner was deferential, quiet and soft-spoken, and he was obviously very much concerned about his son's patently serious predicament. He deplored everything that had happened, especially including the death of the young Bolden boy whom he had liked very well.

His questions of me had to do with his son's present difficulties, what he might expect to occur next, whether there was likely to be a trial, and what, if any, hopes he might reasonably entertain for an agreeable outcome. He also inquired as to whether the boy would be able to have visitors while at Lima State Hospital. He seemed to understand my responses to his specific inquiries and to have a fair appreciation of his son's somewhat dismal prospects. When I told him that I felt sure he would be a welcome visitor at the Lima State facility, and that their medical staff would doubtless want to talk with him also, he promised to arrange to go there the next day.

I subsequently learned from my examination of the Lima State evaluation that he had been as good as his word. The staff notes showed that an interview with the subject's father had occurred on Friday, March 9th.

It was reported to me, during my own conversation with his father, that Charles, Jr. had been born in Pensacola, Florida on October 8th, 1940, the second of Charles and Ruth Kennedy's 5 children. His birth was a difficult one in that it was preceded by a protracted and arduous period of labor; his mother's amniotic sac had ruptured more than 8 hours prior to delivery. That circumstance may have accounted for what was perceived to have been a mild developmental delay. He did not walk until he was nearly two years old and he seemed "a little slow" in learning to talk and to identify familiar objects by name.

The boy had had the usual childhood diseases, including measles, chicken pox and mumps; he'd had considerable difficulty with the latter, probably as a result of having gotten up too soon after the initial siege. His testicles became swollen and he carried a fever of 104 to 105 degrees for a period of 5 to 6 weeks until the swelling subsided. Then, at about age 10, he suffered an hallucination in which he saw worms crawling and wriggling everywhere about him—on the walls, on his clothing and on his parents. The condition had persisted overnight and disappeared by morning.

Charles, Jr. was reared in Pensacola by both his parents until they separated in 1955. He was 14 at the time and remained with his mother until he finally left school, at age 18, after completing only 9 grades. Because he and his mother did not get along well, he followed his father to Springfield, Ohio, where the latter had been living since the separation. He found intermittent employment as a hod carrier for his father and in 1961 fell from a second story scaffolding onto a pile of bricks and suffered a severe head injury. He had bled at the ears for several days and thereafter would sit in a trance-like state, during which he seemed to be confused, and complained of dizziness and persistent headaches.

"Will any of this help support the insanity defense?" Charles, Sr. wanted to know.

"Maybe," I answered. "It's probably too early to say. We'll see what the Lima State shrinks tell us."

In 1961, and against his father's strong advice, Charles, Jr. married Joan Bolden, a mulatto woman who was at least 10 years his senior, divorced, with two sons by her first husband. According to Charles, Sr. she was an alcoholic, mean-tempered and sexually promiscuous. In fact, he said, she had at one time lived in the house next door to his own residence in Springfield and he had had a sexual relationship with her. He had wanted to tell his son about that, but was ultimately unable to do so.

It had not been a good marriage. Both parties drank too much, carried on extra-marital affairs, squabbled over money matters and occasionally assaulted one another. The only bright spot in the situation, the senior Kennedy commented wistfully, was his son's easy, companionate relationship with Joan's sons. He'd brought them to visit often and frequently took them fishing, swimming, and, on at least one occasion, horseback riding. The older of the two boys, Danny, had seemed a particular favorite. He was a truly fine young man, a strong, quick athlete, a good student and active in school affairs and YMCA functions. Charles, Sr. told me that while he had worried that there might be trouble brewing, he had expected that when it came it would involve Joan, rather than one of the boys, especially not Danny. Damn shame about him, he reflected, it really was.

In response to my specific inquiries, Mr. Kennedy said that so far as he was aware, his son's only difficulties with the law involved an arrest for driving while intoxicated while still in Florida and, of course, his recent arrest for threatening conduct directed against Joan. He was generally of a friendly disposition and got along very well with his father and with Mrs. Dean. He was barely able to read and write and had recently failed the written portion of his test for an Ohio driver's license. And, because he lacked any real skills, he'd had difficulty in finding, and keeping, regular employment.

Wilton Crowe, alias Snake-Eye Crowe, had been a long-time friend of the elder Kennedy and appeared to be some 4 or 5 years older. It was easy to see how he had come by his moniker. A tall, spare man, he had bright, piercing eyes that very much resembled the white pips on a pair of black onyx dice. He pretty much confirmed Charles, Sr.'s description of his son's circumstances, his regrettable deficiencies and his relationship with his father and with his step-sons.

Together, the two men recalled for my benefit their peregrinations of Friday evening, January 31st. In company with young Charles, they said, they had stopped first at two colored bars in Springfield, then journeyed to Urbana and had drinks at several more such establishments, and finally arrived at the Elks club in Piqua. They were traveling in Charles, Sr.'s car and he'd been driving; all three had been drinking whiskey, in the bars and in the car. Because he was feeling drunk, Charles, Jr. declined to go into the Elks club; he'd said he'd take a little nap in the car and see them later. It was Charles, Sr.'s recollection that they had later dropped his son off at the Bassett Avenue home. Snake-Eye disagreed, "Don't you remember, man? The boy wasn't in the car when we came out. He'd talked about walking down the street to where he lived, and when he was gone, we just decided that's what he'd done. We didn't see him again that night—and, matter of fact, I ain't seen him since."

Their small disagreement about an essentially insignificant matter served as a bleak reminder to me that there had been only two witnesses to the events that followed. One of them was dead and the other, our client, currently denied any recollection.

AND THEN CAME THE REPORT from Lima State Hospital. Filed with the court on March 26th, it was concise and to the point:

Mr. Kennedy has been observed and examined intensively and has received psychiatric examinations and tests. In our opinion, he understands the nature of the charge to be brought against him and can counsel in his own defense; therefore, he would be considered sane.

Dr. Theodore Reshetylo examined him and will represent the hospital in court if it is necessary for a physician to testify.

No surprise there. However, because we would most certainly need it for purposes of trial, we would insist on the hospital's entire file and the opportunity to review it with Dr. Reshetylo.

Chapter Nine

Sometime over the following weekend, the last weekend of March, Mike Norris re-appeared. Very much in the manner of a fishing cork, suddenly released by an escaping lunker, he simply bobbed up from the depths—of wherever it was he had been.

He telephoned Monday morning. "Tell me, John," he began with mock concern. "Have I been fired yet?"

"Not that I'm aware of," I answered. "You haven't quit, have you?"

"Oh, no," he rejoined. "Not by a damn sight. But I do owe you an apology. I shouldn't have done that to you, and I'm sorry for it. I'll not do it again."

"I know that, Mike. And you don't owe any apologies either—to me or any one else. Everybody's entitled to a few days off now and then."

"Well," he remarked with embarrassment, "I think I just used up my share for the year. I hadn't realized I needed a vacation, but apparently my demons thought otherwise."

"I expect you needed a chance to come down off the Horace Day trial," I offered. "I'm sure that exacted a pretty hefty toll on your reserves." Mike's most renowned courtroom triumph had involved the defense of a prominent Piqua city financial officer on a charge of embezzlement. A high profile case, locally anyway, it had required an exhaustive study of accounting entries and procedures, a mastery of a daunting plethora of sophisticated exhibits and, most importantly, an erudite matching of wits with an impressive array of expert witnesses. Trial to a jury, and the painstaking preparation that preceded it, had required months of intensely stressful attention. Horace Day's acquittal was probably more a tribute to Mike's efforts than it was to his client's innocence. The fact that it had occurred some ten years earlier was ignored by both of us. It was still a convenient rationale.

"That's it," he chortled. "That was a tough case—especially for an old warhorse who generally has trouble keeping track of his own expense account."

"The operative word there being 'old'," I observed.

"We don't die, John. Like the man said, we just fade away. Now, enough of all that foofaraw. Tell me about our Mr. Kennedy."

All right," I agreed. "Have you had a chance to look at all that stuff I sent over?"

"If you're referring to the newspaper accounts, the transcript of the preliminary hearing, copies of the witness statements, court documents, photos and your notes, the answer is yes. The time spent just reading 'all that stuff' seemed longer than a whore's dream. You've put together a pretty good dossier."

"And there's more coming,"I reminded. "The Lima State report was filed last Thursday. As we had anticipated, they found him to be sane and fully able to consult with counsel concerning his defense. I'll see that you get a copy."

"Well, hell," he remarked sarcastically. "Who'd a thunk it? I guess we'll need to look at their files. Maybe even speak with their witch-doctors."

"My thought exactly. And the sooner the better. We'll probably need a court order for a special commissioner to compel production and to depose everybody who participated in his testing and their diagnosis."

"Maybe," Mike drawled thoughtfully, "just maybe, we can do it the easy way. I'd be willing to bet Jimmy DeWeese would consent to an order requiring them to open their files and to discuss their findings with us on an informal basis. Whatta ya' think?"

"It's sure worth a shot. I'll draft an order and we can run it up the flagpole."

With a subtle shift of gears, Mike suggested that our client might well have been returned to the county jail. "If Lima's report got filed last Thursday, our guy probably got shipped directly afterward. And if he's back, we probably need to pay him a visit. See if his recollection's improved. Maybe Lima helped him remember what happened."

WE WERE QUICKLY DISABUSED ON THAT SCORE when we stopped by the jailhouse that afternoon. Charles Kennedy had, indeed, been returned over the week-end, but he still professed to have no recollection whatever concerning the events of January 31st and February 1st.

After we had concluded our distressingly brief interview with our client, I couldn't resist a gentle needle to my co-counsel. "You and Mr. Kennedy seem to be running on parallel time-tables," I mused.

"How's that?" he inquired without having paid much attention to my remark.

"Well," I observed innocuously, "It seems like you've both been away for a month or so, and you both came back to earth over the week-end."

"I guess that's true enough," he conceded with a sheepish grin, "but you have to remember, he's been under a lot of stress, too.

"I'll tell you something else," he added. "If the whole truth be known, I expect we'd find his memory of the last few weeks is a hell of a lot better than mine."

Michael Norris (right), the de facto dean of the trial bar and Horace Day, whose own trial was Norris' most acclaimed courtroom triumph.

OUR NEXT STOP TOOK US TO BOB Huffman's office, not far from my own. He and I were essential contemporaries and shared a common history as assistant prosecutors to Jim DeWeese. The chief difference in that context was that while I had been there first, Bob had remained much longer. And now, because of our prior relationship and the close proximity of our respective offices, we frequently shared a late afternoon cup of coffee and conversation.

Bob Huffman was well above average height, firmly built, and had rugged facial features, mitigated by a pair of keen, sparkling blue eyes. They were probably his best feature. Although he pretended to be unaware of it, he was generally referred to by the female staff-members of the various county offices as 'Bobby Blue Eyes.'

"Come on in, guys," he called out when he saw us enter his reception room. "I figured you'd show up on my radar pretty soon." He took Mike by the hand and pulled him into his office. "Good to see you Mike, it's been awhile." And to me, he said, "You know where it is, John, grab a cup for Mike, too."

Then, after we'd settled in around his desk and worked our way through the amenities, he put on a wry face and offered his condolences.

"Much appreciated, Bob," Mike responded. "But why's that? We haven't lost anybody."

"Not yet, you haven't," quipped Huffman, "but you will. Your client's a goner. First chance you get, you're gonna want to kiss him goodbye."

"Maybe," Mike temporized. "Maybe not."

"What?" Huffman reacted with mock surprise. "You two birds aren't really planning to put up some kind of defense for this Kennedy felon, are you?"

"We're figuring on it," I joined in the dialogue. "Unless you tell us you're ready to dismiss the charges."

Bob Huffman affected a sincere pout. "Now John," he whined, "I think that's hateful. It's just *hateful*."

It was one of his trademark laments. "Here we are; we've got this guy dead to rights, full confession in front of forty witnesses. And now you tell me you're planning to mount some kind of defense? That's just plain *hateful*."

"Life is hard, Bob," I told him. "Some days it's a real bitch."

"I guess I'll have to get used to it," he conceded grudgingly. "What is it you want? Talk about a plea?"

"Too soon," we told him candidly. "We haven't the barest inkling as to what this case is all about. Our client insists he has no present recollection of killing anyone."

"You're kidding, of course?"

"Actually, we're not." I told him. "I haven't said we believe him, but until we can find some way to communicate with him—and vice versa—we're stymied."

"But he's already confessed—to me—and to others...."

"We know that," Mike interrupted. "That's why we're skeptical now. But that's his story and he's sticking to it."

And upon that predicate it was agreed that we would undoubtedly need to access the Lima State files and to review them with the examiners. "I'll get Jim DeWeese to sign an order," Huffman volunteered.

The balance of the afternoon, along with another full pot of coffee, was consumed in the process of reviewing the prosecution's preliminary listing of some twenty potential witnesses and more than a hundred exhibits for use at trial. Included within the list of exhibits were more than 70 photographs, a collection of miscellaneous pieces of bloody glass, a hatchet, a hammer, a club, three all-purpose knives, a hunting knife sheath, a jar of ointment, a bottle of aspirin tablets, a torn and bloody shirt, two canes, two African figurines, four sets of clothing, the defendant's typed statement, a length of bloody gauze, a canvas-like sheet, two pieces of rope, two keys, a tape container, assorted vials of blood samples, and a series of fingerprint comparison charts. "Remember guys," Huffman admonished, "this is only a preliminary list; there'll be more."

THERE WAS NOTHING SINISTER about the timing, but it just happened that two days later—on April Fool's Day—we filed an order, signed by Judge Porter and approved by all counsel, to the effect that:

...Dr. T. J. Reshetylo and the staff members of Lima State Hospital be and they are hereby ordered and authorized to fully discuss with said attorneys for the defendant all matters pertaining to defendant's present mental condition and his mental condition at the time of the commission of the alleged acts and to make available to said attorneys for defendant all files, charts, graphs, reports, test results, x-rays and findings pertaining to said defendant.

Fewer than ten days thereafter the entire Lima State file had been copied and delivered to us by courier. It was voluminous

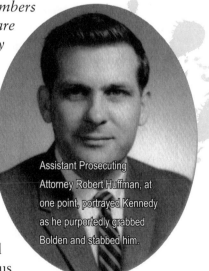

Assistant Prosecuting Attorney Robert Huffman, at one point, portrayed Kennedy as he purportedly grabbed Bolden and stabbed him.

in its bulk, and though we would ultimately find ourselves at issue with some of its conclusions, we had to acknowledge it to have been thorough in its character. Included within the staff evaluation were the results of physical examinations, neurological examinations, electroencephalographic readouts, social service, psychological and psychiatric reports, notes of interviews with former teachers, parents, acquaintances, police officers and officials who had encountered the defendant in one context or another over the course of his personal history, and, of course, an extensive analysis of his level of intelligence and his ability to comprehend his present situation.

Mike and I studied the file by separate turns and then in consultation. We had each highlighted excerpts from the several reports contained within the file as well as from the summary by Dr. Reshetylo. For example:

Physical and neurological examinations are essentially negative. Mental has not revealed any psychotic symptoms. The patient cooperates only superficially, has been trying to confuse the examiners, claiming lack of memory and not remembering anything as far as this offense is concerned. We have evidence from the material in the patient's file that his memory has been selective....

Also noteworthy was the observation that:

The patient's Full-Scale IQ was rated as 77. He appears to be of dull-normal or near moron range of intellectual functioning.

And finally, the official conclusion:

The patient is neither psychotic nor mentally defective, or a sociopath. He is legally sane.

"Hmph!" said Mike when we had completed our review of the Lima State file. "I guess they didn't believe him either."

"That a surprise?" I queried facetiously.

"Not really," he answered. "But it does give me pause."

"How's that?" I asked.

"John," he began, "I think you know with what little regard I hold the pseudo-science of psychiatry. Although I really know better, deep down I can't help but consider it akin to alchemy."

"And?"

"Well," he continued with a grin, "it occurs to me that if those charlatans have concluded that his memory deficiencies are feigned, there may be a good chance they're real. Maybe he can't remember after all."

"Yeah," I agreed sarcastically. "Right."

Chapter Ten

Our discussions with Dr. Reshetylo and his staff proved to be wholly unfruitful. More accurately, they were a total waste of time, an entirely feckless exercise in futility. Nonetheless, the opportunity to test their methodology and their conclusions, prior to trial, was tantamount to the proverbial stone which could not be left unturned.

Pursuant to the authorization granted by the agreed court order, we had arranged to visit with the team of psychiatric/psychological evaluators at the Lima facility on a pleasant afternoon in early April. Mike and I had made the hour-long drive just before the noon hour, grabbed a quick lunch and presented ourselves at the guardhouse just outside the tall chain-link fence which surrounded the entire complex and just beneath the large, intimidating sign which announced that we were at the entrance to the 'Lima State Hospital For the Criminally Insane.' We were efficiently directed to the visitors' parking lot where we were met by a uniformed orderly and promptly escorted to a drearily appointed conference room inside the main administration building. Dr. Reshetylo and his entire staff were already gathered around a plain, institutional-type wooden table on which three massive stacks of files and charts were neatly arrayed.

Together, we spent more than three hours in reviewing their files, test results, summaries and their findings. We found all the participants to be fully responsive to our diverse inquiries, helpful in every respect, and even cordial. We were provided with copies of each and every document requested and nothing, so far as we could ascertain, was withheld. Our session turned out to be more in the nature of a concerned discussion than the adversarial inquisition which we had anticipated.

In the final analysis, however, we could make no inroads on their stated conclusions. Charles Kennedy was entirely sane, they assured us, both in a practical sense and in a legal context. And, not surprisingly, they were also quite adamant in their insistence that Charles Kennedy's claimed loss of memory was a sham.

"Pretty convincing, wouldn't you agree?" I asked Mike as we made our way homeward that evening.

"Absolutely," he acknowledged. "And there's a reason for that. I think they're right on all counts.

"Trouble is," he continued, "we can't afford to agree with them. Right or wrong, we have to take issue with virtually everything they've said."

"I know," I admitted reluctantly. I knew where he was going.

"We don't have anything else. We've pled him not guilty and not guilty by reason of insanity. He's already admitted that he stabbed that kid to death and so long as he continues to deny any recollection, we can't make an argument that he had a legal justification for doing so. That doesn't leave us anything to quibble about except our claim of insanity. There's nothing else out there."

"So what do we do now?" I posed rhetorically.

"I don't think we have many choices," he answered. "We can either convince him to get off this amnesia kick and give us some sort of justification to work with or we'll have to press on with our insanity defense—despite the Lima testimony."

"Or," I appended glumly, "we can plead him guilty. Maybe make a deal for manslaughter."

"Oh, no, we don't," Mike insisted with a wry chuckle. "We 're not gonna do that. You know the defense lawyers' mantra as well as I do. We don't ever plead guilty."

"Yeah, right," I agreed facetiously. "We never plead guilty."

"Besides that, John," he added. "Think of something else. As matters now stand we can't plead him to anything. Not even to simple assault. He'd have to allocute, stand up in open court and admit for the record that he committed a crime, that he knows precisely what he did, and that he had no justification for doing so. Until he gets over his memory lapse, he can't do that and we can't, in good conscience, permit him to do so. What's more, Judge Porter won't let him do it either."

"I think you've just told me I need to keep trying to get him to regain his memory and provide us with some kind of justification," I said, "or to look around for a psychiatrist who's willing to argue with Dr. Reshetylo."

"Or both," he advised.

THREE SEPARATE INTERVIEWS with Charles Kennedy later, I had still made no headway with reference to his claimed memory loss. He was deferential and seemingly cooperative, but he persisted in his claim of amnesia. Even when I told him of our conference with the Lima State people and tried to prepare him for their testimony at trial, he stuck to his guns. He'd sure like to help, he said, and he was trying as hard as he could, but nothing came.

Which, of course, left me with no alternative other than to seize the opposite horn of our dilemma. I would have to find one or more independent psychiatrists who might be willing to become involved in our client's defense and to take issue with the anticipated trial testimony of Dr. Reshetylo.

As it turned out, I had no difficulty whatever in locating an entire stable full of candidates for that particular assignment. The problem was that I couldn't find any such person capable of inspiring a whole lot of confidence—in my judgment anyway. Beginning along about the middle of May, I initiated a series of telephone interviews with some twenty or more psychiatrists from nearby Dayton and Springfield. There was a sameness to each such interview. I would first introduce myself and insist on confidentiality, and then explain our evidentiary problems with reference to our client, his claimed memory lapses, and the Lima State findings, and then inquire as to the doctor's willingness to become involved. The specific questions were whether he would be willing to perform a professional examination of our client and, if he found a legitimate basis to do so, whether he would be willing to testify on his behalf.

The responses which I received were invariably dismaying. After first seeking assurance that they would be properly paid for their time and services, they promised that they could help. To a man, they next posed the same query, "What testimony do you want me to provide? What would you like my findings to be?"

I am quite certain that there were then, in 1964, as there are now, many well-qualified and honorable psychiatrists available for such purposes—but I wasn't having much luck in locating any who fit the description. When I reported my lack of progress to Mike, he couldn't resist a comment to the effect that, "Maybe I should be the one looking for a psychiatrist for our purposes. I expect I've had more experience with whores than you have."

AGAINST THE HOPE that we would eventually make contact with a psychiatrist in whom we could place our confidence, Mike and I filed a motion, on June 3rd, requesting court authority to retain one or more psychiatrists to assist, consult and potentially to testify for us at trial.

Coincidentally, on the same day, Judge Porter filed an order setting our case for trial on Monday, July 27th and directing the clerk to cause a special venire of 75 jurors to be drawn from the jury wheel and summoned for duty that day.

Then, on June 18th, Judge Porter granted our motion to employ psychiatrists:

This matter came before the Court on motion of Michael E. Norris and John E. Fulker, counsel for defendant Charles C. Kennedy, Jr., and it having appeared to the Court from said motion and from the statements of counsel that it will be necessary for counsel to employ the services of independent psychiatrists to examine into and evaluate defendant's mental *condition and ability to form an intent and to testify concerning the same at trial hereof, the Court hereby authorizes said counsel for defendant to employ not more than two qualified psychiatrists for such purpose at a cost not to exceed $100.00 each for such evaluation and $150.00 each per day for testimony at trial of this cause. It is ordered that counsel may be reimbursed for the charges and expenses of said psychiatrists which shall be incurred and paid by them as such counsel.*

Unhappily, we had still failed to locate anyone in whom we could repose even a modicum of confidence.

Five days later, on the 23rd, Judge Porter concluded that the initial panel of 75 potential jurors would prove to be inadequate and he ordered the clerk to draw an additional venire of 50 persons and to summon them to appear for jury duty on July 27th.

Chapter Eleven

The summer of 1964 was a busy time—not only because of the imminence of the Kennedy murder trial and other pending professional exigencies of considerably less importance, but also because of the marriage, in early June, of my wife's younger sister, Gretchen. For no good reason, other than sheer nonsense, my mother had once dubbed her 'Wretched' and it had stuck. Fred Allen, my future brother-in-law, whom I had met for the first time just days before the wedding, was a recent graduate of New York City's Columbia-Presbyterian Medical School and was in process of becoming board-certified as a neurologist.

Because of my own rather persistent pre-occupation with the Kennedy matter, and my sore frustration at being unable to locate a suitable psychiatrist, I complained to him, too long and too loudly, about that which I considered to be a dismal want of integrity on the part of his medical colleagues.

"They're not really my 'colleagues,'" he reminded me dryly. "There is a vast difference between psychiatry and neurology. I acknowledge that both disciplines require a medical degree, but beyond that obvious generality there is no significant nexus between the two fields. You'll have to find some more appropriate brush with which to tar me."

I accepted his rebuke as best I was able, but continued to grouse about my predicament which involved, at the least anyway, a seemingly arcane branch of the medical profession.

"I can understand your chagrin," he commiserated, but I don't see how

I can help." He reflected for a moment, then added, "I can, however, give you a name...."

"I'll be glad for any help I can get," I almost begged. "Old shoes, snake oil, anything at all."

Fred Allen withdrew a ballpoint pen from the inside pocket of his jacket and wrote a name and phone number on his cocktail napkin. "The name is Jim Wall. He's a close friend and mentor of mine—despite the difference in our specialties. He's on the teaching staff at Columbia-Presbyterian and is also engaged in the private practice of psychiatry in New York City. He may have some ideas."

Together we placed a telephone call to Dr. Wall. Fred introduced me and I explained my situation, as well as my dismay and my disenchantment with his Ohio colleagues. He listened patiently to all my plaints, remarked that it was not a perfect world, and offered his advice.

"It occurs to me, John," he said, "that you may not have been looking in the right places. Have you tried Ohio State?"

"Ohio State University?" I asked naively.

"Ohio State University Medical School," he clarified. "They have an excellent psychiatric unit. How far are you from Columbus?"

"We're pretty close, maybe an hour and a half," I answered. "I'm embarrassed at not having considered it myself. I'll check them out in the morning."

"Let me help," he offered. "Dr. Robert Stevenson is one of the best in the mid-west. He's on staff at OSU and also maintains an active practice near the university. And no, he didn't write Treasure Island, Kidnapped, or any of those other stories. But he is a damned good psychiatrist—and a straight shooter to boot."

And before I could express my appreciation, Dr. Wall interjected, almost as an afterthought, "I know him quite well, and if you like, I'll be happy to telephone him first thing tomorrow. Give him a little background and tell him to expect your call."

"Sounds great," I exclaimed with genuine enthusiasm. "My summer just brightened considerably."

"Glad to help," he said. "Tell Fred and Gretchen I'm sorry to miss the wedding."

"We call her 'Wretched'," I told him.

"Fits, doesn't it?" he chuckled.

DR. ROBERT STEVENSON COULD NOT HAVE BEEN more professional, nor more agreeable. He told me that he had spoken with Dr. Wall and that he had, indeed, anticipated my own call. He also told me that he would be happy to interview and to examine Charles Kennedy, report to us concerning his findings, and, if he could do so in good conscience, he would testify in our client's behalf.

"Dr. Wall said that you were not looking for someone whose testimony would be merely convenient to your client's defense, but that you wanted to hear an honest psychiatric opinion as to his mental condition, his limitations and his ability to make the right choices under the extant circumstances."

"Precisely," I answered. "We have no interest in mounting a defense which is predicated on testimony that is simply 'purchased' for the occasion. What we do want is a thoroughly professional, albeit sympathetic, if such be possible, evaluation of our client's mental capacity from a legal standpoint."

I also advised Dr. Stevenson about the financial constraints imposed by the Court with reference to the retention and payment for psychiatric consults and testimony. I was quite certain that he was unaccustomed to accepting employment that clearly promised to entail a far greater expenditure of time and effort than that which the Court had authorized us to pay for, and I needed to warn him at the outset.

"Don't worry about the economics," he said. "It sounds like an interesting study." Then, as though in afterthought, he added, "Besides, Dr. Wall's a good friend of mine."

I STOPPED BY MIKE'S OFFICE the following day to report on my conversation with Dr. Stevenson. He was every bit as gratified by what I told him as I was in the telling of it. As it happened, I had agreed to copy my entire file and ship it to Dr. Stevenson immediately in order that he might review it before interviewing our client. We had also arranged that he come to Troy the following Tuesday afternoon to meet with us in my offices for a preliminary discussion, after which he would spend whatever time he deemed necessary in conference with Charles Kennedy.

"He may not solve all our problems, but I have to feel like he'll be helpful," I mused out loud.

"One thing's sure," Mike agreed. "He sure as hell can't hurt anything. It also sounds like he'll give us an honest opinion—and the aura of professional integrity."

"Mmhmm," I hummed, "and that's refreshing."

Mike lit a cigarette, inhaled deeply and let the smoke out slowly. It was his way of announcing a change of subject. "Something's been bothering me about our game plan and I want you to think about it," he said. "Well, that's not quite accurate either," he amended. "Not so much the game plan—that's almost a given. We don't have many real options there; we'll just have to run with what we've got—plus whatever help the good doctor can provide. What bothers me now is the jury plan."

"How's that, Mike?" I wondered. "Judge Porter's almost doubled the pool. We'll have 125 veniremen to pick from. Seems like that ought to be enough."

With his free hand, Mike thumped his copy of the file. "I spent last weekend re-reading the coroner's description of the stab wounds and the condition of the Bolden kid's body; I also reviewed your memos concerning the sheriff's deputies' reports of what the house looked like, and your own impressions of what you saw when you visited the place. Then, after I'd done all that, I looked at the photos—both those of the body with its gaping wounds and those of the trashed, bloody house."

"Okay."

"Jesus Christ, John, looking at the photos of that kid put me in mind of Julius Caesar at the forum—a 'bleeding piece of earth'—and the house resembled nothing so much as a goddamn abattoir."

It was obvious where he was headed. I should have thought of it myself. "And the question is 'do we really want a jury to see all that blood and gore'?"

"That's what's been eatin' on me since I revisited all that stuff Sunday evening. It's pretty inflammatory," he said. "Let's both sleep on it."

Chapter Twelve

Dr. Stevenson's initial interview with Charles Kennedy proved to be a profound disappointment to all of us. As promised, the good doctor had journeyed to Troy, conducted an afternoon-long session with our client, and then met with Mike and with me to discuss his findings. In essence, his conclusions were pretty much consistent with those of Dr. Reshetylo and his staff.

"I would have to agree that your man is of borderline intelligence, as reported by the Lima examiners. He is, of course, able to function under most circumstances, but," he emphasized, "just barely. And, because of his abnormally low intelligence, I believe it to be very probable that he would be generally incapable of exercising good judgment in stressful situations. However, there is no doubt in my mind that he is fully sane in the ordinary sense of the word. And," he added, "I would have to believe that he was probably equally sane, in that same context, at the time of the commission of his offenses."

"Well, that shoots that defense," Mike conceded glumly.

"Maybe, maybe not," answered Dr. Stevenson. "As I've already said to you, he continues to feign a memory lapse. And that troubles me."

"It troubles us also," I told him. "We're at a total loss as to how to mount a defense without his assistance. We need his version of what actually happened that morning—and why it happened."

"I'm sure," Dr. Stevenson agreed. "His inability—or his unwillingness—to confide in you places the two of you in an untenable position."

"Sure as hell does," Mike grumbled for both of us.

Dr. Stevenson stroked his cheek with his thumb. "Tell you what," he said. "Let me stay on it a while. I can visit with him again, maybe even several times. Maybe I can win his confidence and get him to talk about it."

"It's certainly worth a try," I agreed. "If you're willing to keep trying, we'd appreciate it."

"Absolutely," Mike chimed in. "We're at a total impasse now. If you can just get him to talk with us, we ought to be able to put together some sort of a defense."

THE WARM, BRIGHT DAYS OF JUNE and July passed quickly in their inexorable march towards the trial date and Charles Kennedy had not yet broken his silence concerning the actual events surrounding his having slaughtered his stepson. Mike and I had no choice other than to request a continuance of the trial in order "to fully investigate the charges and to properly prepare" our defense.

"How much time do you need?" Judge Porter inquired when our motion came on for hearing.

"Thirty to sixty days should be sufficient," we assured. And when Bob Huffman made no objection, we were granted the requested extension of time. The order came direct from the bench:

Trial will be continued for a period of not less than thirty nor more than sixty days. The clerk will notify the veniremen and cause the matter to be rescheduled within the requested time.

A hundred fifty prospective jurors, all of whom had been summoned to appear on July 27th, would have to be called off—and subsequently recalled for a date yet to be established. It was a major inconvenience to everyone involved, but one that could not have been avoided. A man's life was at stake.

AND THEN, IN MID-JULY, Dr. Stevenson dropped by unannounced. He had just completed his latest session with our client.

"You know, John," he began tentatively, "None of us has really considered the possibility that your Mr. Kennedy may not be feigning his memory lapse."

"That's true," I acknowledged. "I don't think it's real. And neither does Mike."

"And for that matter," Dr. Stevenson replied, "neither do I. However, because none of us has had any success in persuading him to abandon that which we have considered to be a ruse, it occurs to me that we might owe him—at least for present purposes—the benefit of the doubt."

"If, in fact, there is a doubt," I remarked skeptically. "What do you have in mind?"

"Well, the human mind is a complex and poorly understood phenomenon. On occasion, it has the unique ability to deceive itself, to insulate or to protect itself from an unacceptable reality. I have seen reports in the literature of cases where the mind has actually blocked out— forgotten, if you will—events or images too painful to contemplate. In effect the mind rewrites the history of an event—or denies it entirely—to avoid an unbearable anguish."

"You're not suggesting that to be the case with Charles Kennedy, are you?" I asked.

"Not actually," he answered. "I'd have to admit that in 25 years of practice, I've never encountered a case of autonomic memory repression such as I've described, but I can't, in simple fairness, reject the possibility out-of-hand. I think we need to explore it."

"How do we do that? What do you suggest?"

"Let's try sodium amytal," he posed.

"Truth serum?" I expostulated. "Isn't that the stuff they used in the war to try to get POWs to spew out their secrets? You don't seriously think we can force it out of him, do you?"

"No, no," he laughed. "Truth serum is sodium pentothal. And you're right. It was used, with varying degrees of success to force prisoners of war to give up information which they wanted to withhold. Sodium amytal is a similar drug, but it's used to help a person remember things that his subconscious mind has blocked from his consciousness. Pentothal is a weapon; amytal is an aid."

"So what do we do?"

"You get your client's consent," he instructed. "I'll set it up."

IF I WAS SKEPTICAL ABOUT THE PROCEDURE, Mike was disbelieving. He had pronounced the whole concept to be "stupid" and I didn't disagree; however, neither of us could assign any good reason to resist and, surprisingly, Charles Kennedy had no objection whatever. So we did it.

On an afternoon in early August, two Miami County sheriff's deputies delivered the prisoner, shackled hand and foot, to a pre-reserved room in the psychiatric ward at Dettmer Hospital just north of town. Awaiting his arrival were Mike and I, Dr. Stevenson and a Dr. Chiffiatelli, a local psychiatrist with Dettmer privileges. A pair of hospital attendants were also there to assist as needed.

At Dr. Stevenson's direction, the shackles were removed and Charles Kennedy was stretched out on a metal gurney, to which he was strapped for his own protection, and covered with a light blanket. Then when the deputies had been excused, Dr. Stevenson administered an injection of sodium amytal and waited for the drug to take effect. Within moments Kennedy exhibited obvious signs of sleepiness and as soon as his eyes closed, Dr. Stevenson turned to me.

"You've got about ten minutes, fifteen at the most. Take him through it."

I approached the gurney and began as calmly as I could at what I supposed to be the beginning. "Charles, I want you to go back with me to your place on Bassett Avenue. It's Saturday morning, the first day of February. Last night you and your Dad and Snake-Eye Crow did the bars at Springfield, then at Urbana and finally at Piqua. You didn't go into the Elks Club; you walked on down here to the house and sat down in the big chair in the room with the television. I think maybe you were a little bit drunk and you fell asleep right there in the chair."

Even with his eyes closed, it was apparent to me that Kennedy was with me. He seemed to be accepting the scenario I was attempting to recreate.

"Now remember," I continued, "It's now Saturday morning and you've just waked up. Danny's there with you. You asked him where his mother is and he just said she ain't there. Now you get out of the chair to go wash your hands and face. Danny starts to argue with you, he says you can't wash up there. You're not supposed to be there at all. All of a sudden Danny's got that big wooden figurine, the statue, in his hand and he's just hit you in the head with it, and you've got out of the chair and the two of you are fighting, remember?"

And now it had become obvious that he was remembering. He was reliving it as we went through it together. He became agitated, his arms flailing defensively and his feet scratching at the gurney for purchase. There was no denying that he was engaged in a death struggle. Soon he began to writhe desperately, straining against the body restraints that tethered him to the gurney. His fists opened and closed compulsively and he alternately cowered, covered his body, and slashed outward. All the while he emitted a series of guttural grunts and snarls that demonstrated more powerfully than any words, or even his frantic thrashing about, that he was engaged in a very basic, earthy, mortal combat. This was not feigned; it was stark reality and the man was fighting for his life.

I had long since abandoned my own efforts to help him recreate the events of that fatal day. From the time he first began to fidget and move about, it was eminently patent to all of us that he was fully caught up in the fray and needed no further prompting from me.

And then it was over. As quickly as it had begun, his struggle had ended and he appeared to have entered into a deep sleep. His movements stopped and his muscles relaxed. He lay calmly and harmlessly on top the gurney, his expression serene and his eyes closed. They had not opened during any part of his re-enactment. The whole thing had lasted less than ten minutes.

For a long few minutes we simply watched him, wondering, I suppose, whether there would be anything more, a re-run perhaps. Then Dr. Stevenson said softly, as if not to disturb the man on the gurney, "That's it. That's all of it. He'll sleep for an hour or two and the deputies can return him to his cell. We can go."

"Will he remember any of it after he wakes?" I asked.

"Like it happened yesterday," came the response. "He'll remember it perfectly, and he'll be able to describe it for you. He just demonstrated that his memory loss wasn't feigned. It was real. He'd simply blocked it out. And now," he added unnecessarily, "we've unblocked it."

MIKE AND I PROMISED to interview our client again within a day or two to confirm his ability to confer with us meaningfully, after which we would be in touch with Dr. Stevenson who also wished to interview him in order to properly assess his mental condition at the time of the commission of his crimes. Then we said our goodbyes and made our separate ways homeward.

Mike and I rode together in relative silence. We were both a little shell-shocked. Stunned, actually.

"John," he said as we approached his office, "I've been at this business for over forty years and I confess to you I've never seen anything like what we saw this afternoon. I'd have bet anything I owned that kid was jerking us around like a damned yoyo. I was absolutely, cast-in-stone, dead positive that Charles Kennedy had a perfect recollection of every little detail about everything that happened that day, and that he simply figured that the best defense available to him was a memory lapse."

"And now?" I queried.

"No question about it," he said. "You just saw what I saw. The memory lapse was real to begin with—what'd the doctor call it?—a block? What we just went through was the damnedest thing I ever heard of, but it sure as hell convinced me."

"Me too, Mike," was all I could manage. "Me, too."

Chapter Thirteen

Our next visit with Charles Kennedy, on Friday afternoon that same week, confirmed Dr. Stevenson's confident assurances that our client's memory would be unblocked as a result of his having been induced to relive the experience that had, apparently, precipitated the block in the first instance.

Not only did Charles Kennedy remember—quite vividly—all of the events of that tragic Friday night and Saturday morning, he was unable to get through a reprise of those events without sobbing—at times uncontrollably. He was clearly suffering the pangs of profound and agonizing remorse over the enormity of what he had done to his young stepson, a boy for whom he had harbored an especial fondness. His detailed recapitulation of their argument, the exchange of heated words, threats and demands and his brutal killing of Danny Bolden at the culmination of their savage armed struggle, prompted from time to time by questions from Mike or from me, required nearly two hours to complete. And though his tearful re-telling of it should have been something of a catharsis, it seemed to afford him no significant relief.

We did learn, for the first time ever, that there were actually two knives involved. At one time or another, it seemed, each of the combatants was armed—and both of the knives had belonged to Danny. There was, of course, the hunting knife which our client had wrested away from Danny and with which Danny had been stabbed to death; we'd seen that knife as a part of Bob Huffman's evidentiary arsenal. The other, Charles Kennedy told us, was an entirely different one produced from God-knew-where and actually wielded by Danny at the time the battle ended.

This new information heartened us considerably. Maybe, we speculated hopefully, just maybe, we could make a case for self-defense. The principal problem with that prospect was that there were no witnesses who might confirm our client's story and no second knife had ever been found.

LATER THAT EVENING, MIKE AND I had rehashed all that we'd been told and speculated about some of the new strategies now available to us by reason of Charles Kennedy's recovered memory. Then, just before we broke off our session, Mike adverted to our earlier discussion concerning the potential harm to our client upon the jury's exposure to the sordid, blood-covered crime scene and the coroner's photographs of Danny Bolden's ravaged body.

"We agreed to sleep on it," he reminded. "Have you done so?"

"I don't suppose," I answered obliquely, "there's any chance we could persuade Judge Porter to refuse the prosecution's motion for a jury view of the house ..."

"And to exclude the coroner's photos," Mike finished for me. "Put your money on a snowball in hell, bud; the odds are better."

"It's inflammatory stuff," I argued lamely. "It'll most likely prejudice the jury."

"Of course it will." He answered dourly. "But you know the litany as well as I do. The judge will find that its evidentiary value outweighs any potential prejudicial effect on the jury and it will all go in. The view, the photos and every bloody garment they can lay hands on. It's all 'relevant, competent and probative.' However it might affect the jury, Judge Porter couldn't keep it out if he wanted to."

"I think you've just told me we should waive the jury and consent to have our guy tried to the court," I said. "Did I read that right?"

"Not just to the court," he corrected. "To a *three-judge* court. The law requires it and you can bet Jimmy DeWeese will insist on it."

"Oh?"

"Oh, yeah. I guess you weren't practicing yet when the Dick Knight cases were tried up in Hardin County? That was back in the forties."

"No," I answered. "That was before my time. I was admitted in '53. And, no, I'm not familiar with any cases involving a Dick Knight. What's that about?"

Mike was in high clover now. He was the consummate story-teller and savored each new opportunity to share a tale which he considered to be of value. "You're gonna like this one," he chortled. "It's a classic. Dick Knight was charged with murder one up in Hardin County. Because he didn't have a chance in hell of beating it, he let his lawyer waive a jury and plead him guilty to the trial judge with the expectation that the judge would recommend mercy and sentence him to life imprisonment. The prosecutor agreed and the judge did, indeed, recommend mercy and put Knight away for life.

"Then, while he was in the state pen at Columbus, he got to foolin' around in the prison law library—he had all the time in the world, you know—and he found that the Ohio General Code provides for trial and sentencing by a *three-judge* court in the event of a waiver of trial by jury, and that a *one-judge* court has no authority to accept a plea and make a recommendation of mercy. In other words, his trial was a nullity. Soon's he works that out, he prepares and files a petition for habeas corpus in the Court of Appeals and they order his release. Obviously, since his first trial was a nullity, they have to start all over again, and this time he elects to act as his own lawyer and demands that he be tried to a jury. After all, he had a lawyer the first time around and it looked like he'd misread the law, so Knight figures he's got a better chance without counsel.

"The irony is, this time around the jury finds him guilty and does *not* recommend mercy, so he gets himself the death penalty and they execute the bastard. Talk about 'outa the pan and into the fire!'"

"Or," I laughed, "a little learning can be dangerous?"

"Sure was for Dick Knight. He appealed his conviction and the death sentence all the way to the Supreme Court, but they affirmed, and he ended up in the electric chair."

"All of which means that if we waive—and it sounds like we need to do exactly that—we're looking at a three-judge court..."

"To be appointed by the Supreme Court," Mike appended. "Let's do it."

It was perhaps a week or so later I received a visit from Dr. Stevenson. He had just spent the afternoon with Charles Kennedy and had confirmed with him that his memory was indeed fully restored and that he was now able to discuss the events of February 1st, as well as his own history, in a cogent sequence.

"There is no longer any question in my mind concerning his memory lapse," he said. "It was clearly blocked out."

That conclusion came as no real surprise to me. I anticipated that he would have been convinced from the dramatic signs of the breakthrough which we had observed at Dettmer Hospital last week. My present concerns were focused now on where—and how—we might proceed from here.

"What's your read on the pivotal issue," I wanted to know. "Have you formed an opinion concerning his mental condition at the time of the killing?"

"Mmhmm," he answered thoughtfully. "He was clearly sane—in the customary sense of the word—at the time of the struggle, and at the time he stabbed Danny Bolden to death. I don't think he actually set out to kill the boy, but his actions were not the product of insanity."

"Do you believe, then, that we should abandon our 'insanity' defense?" I asked.

"No, I don't," he said. "I think you can make a very compelling defensive argument in support of your claim of insanity."

"How's that?" I wanted to know. "I thought I just heard you say you believed him to have been completely sane?"

"In the customary sense of the word," he reiterated, "he was certainly sane...."

"But..." I interrupted.

"Doesn't Ohio still follow the so-called M'Naughten Rule?" He asked innocuously, though it was very obvious that he very well knew the answer.

"Absolutely," I answered quickly. "In its purest form—exactly as originally articulated in merry old England over 100 years ago."

"Well then," he paused long enough to extract a small notebook from his briefcase, thumbed to a marked page, and continued, "I've been involved in one or two similar cases over the years. Isn't it a sufficient defense, under M'Naughten, if you can show that your man," he read from the marked page, "'was laboring under such a defect of reason, from disease of the mind, as not to know the nature and quality of the act he was doing...' etc., etc.?"

I confess that I was somewhat abashed to have my psychiatric consultant remind me concerning the law of Ohio, but I was certainly willing to listen. "Yes, that's my understanding of the rule," I answered.

"And, isn't it also a recently adopted corollary to the rule that he may be exonerated if he can show that, even knowing the nature and quality of his act, that it was wrong," Dr. Stevenson consulted another passage in his notebook, "that he had not the capacity to reject the wrong and to embrace the right course of action?"

"I believe that's a correct statement," I conceded sheepishly. I should have been advising him concerning the implications and ramifications of the law as it pertained to the defense of insanity, not the converse. However, I liked where he was headed and was more than willing to follow along.

"In that case," he concluded, "I think I can, honestly and in good conscience, support an argument to the effect that your client was, at the time of the homicide, laboring under such a defect of mind as to be totally unaware of the nature and quality of his actions, and that, even if he did know, he lacked the ability to reject the course he took. In other words," he recapitulated, "in simplistic terms, he simply couldn't help himself."

MIKE AND I NEXT ARRANGED a conference with Judge Porter, Jim DeWeese and Bob Huffman. We advised concerning our decision to waive a jury trial and requested that Charles Kennedy be tried before a three-judge court.

Jim DeWeese spoke that which was in everybody's mind, "That's probably a wise course, guys. I doubt very much that a jury could remain unaffected—or truly impartial—after they see some of the gruesome exhibits we're set to offer."

And, when a general agreement had been expressed, he added, "And it really doesn't matter to us. We expect a conviction either way."

Bob Huffman feigned a mock grimace and cracked, "That's easy for you to say, Jim. I'm the poor bloke who's got to try this thing."

"That's right," DeWeese mocked him playfully. "And I expect you to win it."

TWO DAYS LATER, ON AUGUST 20TH, we received notice that the case had been assigned for trial to a three-judge court consisting of the Hon. John M. Kiracofe of nearby Eaton, the Hon. Howard G. Ely of Greenville, and the Hon. Huber Beery of Sidney, all of whom had been specially appointed for the purpose by the Supreme Court. Trial would begin on Friday, August 28th.

Chapter Fourteen

Because of my total preoccupation with matters pertaining to the defense of Charles Kennedy, the summer of 1964 seems, at least in retrospect, to have passed very quickly. I remember that it was hot and that it was dry for long periods. People worried about drought. And yet the same climactic conditions that gave rise to those concerns also produced an inordinate number of bright, sunny days followed by cooler, but still pleasantly warm, evenings. It was a good time to be alive.

And there were, indeed, events and activities—quite apart from the matter of *The State of Ohio vs. Charles Kennedy*—to command our attention and to invite our participation. Stated otherwise, the world continued to turn; life went on.

Because of the enactment, by Congress, of the Civil Rights Act of 1964 and the extensive voter registration campaigns, with the attendant civil unrest and disorder spawned by that legislation, particularly in the South, this year's summertide season came to be known as Freedom Summer. It would be impossible, even today, to ignore the events and the widespread impact on our history, of Freedom Summer.

And, on another front, not entirely unrelated to the social upheaval produced by the nation's struggle for racial equality, our two major parties had held their respective national conventions and had crafted an exciting election contest for the Presidency between incumbent Lyndon Baines Johnson and Senator Barry Goldwater. The country's growing frustration with the progress of the Vietnam campaign would inevitably become a pivotal issue long before the polls opened on November 3rd. All of which was equally fraught with the impact of historical significance.

It would also have been difficult to ignore, that same summer of 1964, the release of convicted wife-slayer Dr. Sam Sheppard from prison and his subsequent marriage to Adrianne Tenbenjohanns, Cassius Clay's seeming reluctance to grant Sonny Liston a rematch for the heavyweight title he'd lost to Clay in February, and the stunning performance of Miami County's own Bob Schul in winning a gold medal in the 5000 meter run at the Olympic Games in Tokyo.

However hectic matters were that summer, there was still time and opportunity for personal and family pursuits. Nancy and I found time, in early July, for our annual canoe trip, this time an exhilarating run down Michigan's Au Sable River, and then, in August, we treated ourselves, and our two sons, to a trip to the World's Fair at Flushing Meadows. And, as might be imagined, while in the New York vicinity we also enjoyed a visit with the newly-weds, Fred and Wretched Allen, who were still residing in the city during the completion of Fred's residency at Columbia Presbyterian. That

Prosecuting Attorney Jim DeWeese set the tone: "We expect a conviction either way...."

visit paid an additional and unexpected dividend in that we were able to couple it with an evening with Dr. Jim Wall, the psychiatrist friend to whom Fred had referred me earlier in the summer.

I found both Dr. Wall and his attractive wife to be charming, eminently sophisticated and exceptionally congenial in every sense of the description. Over drinks and dinner, the conversation was sprightly and intensely enjoyable. I may, however, have spoiled the prevailing holiday-like ambience and spread the proverbial wet blanket over the affair by broaching the subject of my star defendant's misdeeds, his mental deficiencies, and Dr. Stevenson's anticipated opinion testimony on his behalf. Dr. Wall told me that he was happy to learn that he had been able to disabuse me of my skepticism concerning his professional colleagues and that his own referral had been helpful. "You need to know," he tweaked jovially, "that we're not all whores."

He was most intrigued, I discovered, by Charles Kennedy's startling recovery from his memory lapse under the influence of sodium amytal. He had, of course, read of such cases, but had never actually seen it first hand. "Then it's not all anecdotal," he said. "It would seem that your client's experience confirms the phenomenon. I expect Bob Stevenson will be doing a paper on the subject—for the journal, that is. We've always known of the mind's capability for blocking out that which is too painful for it to accept or to process—just as your client has done—but we've not always enjoyed a very high degree of success in getting past the block. Often, after time, the repressed memories will come to the patient, either gradually or, most frequently, in a sudden rush. But I've not seen anything quite like what you've described. You can be sure I'll be calling Bob about it in the morning."

By the time our evening ended—and we'd probably bored everyone else to tears—I had described Charles Kennedy's history, the details of his offenses, and Dr. Stevenson's opinions, analyses and suggestions as best I could. For his own part, Dr. Wall expressed his own concurrence with his colleague's conclusions and his anticipated testimony. He was, of course, quite conversant with the so-called M'Naughten Rule as it was applied in virtually every Anglo-American jurisdiction.

"It's been broadened somewhat from the original, you know," he remarked.

"Actually, I don't know that," I admitted. "I'm only familiar with it as it is currently applied by the Ohio courts."

"And that is all you really need to know," he said. "But I find it interesting, from a purely academic standpoint, that the Rule as originally articulated by the judges back in 1843 did not include the concept of 'irresistible impulse.' These days, by judicial interpretation, most states have appended to the original statement of the Rule language to the effect that the insanity defense will hold even if the perpetrator knew that his acts were wrong, but was powerless to resist committing them."

"And that's good," I noted. "At least from my client's standpoint."

"I think it's appropriate," he added deliberately, "in most cases...and if properly applied to the facts."

Chapter Fifteen

Actually, the August 28th trial date had been threaded into the court schedule before Mike and I had informed Judge Porter of our decision to waive a jury. It had been Judge Porter's intention that we should begin the process of jury selection on Friday, the 28th and continue on through Saturday, and even into Sunday if necessary in order to have an acceptable panel in place before court was adjourned for the week-end. That would have permitted us to take opening statements and to view the premises on Monday morning and begin the actual presentation of evidence in the afternoon. Total trial time had been estimated at two weeks and Judge Porter thought we might get through it more efficiently with a Friday, Saturday, and possibly Sunday, running start. Then, when advised of the jury waiver, he'd called off the 125 jurors who had been summoned, and kept the trial date.

The three trial judges had other ideas. Recognizing that we'd not be needing the time for jury selection—and having received very short notice of their own special assignments by the Supreme Court—they found it to be convenient to all concerned to defer the commencement of trial until Monday, the 31st. Their only requirement was that a written waiver of the defendant's right to a jury, signed by the defendant himself, be filed forthwith. Mike and I accomplished that very promptly and were really quite content to have the weekend to conclude our final trial preparations.

AND THEN, ON MONDAY MORNING, after what had seemed at the time to be an incredibly short abeyance, trial began in earnest. As a first order of business, Presiding Judge John Kiracofe required the defendant Charles Kennedy to re-affirm, in open court and in writing, his voluntary waiver of the constitutionally prescribed right to trial by a jury of his peers and his agreement to be tried by a three-judge panel. He took great pains to explain both the significance of the right and the implications of the waiver. Finally, after all three members of the panel were satisfied that the defendant fully understood his rights and that his decision to waive those rights was both voluntary and knowingly taken, the waiver was accepted. The court was not taking any chances with this one.

Bob Huffman opened for the state. Because of the absence of a jury, his remarks could be simple, direct and to the point. There was no need to educate the panel of judges to the nuances of courtroom procedure, the specific elements of the crime charged, legal concepts such as the burden of proof and the weight of the evidence or other matters with which a jury of laymen needs to become acquainted. In plain, concise and artful language Huffman advised the panel that the state would prove, beyond a reasonable doubt, that the defendant Charles Kennedy had stabbed his 13 year-old stepson to death on February 1ˢᵗ, 1964, at Piqua, in Miami County, Ohio, and that he had done so without excuse or justification, but purposely and with premeditated malice. The evidence, Huffman promised, when spread before the court would mandate their verdict of murder in the first degree.

My own opening, for the defense, was yet more brief than Huffman's. Defendant Kennedy would not deny that he had caused the death of Danny Bolden at the time and place charged by the state. Neither would he deny that the instrument with which he had done so was the knife which would be offered into evidence by the state. However, I charged the panel, the state would not be able to prove, by the requisite quantum of evidence, the essential elements of murder in the first degree, i.e. intention, malice and premeditation. Furthermore, I added, the defendant would show, by a preponderance of the evidence, that Charles Kennedy was fully justified in taking the boy's life in defense of his own and that he was powerless to prevent both his actions and the result of those actions, which had been provoked and escalated by the decedent himself.

Total elapsed time for both opening statements was something less than 10 minutes—certainly not an all-time record for brevity, but very probably very near the mark for first degree murder trials.

The balance of the morning session was devoted to a visit to the Bassett Avenue crime scene by all the participants in the proceedings. The three judges shared a ride with Helen Foley, the very efficient court reporter who was, herself, by virtue of longevity and a reputation for flawless efficiency, already something of a local legend. Charles Kennedy was driven in a sheriff's cruiser, cuffed and shackled for the adventure, by Chief Deputy McMaken and two other deputies; Bob Huffman, Mike Norris and I rode together in my personal automobile, and the remaining staff members were transported by bailiff Paul Braunschweiger.

The procedure for the crime scene view was greatly simplified by the non-presence of a jury. Had a jury been at hand, the lawyers would have been prevented from any form of direct communication with its members. If we had wanted to direct their attention to any specific area or particular feature, we should have had to request that the bailiff instruct the jurors accordingly. Without their presence, the lawyers and the judges were free to move about the premises together and to point out to one another those specifics and particulars which we deemed to be of especial interest or significance.

As might have been expected, we, the lawyers and judges, moved through the house and grounds as a unit, noting and remarking about the condition of the several rooms, the wrecked furniture, the blood-stained furniture and the blood-spattered walls. I experienced a well-concealed shudder as I contemplated the savagery of the struggle which had produced such total chaos and tried to imagine the impact this particular scene would have had on a jury. There was no question in my mind that we had called that one right.

THE PRESENTATION OF EVIDENCE BEGAN RIGHT AFTER LUNCH. The first witness for the state was 14-year-old Keith Bolden. He was Danny Bolden's first cousin and resided on Bassett Avenue, just a few doors down the street. It was he who had actually discovered Danny's torn and savaged body lying on the ground outside the broken window of his mother's home on the morning of February 1st. In response to Bob Huffman's gentle questioning he told the panel how it was that he had happened on the scene that day, what it was that had first attracted his attention, and his own horrified reaction to the gruesome sight that presented itself upon his closer examination. His descriptions were devastatingly graphic and were more than sufficient to set the stage, and the mood, for the evidence which would ultimately follow. We had virtually no cross-examination.

Then came Dr. William N. Adkins, the county coroner. He testified concerning his examinations of Danny's body, the first of which was a superficial post-mortem, followed by a thorough and medically definitive autopsy to determine the precise cause of death. Dr. Adkins told the panel that more than a few of the wounds which he had observed were each sufficient to have caused the boy's death, but that he believed that the fatal wound was a four-inch laceration of the aorta, very near the heart. He described a considerable number of other wounds to the chest and to the back. The back wounds, he said were deep slashes, not likely to have been fatal, but probably inflicted first.

When asked about the deep stab wounds to the chest, Dr. Adkins spoke in terms of the positional relationship of the assailant and the victim, the point and angle of entry, and the probable course of the knife stroke.

"Do you have an opinion as to how such wounds were inflicted?" asked Huffman.

"Yes sir, I do," came the response.

Chief Deputy McMaken had been seated at the prosecutor's side as the state's trial representative. At a signal from Huffman he rose from his chair and stepped to the center of the courtroom. Bob Huffman then produced a rubber knife, approached the deputy from the rear, wrapped his own left hand and arm about his neck in a firm grasp and, in slow motion, slashed with his right over the deputy's right shoulder and downward into his chest. "Like this?" he asked.

Dr. Adkins reflected for a moment before he answered, "Yes sir, that's my opinion."

And, of course, before he let him go, Huffman offered into evidence an impressive stack of photos taken prior to, and even during, the coroner's autopsy. In vivid color, they were shockingly graphic and daunting to behold. We objected as a matter of course, but were properly overruled. There was no legitimate basis to exclude them from the skein of evidence.

Mike and I had anticipated Dr. Adkins' stated opinion as to the manner in which the wounds had been inflicted. We had agreed that we simply could not allow that version, as re-enacted by the prosecutor and his deputy, and confirmed by the witness, to go unchallenged. However horrible the actual event had been, the scenario we had just witnessed made it seem still worse than we believed it had been.

So it was that after a series of preliminary questions on cross-examination, we presented our own portrayal of the manner in which the wounds to Danny Bolden's chest might just as easily have been inflicted. With Bob Huffman's permission, I first availed myself of his rubber knife, held it in my own right hand and lay down, flat on my back, in the center of the courtroom floor. With no further ceremony, Mike left his chair at the counsel table and took up a position directly on top of me, his knees on the floor astride and holding me down with the weight of his body. He grasped my throat with his left hand and drew back his right as though to strike at me. We freeze-framed in that tableau while I asked Dr. Adkins to assume, for the moment, that the combatants had been positioned as we were at that moment, with Danny Bolden on top of Charles Kennedy.

Then, also in slow motion, I pretended to stab Mike in the chest with an overhand stroke. "Doctor, would not the delivery of the wounds to the victim's chest from this position and in the manner which I am now demonstrating be equally consistent with your findings as to the angle of entry and the course of the stroke as the version postulated by Mr. Huffman?"

After no more than a moment's hesitation, Dr. Adkins answered readily, "Absolutely. I hadn't really considered the matter from that aspect. One possibility is just as likely as the other. I apologize to the court for any confusion I may have caused on that score."

It was all we could have hoped to accomplish and the witness was promptly excused.

ALL OF THE LOCAL NEWSPAPERS REPORTED on our separate re-enactments during the course of the coroner's testimony. I was especially intrigued by excerpts from Tuesday morning's reportage by the *Dayton Journal Herald*:

First day of the trial resembled the last act of Hamlet as Prosecutor Robert Huffman represented Kennedy grabbing Bolden from behind and stabbing him. That demonstration was followed by a defense demonstration in which the defendant was represented as lying on the floor with the Bolden youth (who weighed 165 pounds) on top of him. Defense attorneys John Fulker and Michael Norris staged their rendition of the death scene and struggled on the courtroom floor slashing through the air with a rubber knife. County coroner Dr. William Adkins testified the youth could have sustained the wounds under either of the two scenarios.

EDWARD HOPKINS WAS A VETERAN FORENSIC SCIENTIST with the Ohio Bureau of Criminal Investigations, colloquially known simply as the BCI. He was called as the second witness for the state and his testimony was, for the most part, both canned and perfunctory. He told the panel of judges that he had examined blood stains found on various items of clothing owned by Danny Bolden, David Love and the defendant Charles Kennedy. He had also performed chemical analyses on a number of the other artifacts contained in the prosecution's evidentiary arsenal and his findings fully supported the charges lodged against our client. There were, of course, no surprises from this witness and his testimony, though an essential part of the state's *prima facie* case, had no real significance from our standpoint. We had already acknowledged the fact of Charles Kennedy's having killed Danny Bolden and having kidnapped David Love. It would have been pointless to take issue with Mr. Hopkins' testimony. We waived cross-examination and the witness was excused.

Bob Huffman next called Wilton 'Snake-Eye' Crow to the stand and led him painstakingly through a description of his meanderings, in company with the defendant and his father, on the evening of Friday, January 31st. He admitted that all three had consumed an inordinate amount of whiskey as they visited one bar after another in Springfield, Urbana and Piqua. They had also had several bottles with them in the car and were thus able to keep "well-lubricated" even as they drove from one oasis to another.

In a brief cross-examination of Snake-Eye Crow, we were able to elicit a favorable picture of Charles Kennedy as a friendly, easy-going young man with no known penchant for violence. We also made the point that the defendant got along well with just about everyone, most especially including his two stepsons, for whom he seemed to care very deeply.

"This ain't something he'd a ever done if he was in his right mind," Snake-Eye Crow remarked gratuitously.

THEN CAME DEPUTY SGT. WILLIAM KISER with the written statement he'd taken from Kennedy at Mercy Hospital on February 1st. Although the statement was unsigned, Deputy Kiser asserted that he had accurately transcribed the defendant's spontaneous "confession" precisely as given in the presence of prosecutor Huffman, Chief Deputy McMaken and a half dozen other officers.

Quoting directly from the statement, Deputy Kiser testified that Kennedy had told him that he had gotten "high" the night before, had left his father and Snake-Eye, and had walked down the street to his wife's home on Basset Avenue. There was no one there when he arrived, so he simply settled into a comfortable chair and went to sleep. He was awakened Saturday morning by his stepson, Danny Bolden, who seemed to be angry at him and told him to leave the house. Kennedy had said he'd go as soon as he had washed up a bit. The answer didn't seem to have suited the boy because he next struck Kennedy in the back of the head with a wooden figurine. A struggle ensued and Danny picked up a knife and threatened to attack. According to the statement Kennedy wrested the knife away and stabbed at him with it until the boy jumped out the window.

Kennedy had said that he next went to the home of David Love and told him to "crank up" his automobile. He said that Love then consented to accompany him to Springfield where they parted company.

DAVID LOVE, AGED 87, appeared for the prosecution and vehemently denied that he had made the trip voluntarily. He said that Kennedy had forced his way into his home, struck him in the head with a weapon of sorts, tied him up and forced him—at knife-point—into his own car for the trip to Springfield. Kennedy had driven and, in the course of their journey had said to him, "I killed Danny and now I'm gonna do away with you." And, as if to demonstrate his intention to do so, he struck the old man another savage blow to the head. Love concluded by stating that he had been discovered later that day, still in his car and virtually unconscious, in a parking lot in Springfield.

Bob Huffman had intended to conclude the state's case with the testimony of Joan Kennedy, Danny Bolden's mother and Charles Kennedy's wife. Over our strong objections, she was permitted to testify that Charles had threatened to kill her on several occasions over the course of their marriage. Once, she said, he had cut a cord from a venetian blind, snapped it at her in a menacing way and told her she should "call my children in here, it'd be the last chance I'd get to talk with them."

Then, as a part of winding up the presentation of the prosecution's evidence, it was agreed that the physical exhibits, blood samples, photos and other non-controversial items, all of which we had seen before, might be admitted into evidence by stipulation of counsel. That meant that it would not be necessary for such items, particularly the photos, to be formally authenticated by a live witness who could identify each item and confirm its provenance.

"One other thing, guys," said Bob Huffman when we had agreed concerning the stipulations. "I've got one more photograph we need to talk about. You haven't seen this one—and neither had I until just a moment ago. Take a look at this." He handed us an 8x10 glossy that purported to depict the crime scene. Danny Bolden's body was prominently distinguishable, covered with a rude blanket and lying on the ground where it had been discovered. Many of the early arrivals were readily identifiable, as was the scene itself. We'd already seen dozens of such photographs and hadn't picked up on anything of especial significance.

Mike found it first. "Mother of God," he breathed, almost reverently. "There's the second knife." And indeed there it was. In the near foreground of the picture, lying in the middle of a small patch of brown grass, but clearly discernible, was an open knife. It actually appeared to be a hunting knife. It was most certainly not the knife that had taken the life of Danny Bolden. That knife had been found in David Love's automobile just hours after the homicide. The one we were looking at now—in the photograph—had never come to the attention of the authorities. If it had been discovered—

and it most certainly had been—the discovery had not been reported.

Ever since his memory had been restored, our client had steadfastly insisted that there had been a second knife. He had taken the first one away from Danny, he said, but Danny had immediately armed himself with another and had used it to attack him again. But until this very moment, there had been no proof—other than Charles Kennedy's insistence—of the existence of this second knife. Other knives, including those of the hunting variety, had been found in the house, but none was ever located anywhere near the body or in such a circumstance as to be implicated.

"That's sure what it looks like to me," Huffman agreed. "One of the newspaper photographers just brought it to me during the last recess. He said he'd taken over a hundred shots and he hadn't actually developed them all. He gave us those he thought would be useful and we showed them to you. They're already in evidence. Then after trial began, he became interested and decided to develop the rest of them. He found this and brought it straight to me."

"And you're ready to rest your case?" Mike speculated tentatively.

"Yes," answered Huffman. "But I don't have to. How do you want to handle this?"

Mike and I conferred briefly, then I suggested to Huffman, "How about if you offer the photo as a part of your evidence? That'll give it the same level of dignity as the rest of the exhibits. Maybe you could even put your photographer on the stand so he can explain how it happened to come to light."

"I can do that," Huffman agreed. "Fair's fair."

HERE AGAIN, THE DAYTON JOURNAL HERALD said it best. In its account of the state's final witness the reporter appreciated the full significance of the discovery:

A mystery photo—which tends to imply that a 13-year-old boy who was stabbed to death February 1 may have been armed with a knife—was revealed yesterday in the trial of the boy's stepfather charged with first degree murder. The picture was taken near the body of the boy by a Piqua news photographer. The photo shows what attorneys say "appears to be a knife" lying on the ground. Marshal Julian testified that he took the picture as he walked away from the body. Julian said he did not see a knife and wasn't aware that the negative showed what appears to be a knife until Miami County sheriff's deputies pointed it out.

Chapter Seventeen

Bob Huffman had rested the state's case against Charles Kennedy just after the lunch break Wednesday, September 2nd. Although he had subpoenaed a total of 31 witnesses, he ultimately determined to call only six to the stand for testimony. Marshal Julian, whom he called at our request, made a total of seven prosecution witnesses.

And, in accordance with standard practice—more ritualistic than meaningful—Mike and I moved the court for dismissal of all charges on the grounds that the state had failed to make even a *prima facie* case against the defendant as to either of the crimes alleged, i.e., murder in the first degree and kidnapping. Stated otherwise, we claimed that the state had failed to offer at least some credible evidence sufficient to sustain each of the elements necessary to ground a conviction on either charge. Although the motion was ridiculous on its face, we were virtually constrained to interpose it at this juncture as a matter of practice. It was just one of those things that lawyers do "to protect the record." In that which can only be seen as a totally feckless effort in futility, we even argued the claimed merits of the motion.

Although Presiding Judge John Kiracofe assigned a greater dignity to our motion than that to which it was properly entitled with his announcement that the panel would adjourn to chambers to consider the motion, we were not the least encouraged. There was no chance our motion would be sustained and everyone in the courtroom knew it.

SOME 45 MINUTES LATER we were summoned back into the arena to learn that the court, after careful consideration, had determined to overrule the defendant's motion. The trial would proceed and the defense should present its evidence.

We began with the defendant himself and led him, painstakingly, through the history of his life, from his childhood in Florida as the product of a broken home, his difficulties in school and his move to Ohio to join his father. We talked about his inability to find and keep a job, his lack of skills or training and his essential ineptitude in social situations. We had him describe the incident that had occurred when he was a young boy, still living with both parents, when he awoke in the middle of the night and imagined that his bedroom, bath and his own entire body were covered with teeming, wriggling worms. The delusion had lasted throughout a long night spent in his parents' bed and in the morning the worms were gone. He described a head injury he had sustained from a fall from a scaffolding and lit on a pile of bricks. He had bled profusely from both ears and had been hospitalized for several days.

We had him tell the court about his relationship with his father, his marriage to Joan and his affection for her two sons. They'd had their problems he said, he and Joan, because of her drinking and her promiscuity, but he would never have harmed her in any way. And he certainly would never have intended any injury to either of the two boys.

He acknowledged his own drinking problem, but said he was trying to get that under control. All he had ever really wanted, he told the judges, was to be a good husband to Joan and a father to the boys.

As to the events surrounding his fight with Danny, his account didn't differ from that which had already been related except that he insisted that he had not been the aggressor in any sense of the word, that after he had taken away Danny's knife, the boy had produced another one, from his jacket pocket, and had used it to renew his attack against him. Charles had only tried to protect himself and had never meant to kill, or even to injure, anybody. He had not, he said, known that he had hurt Danny, let alone taken his life, until he later saw blood on his own shirt; that was when the realization of what he'd done came to him and when it did, he was so devastated he slit his own wrist with a razor. "I wanted to hurt myself for hurting him," he moaned despairingly.

It took a great deal longer to elicit Charles Kennedy's testimony than it has to recount it here. We consumed the balance of the afternoon and most of Thursday morning in the development of his history and his account of the homicide and his subsequent flight, in company with a willing David Love, to Springfield. His testimony was not only time-consuming, it was also tedious. There came a time during Bob Huffman's extensive cross-examination when all three members of the panel appeared to be soundly asleep. Mike nudged me gently to call my attention to the fact that all three had their eyes closed. When I nodded my recognition of the fact, he whispered mischievously, "Watch this."

And with that, he leaned forward, placed his elbow on the counsel table next to a stack of law books and rested his head in his uplifted hand; then slowly he allowed his hand and elbow to slide across the table so as to push the books over the edge. When the heavy law-books hit the floor with a startling crash, I saw three pairs of judicial eyelids snap open like spring-wound window shades. Then, while the embarrassed judges recovered their composure and addressed themselves once more to matters at hand, Mike stifled a grin and whispered only that, "I think we now have the court's full attention."

We next called the defendant's father, Charles, Sr., to the stand to confirm and to elaborate on his son's developmental delay, his obvious intellectual and social handicaps, his wriggly worms delusion, and the head injury and possible concussion sustained as a result of a construction site accident. He also confirmed the story told by his friend Snake-Eye Crow concerning their travels and their drinking activities on Friday evening, January 31st.

And, over Bob Huffman's objection, we were permitted to read the deposition of Mary Dean. Because of her advanced age and physical debility she was unable to appear in court for live testimony and we had arranged to take her testimony before Helen Foley, the official court reporter, some weeks before the trial. There was nothing really new to be learned from Mrs. Dean except that we had been able to wring from the deposition her statements to the effect that when she saw Charles that Saturday she thought he looked "kind of off," "He didn't seem right," and he had a "crazy look about him."

Friday was to be the 5th day of trial and both court and counsel recognized that we would not be able to complete the presentation of evidence that day. It was pretty much a given that we would need a special Saturday session to finish. Holding over until Monday was not an option because two of the judges had other commitments in their own counties.

When I entered the courtroom that morning I was surprised to see my co-counsel handsomely decked out in an obviously new and uncharacteristically sporty outfit, plaid slacks, yellow tie and a kelly green jacket.

"Wow!" I exclaimed. "What's with the new threads?"

"It's your fault," he growled with his customary good nature. "Yesterday morning you came in here complaining that if we didn't finish this damn thing soon you were gonna run out of fresh clothes. Remember that?"

"Well, yeah," I answered, "but...."

"That's right," he interrupted before I could finish. "That reminded me that I've worn the same dark suit to court every day this week—and it embarrassed me. So I made a quick trip to Longendelpher's and bought myself a whole new set of clothes. And," he gestured grandly at the bright array of colors, "I wanted to make damn sure you'd notice."

THE TESTIMONY OF THE DEFENDANT, his father and Mrs. Dean, while necessary, competent and relevant, had been primarily intended to serve as both prelude and predicate for the expert, opinion evidence of Dr. Robert Stevenson. His presence on the stand was, at once, imposing and professional. Exceptionally suave and collegial in both appearance and manner, he commanded deference to his qualifications and confidence in his judgment.

In response to my questioning, he sketched out his *curriculum vitae*, his education, background and experience. That we go through that exercise is necessary in order that the court may hear and consider his professional opinions as an aid to their decision-making process. In essence, we use the witness's resumé to qualify him as an expert in his specialty discipline.

"And, at the present time, you are board-certified in the field of psychiatry, with an active practice in Columbus, Ohio, is that correct?" I inquired.

"That's correct. Yes sir."

"You are also a member of the teaching staff at Ohio State University and you enjoy staff privileges at two separate hospitals in Columbus?"

"Yes sir."

Bob Huffman was satisfied and conceded the point. "The state will stipulate to the doctor's credentials," he announced.

I had entertained no doubt that, if asked, Bob Huffman would have stipulated at the outset, but I had not asked him to do so. I wanted to acquaint the panel first-hand with the doctor's rather impressive *bona fides*.

"Dr. Stevenson, did you, at my request, have occasion to examine the defendant Charles Kennedy?" I asked.

"I did."

"And, in that connection, did you also have an opportunity to review any written materials concerning the defendant?"

"I did."

"Please tell the court what your examination of the defendant and your review of the materials consisted of," I directed.

To which Dr. Stevenson described his interviews with Charles Kennedy, his documented memory lapse and its subsequent restoration. He also detailed his review of the Lima State tests, reports and evaluations, witness statements which I had provided, and virtually every other document or memorandum concerning the defendant and the specific acts with which he had been charged.

"In the process of your review of the Lima State files, did you note Dr.

Reshetylo's findings concerning the defendant's mental condition?"

"I did. He found the defendant to be sane."

"At the time of his examination?" I asked.

"Yes sir, that was his conclusion."

"Doctor, did you consider that conclusion to be appropriate?"

"Yes, I did," Dr. Stevenson responded. "He certainly appeared to be fully sane at the time of my examinations."

I would have liked to ask Dr. Stevenson about his opinion as to the defendant's state of mind at the time of the commission of the offenses for which he was on trial, but because of the rules of evidence then in force, that direct line of approach was impermissible. Because Dr. Stevenson had no first-hand knowledge concerning the events in question—he had not, of course, been personally present when they occurred—any information concerning those events could have come to him only by way of hearsay and he could neither testify nor render an opinion based on anything he had learned by virtue of that strictly proscribed avenue. The rationale was simply that a witness, expert witnesses included, could testify only as to matters they had actually seen and observed.

And yet, because opinion evidence concerning matters outside, or beyond, the scope of common experience can often be of assistance to the trier of fact in arriving at a just result, it was universally conceded that it should be heard. For that reason the use of the so-called hypothetical question had long since evolved as a method by which trial lawyers might present—in acceptable form—the opinion testimony of a person properly qualified to testify as an expert in a particular field of study or endeavor. Although we could not ask the expert his opinion about a specific person or circumstance, we were quite at liberty to inquire about a hypothetical situation which exactly conformed to that under consideration. The only constraint was that there must have been, at the time the question is posed, some evidence as to each fact the witness is asked to assume.

My next series of questions, then, were predicated on a long and tedious enumeration of assumptions which were intended to describe, in infinite detail, the defense theory of the case and the evidence before the court. "Dr. Stevenson," I began, "for the purposes of my next line of inquiry I will ask you to assume a purely hypothetical man whose history, background, education, intellectual limitations, life experiences and personality traits are precisely similar to those of the defendant Charles Kennedy, Jr. as you have come to know them to be—from any of the materials which you have reviewed or from your own examinations of the defendant himself. Can you do that?"

"Yes sir. I can," answered the witness.

"Assume further, if you will, that this hypothetical man, on the evening of Friday, January 31st, 1964, in the company of his father and another man, visits a number of bars in Springfield, Urbana and Piqua, Ohio, and that all three of the men are also drinking whiskey in the father's automobile; assume also that the hypothetical man allows himself to become thoroughly inebriated and that he leaves his father and the other man and walks a few blocks down the street, enters his wife's home on Bassett Avenue in Piqua, and falls asleep in a chair; that he is rudely awakened the following morning by his 13-year-old stepson and ordered to leave the premises, that he agrees to do so as soon as he has washed up and that he is thereafter struck in the head with a heavy wooden figurine; that a violent struggle ensues during which his stepson, a well-developed 165-pound athlete, produces a hunting knife and attempts to injure him. Are you with me, Doctor?"

"Yes sir, I am."

"I will ask you to assume further that during the course of the struggle, our hypothetical man manages to take the hunting knife from his stepson and that the boy immediately arms himself with yet another knife and resumes the attack...."

The litany of assumptions which I asked the doctor to accept dragged on almost interminably. It included everything we knew about the struggle, the observed number of knife wounds, the cause of death, the abduction of David Love, the defendant's flight to Springfield, his attempts against his own life, his remarks to Mrs. Dean, his apprehension at her home, his subsequent statements to the authorities, his memory lapse and its later recovery, his evaluation by the Lima State personnel and just about every conceivable fact concerning which there was a shred of evidence in the record.

My mother had attended the trial on that particular day. She just happened to note that I had droned on for more than 40 minutes in setting out the list of assumptions upon which my further inquiries were to be predicated. Nonetheless, she told me later, she had very much enjoyed my "speech." I suspect that she had an imperfect understanding of what it was she had heard.

Finally, and thankfully, finished with the intensely tiresome enumeration of each of the several facts to be assumed with reference to our hypothetical man, I was in a position to proceed with that part of Dr. Stevenson's examination which I considered to be crucial to the defense.

"Based solely on those facts which I have asked you to assume, Doctor," I queried, "do you have an opinion as to the state of mind in which this hypothetical man acted at the time of his struggle with his stepson?"

"I do," came the anticipated response.

"In your opinion as a board-certified psychiatrist, at the moment our hypothetical man inflicted the knife wounds on his stepson, did he have the ability to choose the right action and to reject that which was wrong?" I asked as though I were unsure what the answer might be.

"It is my professional opinion that he did not have that ability," asserted Dr. Stevenson. "At the time those wounds were actually inflicted, your hypothetical man was not in a state of mind to determine what was the right thing to do. Neither would he have had the ability to resist the instinctive impulse to retaliate aggressively—and, as occurred in your hypothetical, to take the life of his assailant."

And in standard fashion, virtually scripted in advance, I continued my quest, "Doctor, please tell the panel those considerations upon which you base that opinion."

"In the first instance, the hypothetical man you have posited was of profoundly sub-normal intelligence, barely able to cope with life's exigencies under the best of circumstances. Added to the mix is the fact that he had just awakened and would not therefore have been fully oriented to time and place, and, of course, he found himself, almost immediately, locked in a mortal combat. Under those circumstances, I would not have expected him to have realized what he had done until some time after the event. I think, in fact, that one of the assumptions I was asked to accept was that our hypothetical man did not realize that he had hurt or killed his stepson until much later, and when he did so, he twice attempted to take his own life.

"The actions and the reactions of your hypothetical man are not those of a person who premeditates the killing of another human being."

BOB HUFFMAN HAD INTERPOSED AN OBJECTION to both the questions and the answers given with reference to our hypothetical man, who in fact was a mirror image of the defendant Charles Kennedy, but his objections were, in fact, purely perfunctory and were promptly overruled. He fared little better on cross-examination. Dr. Stevenson's professional credentials were impeccable and his testimony had been entirely fair, reasonable, and for that reason, unassailable.

As it happened, after the defense rested its case with Dr. Stevenson's testimony, Bob Huffman called Dr. Reshetylo as a rebuttal witness, only to hear him agree with Dr. Stevenson.

The evidence was in.

Chapter Eighteen

All that remained to be done now was to dispose of the defense motions for dismissal, which were perfunctorily and fecklessly renewed as a matter of standard practice, the perorations of counsel (final argument), submission of the case to the court, deliberation by the three judges and, of course, the verdict. It seemed clear enough that all of these matters could be concluded in a single session, so it was determined by consensus of court and counsel—as well as the defendant himself—to make Saturday the final day of trial.

As a first order of business that morning, the anticipated defense motions were made, argued disingenuously, and summarily overruled from the bench. We could proceed to oral argument. Bob Huffman's summation of the evidence was a classic prosecutorial review and analysis of all the evidence which tended, in any way, to incriminate our client. Most of it was entirely superfluous because there were no issues whatever as to who had killed Danny Bolden, when and where it had happened, or, for the most part, why it had happened. Nonetheless, Huffman wanted to make sure the court recognized that he had covered—and proved beyond a reasonable doubt—each of the essential elements of murder in the first degree. And, of course, he had done so. It remained only for us to try to deflect the thrust of the state's case by showing either that the killing was justified or that the defendant was in such an impaired state of mind that he was unable to restrain himself from acting as he did.

Huffman's argument took something just over an hour. My own summation consumed perhaps an hour and a half. I laid particular emphasis on the discovery of the second knife, which tended to corroborate Charles Kennedy's version of the struggle and supported his claims, both of self-defense and irresistible compulsion. I reviewed the time-honored M'Naughten Rule and its several relevant ramifications, the psychiatric testimony offered by Dr. Stevenson, the social, psychological and intellectual limitations of the defendant, and concluded by reminding the court that the state's own expert, Dr. Reshetylo, had entirely agreed with Dr. Stevenson as to the issue of the defendant's inability to reject the course of action which he ultimately chose.

Bob Huffman had the final word. In a ten-minute rebuttal, he argued that the mere presence of a second knife near Danny Bolden's body could not support a judicial finding that his death had been provoked by his own aggression and that our 'pseudo-scientific' claims of irresistible impulse were in reality nothing more than a "God made me do it" excuse for murder.

Presiding Judge John Kiracofe conferred briefly with the other members of the panel and announced that the judges would retire to chambers to deliberate the issues; court would be in recess for one hour.

IT WAS LUNCHTIME, so as soon as the judges had left the courtroom and Charles Kennedy had been escorted back to the jailhouse, Mike and I betook ourselves across Main Street to the locally prominent Flash Restaurant. Little more than a hole in the wall carved out of the vestigial remains of the 120-year old former courthouse, the Flash was locally prominent only because of its proximity to the 'new' courthouse and to the offices of virtually every lawyer in town. Even so, because this was the Saturday before Labor Day, most of the downtown people had closed up shop for the long week-end, and the place was virtually deserted.

We picked a table in the elevated section at the rear of the restaurant and made small talk with Katherine McNeil, while studiously watching her pour out three cups of steaming coffee, one for Mike, one for me, and, as a matter of course on a slow day, one for herself. Katherine was the owner-operator of the Flash and was on friendly terms with all her regulars, so it was natural for her to join us for coffee and conversation.

"Well," she asked casually, "Are you finished yet?"

"You're asking whether we're finished? Or whether our case is finished?" Mike wanted to know. Then, before she could respond, he continued. "Actually, Katherine, the answer is 'both.' Our case is all over except for the verdict, which we expect in an hour or so, and the two of us are pretty well spent after a long, hard week of trial."

"And the verdict you're expecting is?"

"Katey," I interjected, "that's probably the toughest question I've heard all week—and we've heard some really tough ones." Because she was the mother of one of my best friends, and a classmate to boot, I'd been mooching my morning coffee from Katherine McNeil since high school days. Their house was located directly on my route to school and I'd made it a habit to stop by for coffee and walk along with her son Dick the rest of the way to the schoolhouse. So, while she was 'Katherine' to Mike, she'd always been 'Katey' to me.

"Actually, Katherine, there are four possibilities." Mike addressed the question. "The judges might find our client guilty of murder in the first degree, God forbid; they could also find him guilty of murder in the second degree or of simple manslaughter—or they could acquit him altogether."

"Which ain't very likely," I appended quickly.

"Not likely at all," Mike agreed. "But then I don't really expect them to come back with first degree either. I think we've cast some reasonable doubt on the issues of premeditation and intent. I think we're looking at either second degree or manslaughter, depending on how much the judges buy of what we've been trying to sell."

"I think you're right," I said. "On all counts. What's more, I think Bob Huffman sees it the same way. You'll have noticed he didn't ask for the death penalty."

"IT IS THE DECISION OF THE COURT that the Defendant Charles C. Kennedy, Jr., is guilty of murder in the second degree," announced Judge Kiracofe in solemn tones. "Does the defendant have anything to say as to why sentence should not be imposed?"

There was nothing to be said and there would be no pre-sentence investigation, recommendation by the Probation Department, or any other consideration. The statute then in effect mandated the penalty for murder two. "No, your honor. The defendant stands mute," I answered as the three us stood together at the counsel table to receive both the verdict and the sentence of the court.

"Very well," acknowledged Judge Kiracofe. "Charles Kennedy, Jr., it is the sentence of this court that you be taken forthwith to the Ohio State Penitentiary at Columbus and confined there for the term of your natural life. This court stands adjourned."

Charles Kennedy took the verdict and the resultant life sentence as equably as he had accepted every other aspect of the process, from his arrest, through all our conferences along the way, and through the trial itself. It was as though he had divined the outcome from the very beginning and had fully expected the ultimate outcome. He offered his hand to both of us, in turn, and thanked us for our efforts in his behalf. "Don't worry about me none," he said. "I be all right. Might even make some new friends over there."

Then, after receiving our own goodbyes and well-wishes, he turned to the team of deputies, extended his wrists for re-shackling, and accompanied his escort out of the courtroom for his return to the county jail and his ultimate removal to the penitentiary.

The panel of judges had remained in their leather swivel chairs at the bench during the defendant's leave-taking. They had anticipated that there would be a short wrap-up conference with the attorneys. Bob Huffman took a moment to exchange congratulations with Mike and me, then accepted our own reciprocal expressions to him. It had, after all, been a draw. He had contended for murder one, and we had hoped for manslaughter. Murder two was about half-way in-between our respective positions.

In accordance with custom, the three judges also offered their own compliments to all of us concerning the manner in which the case had been presented; for our own part we thanked them for their willingness to serve and for their attentiveness to the evidence. Those amenities out of the way, Judge Kiracofe described their deliberations, "It was a difficult choice between murder two and manslaughter," he said. "I expect you've already worked that out."

And, of course, we had. "Did not the existence of the second knife weigh in your deliberations?" I asked.

"Very much so," answered Judge Kiracofe. "First off, we were not all convinced that the object depicted in the photograph was actually a knife. Judge Eley was firmly convinced that it showed a standard type hunting knife, Judge Beery believed just as strongly that what we were looking at was nothing more than an aberration in the photographic process, and I was effectively undecided. Were I to hazard a guess, I would have agreed with Judge Eley. As it happens, however, we finally decided that even if there were a second knife and your defendant found himself in a self-defensive posture, he employed far more force, deadly force, than that which was necessary to defend himself."

"Overkill," I commented.

"Precisely," added Judge Eley, who was a tough-minded former marine and a no-nonsense judge. "Both literally and figuratively."

"And our irresistible impulse defense?" queried Mike.

Judge Kiracofe was ready for that one. "We were very impressed with your psychiatrist, Dr. Stevenson, and with his testimony. He made a good case for your argument that the defendant, compromised as he was, did not have the ability to restrain himself from stabbing the Bolton boy to death..."

"But?" prompted Mike.

"But we were simply unwilling to extend the M'Naughten Rule far enough to allow the defendant's rage, whatever its cause, to excuse him altogether. We did conclude, however, that the evidence, under the Rule, was adequate to eliminate the element of premeditation from the defendant's conduct," explained Judge Kiracofe.

"Thus second degree," concluded Mike.

"Correct," pronounced Judge Eley. "And you can thank your psychiatrist for that."

Author's Note

During that time in my career at the bar when I was engaged in an active criminal practice, I was frequently asked by some of my more outspoken personal friends how it was that I could bring myself to defend persons accused of truly heinous, criminal acts, particularly when there was little or no room for any doubt concerning their guilt or innocence. How could I look at myself in the mirror? How could I sleep at night?

I routinely answered those questions to the effect that I slept very well, thank you. I was simply doing my job, fulfilling the role assigned to defense counsel by our system of criminal justice. I pointed out that it was not for me to determine my client's guilt or innocence—or to mete out an appropriate punishment for his offenses. That's what judges and juries are for. My function was to serve as a leavening influence, a balance between the prosecution's zeal to convict and the system's interest in the protection of persons accused of activities proscribed as criminal. And in the performance of that function, I felt it to be my solemn duty to the defendant—and to our system of laws—to make all of the arguments and to take all of the measures on his behalf which the defendant might make and take for himself if he possessed my training and experience. I had, after all, taken an oath to do so.

That did not mean, of course, that I condoned the criminal conduct involved or that I needed to empathize with—or even to like—my client. It meant only that I was to advocate his cause and to mount for him the best defense available.

In the case of Charles Kennedy, I confess that, despite the thoroughly atavistic savagery of his brutal slaying of Danny Bolden, I nonetheless came to feel a genuine sympathy for him. If ever one existed, here was a clear case where an unfortunate—lamentable, actually—combination of inherent limitations, genetic, intellectual, environmental and social, had virtually predestined the course of conduct which ultimately ended one life and blasted another.

And so, for all those reasons, I was not entirely comfortable with the prospect of Charles Kennedy's being confined in a cage, like an animal, for the rest of his life. I managed to assuage my dismay in that regard, however, in contemplating that the structured life of a prison inmate and the assurance of regular meals, medical attention and minimal creature comforts might actually be a benefit to him. I also recognized that his custodial confinement might well provide the best possible assurance that those same forces which had already combined to produce one tragedy might not synergize to produce yet another.

As it happened, Charles Kennedy seems to have fared very well at the Ohio State Penitentiary and he was released on parole in April of 1975 after serving some ten and a half years of his life sentence.

Acknowledgments

Over the course of the last twenty-five years or so I have had occasion to examine into the circumstances involved in eight separate, selected homicides committed in Miami County, Ohio, during the two hundred years of its existence as a political subdivision. That exercise has, of course, entailed an attempted re-creation of the real-life, high-stakes dramas which were played out in the local courtrooms when the perpetrators of those homicides were subsequently brought to trial on charges of first degree murder.

The eight cases were selected, however subjectively, because I considered them to be unique—in some particular or another—and therefore readily distinguishable from the commonplace, run-of-the-mill killings of one person by another and the customarily banal trial proceedings which necessarily follow in order that the state and the families of the victims might achieve some measure of justice—and closure. Some of my cases were chosen because of their high profile, and the intense public attention they commanded; others, because of some exceptional feature, nuance or wrinkle which I felt set them apart from the bathetic norm. In retrospect, I note that while each of the eight perpetrators was clearly guilty of some degree of criminal homicide, only six were actually convicted. Two were totally exonerated, and of the six who were convicted, only one was executed. One died in prison, and the remaining four were released after serving hard time.

I have taken a great deal of pleasure in researching and presenting these several cases. I truly found them to be unique in their separate characteristics and I was interested in the process of the trials as only a trial lawyer can be. And so, in some sort of circuitous way, I consider myself indebted to the participants in these several tableaux, the perpetrators, the lawyers and even the victims, for their respective contributions to the common lore.

Lest I be misunderstood, let me hasten to articulate that I have not intended to glorify, sensationalize, or to condone, in any way, the conduct of any of the perpetrators whose stories I have presented. I consider that murder, per se, is trite. The willful taking of a human life, without a compelling justification, is the ultimate obscenity. Nonetheless, and despite that universally held perception, human nature cannot be denied. We are, all of us, intrigued to a greater or lesser extent, by capital cases, those instances where the actors actually play for all the marbles.

Quite apart from any subtle obligations which I may owe to the participants, I need to acknowledge the contributions of a great many people, friends really, who have provided valuable assistance to me in the production of this latest exposition. Pony Favorite's grandson, Russell (Bussie) Favorite was good enough to share with me his personal recollections of the family traditions concerning the murder of his kinsman and to provide copies of photographs of some of the principals involved in that affair. Doug Enyeart reviewed his grandfather's scrapbook with me and lent me several photographs and other materials pertaining to Harley Enyeart, and Karol Kerr McCarthy made available to me a scrapbook and photographs of her father, former prosecutor Ellis W. Kerr. Local Historical Library Archivist Patrick Kennedy and former Archivist Juda Moyer could not have been more responsive to my frequent, and doubtless annoying, requests for isolated and esoteric bits of information. I am also indebted to the Troy-Miami County Public Library for copies of contemporary newspaper accounts and photographs which I have abstracted from its micro-fiche records. The assistance, together with the many accommodations of all these persons, has been most helpful and is greatly appreciated.

My good friend, former classmate and longtime secretary, Martha Crouse, suffered stoutly through the various stages of production of my prior works and helped me with the initial phases of this effort as well. Alas, however, I seem to have worn her out, and she retired a short time ago. Happily, my current secretary, Carolyn Benzies, stepped immediately into the breach and helped me through the project. That help has consisted of transcription, typing, word-processing, organizing, editing and a thousand other functions that I can barely comprehend—and most certainly cannot describe. I could hardly fail to appreciate her invaluable support and assistance. I can only hope I haven't worn her out as I did Mrs. C.

J.E.F

254 *Shards, Pellets & Knives, Oh My!*

A practicing attorney for more than fifty years,
John Fulker is uniquely qualified, by experience and insight,
to re-create the circumstances and the drama involved in these
actual episodes. His research of court records and contemporary
accounts, coupled with personal interviews and his own personal
recollections, has enabled him to select and to present each
of his cases with understanding, empathy and,
above all, an elegant writing style.